The New Magic of Microwave Cookbook

Magic Chef®

Publication Arts, Inc.
5700 Green Circle Drive
Minnetonka, Minnesota 55343

We're glad you've chosen Magic Chef as your microwave oven. We think you'll be glad, too, when you see the new ideas Magic Chef has put into microwave ovens. Ideas like heat control, quick defrosting, slow cook capabilities, multi-meal cooking, automatic temperature control and many more. All great ideas that make microwave cooking the most versatile cooking method in existence, enabling you to prepare favorite traditional dishes as well as many modern-day meals in just minutes.

For those of you who have never used a microwave oven before, try out this cookbook's mini-course illustrating the basic techniques of microwave cookery. You also will find the introductory pages on utensils and procedures very helpful. Take a look at the photos to get an idea of the many taste-tempting dishes you can prepare with your microwave oven.

The recipes and techniques included in this book were tested by our own professional staff of home economists as well as by homemakers. All the foods shown in the photos were prepared from the recipes in this book. They were photographed just as they came out of the microwave oven... without any special treatment. These are the same recipes you will enjoy preparing and serving every day for family meals and for special occasions.

Magic Chef is proud of its long standing reputation as the oven of "cooking experts". We want you to become as "expert" as possible in microwave cookery. Your new oven along with this cookbook will get you off to a great start.

If you have any questions or need additional assistance, please write me.

Joanne Crocker

Joanne Crocker
Magic Chef, Microwave Division
P.O. Box 2369
Anniston, Alabama 36202

A special thanks to
Patty Harper Sheffield
and Debra Lacey.

Published by Publication Arts, Minnetonka, MN.

Library of Congress Catalog Card Number: 80-82151.

Contents

The Magic of Microwave

Almost everyone knows that microwave cooking is fast. Saving time is generally the first reason for buying a microwave oven. But microwave does a lot more than save cooking time. Foods cooked by microwave retain their natural flavor. You use less seasoning in microwave cooking because seasonings don't cook away.

Microwave cooking saves nutrients: foods with a high natural moisture content need little or no water, others use far less than conventional cooking. Foods cook in their own natural juices, which enhances flavor.

A microwave oven saves energy: not only because it cooks faster, but because it doesn't consume energy heating up, or waste it cooling down.

Microwave cooking lets you keep your cool. The kitchen doesn't heat up: even the oven doesn't heat up. As for the cook…you'll be unhurried, unworried, with more time for your family, your friends and yourself.

Microwave makes your freezer more convenient. No more worry if you forgot to defrost the meat. You can defrost and cook in about the same time or less than you are used to cooking in. If you grow your own vegetables, or freeze vegetables in season, microwave can help prepare small portions for the freezer, then defrost and cook them in the same container.

Every cook knows that preparing a meal is only half the battle. Microwave cooking saves clean-up time, too. Many of your favorite serving dishes can be used to mix and cook as well as serve. You can even cook on disposable plates for an absolutely no-clean-up meal. Spatters and spills don't bake on with a microwave oven, so it's easy to keep the oven clean.

What is Microwave Energy

Electrical energy is transformed into electro-magnetic energy or microwave energy by a tube called a magnetron. This tube is like a broadcasting station sending out waves of high frequency energy in the cavity of the microwave oven where they are reflected off the metallic side walls, floor and ceiling of the oven and are eventually absorbed by the food. This electro-magnetic energy causes the molecules of the food to agitate. This agitation produces friction which in turn causes it to cook. Because all the heat is produced in the food itself no heat is wasted in preheating the oven or heating the utensils. Microwaves are high frequency radio waves, they cannot cause a chemical change or a breakdown in your foods.

How Microwave Cooks

Microwaves react differently with different substances.

1. They are *reflected* by metal or foil, just as light is reflected by a mirror. The cooking cavity and door are made of metal in order to contain the energy and reflect it back to the food. Any metal in the oven will reflect or bounce energy. The cooking shelf is positioned in the oven to take best advantage of the reflected energy.

2. Microwaves pass *through* certain substances, such as paper, plastic, glass and ceramic, as light passes through a window. These materials may warm up eventually, as heat transfers from the food to them.

3. Microwaves are absorbed by food and liquids, causing the molecules of the food to agitate, produce friction and in turn heat. Microwaves penetrate about ½ to 1½-inches, depending on the density of the food and after that heating occurs through transference or conduction.

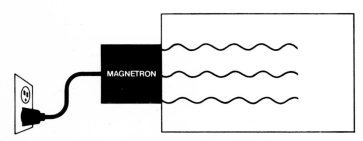

Electrical energy is transformed into high frequency radio waves.

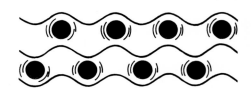

The radio waves agitate the food molecules causing heat by friction.

How Heat Control Works

Your conventional oven gives you a variety of temperatures on which to cook. After you select the temperature setting, your oven preheats to the desired temperature, then goes on and off to maintain that temperature level. If you wish to choose a lower level, or turn it off, it will retain heat as it "coasts" to cool. Heat control microwave ovens are never preheated and respond to changes instantly.

The earliest microwave ovens had one setting. ON. Energy was constant, and cooking was regulated only by time. Rest periods were needed for food to "equalize" or transfer heat to the interior, especially in defrosting, where the outside might cook before the inside was defrosted. This technique was also necessary for many foods which require a slower, more gentle cooking.

The defrost setting on a microwave oven provides controlled cycling of microwave energy. As the food is defrosting this cycling effect permits the cold areas in the center of the food to equalize in temperature with the warmer outer areas of the food, thus preventing the outer areas from rising in temperature too fast and starting to cook before the food is completely defrosted.

Other heat control settings provide different levels of heat or energy just like your conventional range and oven. Just as everything you cook conventionally does not cook best on HIGH or 500° F, not everything you cook in your microwave oven will cook best on HIGH. Many foods need slightly longer and lower heat or energy settings, such as SIMMER, to allow flavors to develop and tenderizing to occur. Lower heat or energy settings such as WARM can be used just for keeping things warm without additional cooking, or for such things as softening butter or cheese. As quantities of food to be microwaved or defrosted increase or decrease, many times a higher or lower heat or energy level is necessary to provide for the best results.

The faster these cycles and the more settings available on a microwave oven, the more control you have. Solid state heat control provides a number of settings from 1 to 10 with shorter and more frequent pulses of energy to give precise cooking performance.

Precautions to Avoid Possible Exposure to Excessive Microwave Energy

(a) Do not attempt to operate this oven with the door open since open-door operation can result in harmful exposure to microwave energy. It is important not to defeat or tamper with the safety interlocks.

(b) Do not place any object between the oven front face and the door or allow soil or cleaner residue to accumulate on sealing surfaces.

(c) Do not operate the oven if it is damaged. It is particularly important that the oven door close properly and that there is no damage to the: (1) Door (bent), (2) Hinges and latches (broken or loosened), (3) Door seals and sealing surfaces.

(d) The oven should not be adjusted or repaired by anyone except properly qualified service personnel.

The above is printed in compliance with the Food and Drug Administration, Department of Health, Education, and Welfare, Performance Standards for Microwave and Radio Frequency Emitting Products, 21 CFR 1030.10.

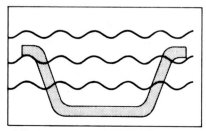

Microwaves pass through some materials like glass and paper.

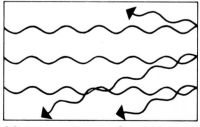

Microwaves are reflected by metal.

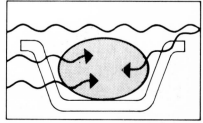

Microwaves only penetrate food and cause heat by agitation.

How To Use This Cookbook

American lifestyles are changing rapidly. People don't have hours to spend cooking meals, nor do they have time for cleaning up a sink full of dirty pots and pans. But microwave helps solve these problems and many more.

This cookbook is designed to help you make the best possible use of your microwave oven...as a time and budget-saver, as an efficient teammate for the freezer and as a means of accommodating varied mealtime schedules.

For new owners of microwave ovens, the chapters on cooking utensils and techniques will be especially helpful. Also, there's a mini-course on microwave cooking which features pictures and step-by-step directions to help you learn to cook with microwave through experience. That's the section called Let's Get Started.

HOW TO READ THE RECIPES

All recipes in this cookbook are set up as follows:

NAME OF RECIPE

Number of servings
Microwave cooking utensils needed

Ingredients listed in order of use

Procedures include covering, stirring, times, heat control settings, changes in settings and testing for doneness. An explanation of each of these key components follows:

Number of Servings. Most of the recipes are for 4 to 6 servings. For fewer servings, cut the recipe ingredients and cooking time in half. Check for doneness and add more time if necessary.

Throughout the cookbook, easy-to-find symbols identify recipes which are suited to particular cooking styles. Some recipes carry more than one symbol.

HOW TO USE THE COOKING STYLE SYMBOLS

 Microwave Show-offs

The "magic" will be evident in anything cooked in the microwave oven. There are certain recipes, however, which show off microwave's difference dramatically. These dishes are noted with the special show-off symbol.

 The Microwave/Freezer Team

Many people wisely use the microwave as a "flash defroster", but it can be much more than that. The Microwave/Freezer symbol indicates recipes which freeze beautifully. Make a double recipe, serving one now and freezing the other. Prepare your own TV dinners with plastic or paper plates or shallow foil trays. Use boil-in-bags to freeze leftovers in single portions for faster freezing and reheating. Prepare vegetables as they will be served...whole, halved, sliced or diced. Then under-cook slightly, freeze and add later to favorite dishes.

 No Time to Cook

For people who have little time to cook, recipes with this symbol are ideal. They are all quick to prepare, require minimal clean-up and use ingredients that can be kept on hand in the freezer, refrigerator or cupboard.

 Leftovers

Microwave reheats foods without flavor or quality loss so that leftovers don't taste leftover. Large quantities can be prepared with the extra portions being reheated the next day for "fresh cooked" flavor or made into frozen entrees or dinners. Certain recipes in this cookbook plan for leftovers. Some start with cooked meat, while others offer a second-meal variation.

OUR MICROWAVE RECIPES FOR YOUR MICROWAVE OVEN

These recipes were developed for heat control microwave ovens with 600-650 watts of power. But every one of them can be adapted to any microwave oven. One point to remember: "High" settings in this book indicate that you are using the full power of 600-650 watts. A setting of '9' means 90% of 600-650 watts, and '5' means 50% of 600-650 watts or about 300-325 watts.

IF YOUR HEAT CONTROL OVEN IS NOT OURS

This test shows how to match any oven's settings with the settings in this book: Fill a 2-cup measure with cold water. Take the temperature of the water. Microwave 1 minute on High. Take the temperature again. Write down the difference. When the measuring cup cools, use fresh water and make the test again at another setting. Now, divide the temperature difference on the second setting by the temperature difference on the High setting.

Example:

	Test on High	2nd Test
Temperature after heating	95°	77.5°
Starting water temperature	-60°	-60°
Difference	35°	17.5°

Second difference divided by first difference equals 5.

The answer in this example is 5. Therefore, whenever a recipe in this book calls for a setting of '5', you will use your oven's setting which you have just tested...no matter what that setting is called. Using this procedure, you can test all your settings and make a list of the corresponding setting.

IF YOUR OVEN HAS AN ON (HIGH) SETTING ONLY

In this case power levels can't be adjusted so cooking times must be adjusted instead. For a recipe with a setting of '5', instead of cutting the heat to 50%, cut the time to 50%. When the directions say to cook at '6', use 60% of the recommended time. For times longer than 2 minutes, watch foods carefully and turn, stir, rearrange or rest as you think appropriate.

IF YOUR OVEN HAS LOWER POWER

If an oven's power is 400 to 500 watts, its power level on High is just right for recipes in this book that call for setting of '7' or '8'. When a recipe calls for High, cook it a bit longer than the recommended time. If it calls for a setting lower than '7', shorten the cooking times. All the recipes include doneness tests, so you'll be able to judge timing.

Read your own Care and Use manual. Follow manufacturer's instructions regarding the use of metal in your oven. Also, check the pattern of turning, stirring or rotating recommended by your manufacturer.

THE MAGIC OF MICROWAVING
Make-ahead Meals

There are times when it's more convenient to prepare a meal in advance and reheat at serving time. When reheating in the microwave:

Heat dense foods like baked beans and mashed potatoes first, as they retain heat longer than other foods.

To speed heating, cover the dish and stir occasionally.

Larger quantities take longer to reheat as do foods that have been refrigerated.

Reheat roasts whole and turn several times during heating.

Layer slices of meat on a platter, cover with waxed paper and reheat.

Split-shift Dining

Food can be arranged on individual plates, enabling everyone to have a good hot meal when it's convenient. To arrange food on the plates:

Place food in a thin layer for faster heating.

For even heating, place slow-to-heat items like meat and mashed potatoes around the outside of the plate.

Make a depression in the center of dense foods like baked beans and mashed potatoes.

Put quick-heating foods like peas in the center of the plate.

Arrange irregularly-shaped foods like chicken legs with the thickest parts to the outside.

A sauce over the meat will keep it from drying out while waiting for the dinner.

To reheat the prepared plate:

Start with a short time and add time if needed.

When the plate's bottom feels warm, foods have heated enough to transfer their warmth to the plate, and the meal is ready to serve.

Company's Coming

An entire party menu can be prepared in advance and cooked or reheated in the microwave just at serving time. Also, the microwave and conventional ovens can team up with each being used to its best advantage.

Microwave Cooking Utensils

Microwave Cooking Utensils. Microwave allows use of varied cooking utensils never possible before. Paper plates and napkins, china and glass...all are great for the microwave. While metal pots and pans are not recommended, it won't be necessary to buy a whole new set of cookware. Many things you already own will go into the microwave and on to the table, saving both serving and clean-up time. This chapter describes the kinds of cooking utensils that are appropriate for the microwave.

In this cookbook, the cooking utensils needed are listed at the upper right of each recipe. If the suggested size container is not readily available, a larger one may be substituted, although cooking time may be affected. Using a smaller size dish is not recommended because foods which boil need room to expand. And remember that none of the utensils used should rub against the oven door or sides during cooking.

Metal. Some metal can be used in microwave ovens, but an understanding of do's and don'ts is necessary. Do not use metal pots, pans and baking sheets; dishes trimmed with gold or silver; glass or ceramic utensils with metal screws, bands or handles. When cooking or defrosting in plastic bags, remove bands or handles. When cooking or defrosting in plastic bags, remove metal ties. Since metal reflects microwave energy, there will be no heat at the metal surface, thus creating uneven heating patterns. Metal containers may create conditions which can cause a static discharge within the oven. It won't hurt you, but it may deface the oven.

Usable Metal. If your oven is not one of ours, consult your Use and Care manual before using any metal. Even where metal is permitted, it will slow cooking, and other materials may be more desirable.

Here are some metals that are allowed in our ovens and in some other oven brands. Small pieces or strips of aluminum foil may be used to shield the thin ends of roasts, tips of chicken wings and legs, or any parts which might over-cook before the thicker parts are done. Our recipes will tell when the foil should be removed for even cooking. With a frozen turkey, remove the metal clamp on the legs after defrosting in the microwave and before cooking. Metal skewers and metal roasting pans can be used when there is a large amount of food in proportion to metal. Shallow (¾-inch) TV dinner trays may be heated by microwave, but the foil cover should be replaced with waxed paper or plastic wrap. To heat a TV dinner faster, remove the contents from the metal tray and arrange on an ordinary (non-metallic) dinner plate. In the Convenience section of this cookbook, there are numerous suggestions for heating many products normally purchased in foil containers.

Glass, China and Pottery. Food can be heated to serving temperatures right in their own serving dishes, platters or plates. Warm dessert in a glass dish, or heat coffee right in the cup. Use glass mixing bowls, glass measuring cups and glass baking dishes. China and glass are not affected by microwave as long as they have no metallic trim. Dishes designed for the conventional oven — such as stoneware, porcelain souffle dishes and pottery casseroles — work well in the microwave unless they have metal in their glaze or composition. Delicate glassware, china and lacquerware are not recommended for microwave oven use.

Examples of suitable ovenware are the French Chef line by Marsh Industries, Temperware by Lenox and Casual China by Franciscan.

It's a good idea to test any dish for suitability. Place empty dish in oven. Microwave 1 minute on High. If the dish becomes warm, do not use in microwave oven. If the dish becomes lukewarm it is suitable for heating but not cooking. If dish remains cool it can be used for cooking.

Oven Glass/Glass Ceramic. These materials are excellent for microwave unless they have metal trim or metal parts such as clamps, screws or handles. Manufacturers are adding new items all the time. Check for labels such as "Good for Microwave", "Freezer-to-Oven" or "Oven-Proof". Fire King cookware by Anchor Hocking, Pyrex and Creative Glass by Corning, Glassbake by Jeanette Glass, Glass Ovenware by Heller Designs, Inc., and Heat-proof cookware by Federal Glass are examples of oven glass. Teflon-coated oven glass can be used in the microwave oven without changing cooking time.

There are many new and exciting plastic utensils being sold and promoted for microwave cooking. They come in new shapes, sizes and designs to give you more flexibility in microwaving. When selecting plastic cookware, it is important you understand the limitations of the particular type of plastic you are considering. Some of these utensils can withstand temperatures up to 400°F and may be suited for use in the conventional oven as well. These utensils are made from a thermoset plastic material. Examples of this type of cookware are Microware® by Anchor Hocking and Nordic Ware's® microwave cookware.

Other plastic utensils have different heat tolerances. Those made from polysolfone material generally can withstand temperatures up to 300°F. Examples of this type of cookware are those made by M.C.E., Tara, Eagle, Bangor and Fleet. It's important when selecting plastic cookware to carefully read the label. Make sure it has been designed for microwave cooking and follow the manufacturer's instructions carefully.

Plastic roasting racks hold the meat out of its juices to let you roast your meat without stewing it. Cupcakers and muffin pans are convenient utensils for handling muffins, cupcakes and some of them can even be used for poaching eggs. Special bacon racks allow you to microwave bacon easily and retain the bacon fat, if you wish. Ring molds come in fluted designs, as well as straight sides, letting you make fancy cakes, meatloaves, and vegetable molds. Individual dishes have been designed to cook perfect hamburger patties every time. Cooking sheets and baking trays make convenient pans for many microwave cooking applications. High-sided cake pans have been designed for cake mixes which rise higher in the microwave oven. Special microwave popcorn poppers allow you to pop popcorn quickly and easily in your microwave.

Straw and Wood. These materials can be used for quick warm-ups, such as heating rolls or Baked Alaska. Large wooden items may dry out and crack with prolonged heat.

Utensils *continued*

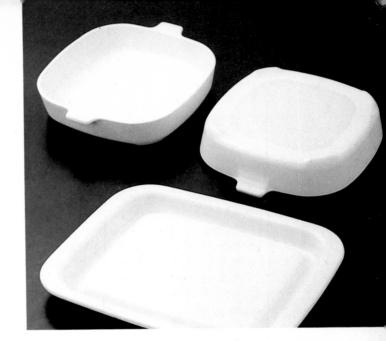

Browning dishes. The browning dish was designed for foods which cook too quickly in the microwave to develop a browned surface. A special coating on the bottom of the dish becomes hot enough to brown foods. Browning dishes are available in several styles including a platter which is ideal for foods which won't slide or develop juices, a grill designed to allow for fat drain-off, plus browning casseroles in varied sizes. Generally browning dishes have short legs so that they can be safely placed on formica countertops when hot. When using a browning dish, follow the manufacturer's instructions carefully.

Never use a plastic spatula in the browning dish as it will melt. Do not set hot browning dishes on plastic table cloths.

Plastic Tableware. Plastic foam cups and dishes or dishwasher-safe plastic containers can be used for low-heat microwave cooking and reheating. Even safe containers, however, may develop burned spots or distortion with foods high in fat or sugar content. Melamine plastics are not microwave-oven-safe; Melmac plastics are, but may discolor.

To test plastic dishes, place ¼-cup water in dish and bring to boil in microwave. Then check for distortion where the hot water came in contact with the plastic. Also, notice any discernable odors.

Non-Stretch Plastic Wrap and Plastic Bags. This may be used on dishes which do not have suitable covers. Foods may be cooked directly in oven-wrap or boil-in-bags without foil strips or metal ties. (Substitute string for metal ties when sealing.) Boil-in-bags should be pierced or slit so that steam can escape during cooking. Also, be careful of escaping steam when plastic wrap is removed. Thin plastic sandwich bags and freezer bags are not recommended.

Paper. For reheating and for low-heat or short term cooking, paper products become useful microwave cooking utensils. Use paper towels or waxed paper to absorb grease or moisture when heating rolls or baking potatoes. They also are good covers for reheating dishes and casseroles. Paper towels and waxed paper prevent splatters without sealing or steaming foods.

Paper plates do vary in their effectiveness for microwave, and some manufacturers of plastic-coated plates are now labeling their products for microwave. Uncoated paper plates are fine for something like a warm sandwich, but a moist food like spaghetti will make these plates soggy. Wax-coated dishes may melt in the microwave. When heating coffee, use "hot cups" as you normally would for a hot beverage.

Paper cartons and freezer wrap can be left around foods during defrosting. However, check for metal ends, ties on bags and for foil-lined paper bags.

11

Let's Get Started *a mini-course in microwave cooking*

For those new to microwave cooking, this chapter offers some quick and easy dishes to try right away. It illustrates the basic cooking methods and terms explained in the sections on microwave utensils and cooking techniques. You'll have a chance to get acquainted with your new oven and, at the same time, see some of the magic of microwave in action.

Instant Coffee, Tea or Cocoa. Microwave heats small amounts of liquid in about half the time of the average range burner. Three servings of coffee heat faster in individual cups than they do in a single large container.

Fill a hot beverage or foam cup, or a regular coffee cup (no metal trim) with hot tap water. MICROWAVE 1 to 2 MINUTES on HIGH, or until water is steaming hot. Add instant coffee, tea or cocoa to taste. Stir. Notice, while water is steaming hot or boiling, the handle of the cup remains cool, unless decorated with shiny metallic glaze.

Cold perked coffee can be reheated as needed, for a fresh, just-perked taste.

Demonstrates: speed, heating in a cup, reheating and warming against metal (see utensil chapter).

Warm Rolls. Rolls warm quickly in the microwave oven. If rolls are over heated they become hard or tough. Be careful when heating sweet rolls; sugar or fruit filling becomes very hot. You may burn your tongue.

Place roll on a paper napkin to double as a plate and absorb moisture. If roll is placed directly on a plate, trapped steam will make the bottom of the roll soggy. MICROWAVE 10 to 15 SECONDS on HIGH. When surface is barely warm, interior will be hot, a pat of butter placed on the warm roll will begin to melt. When heating more than one roll, add ⅔ of original time for each additional roll.

Demonstrates: warming, heating properties of sugar and use of paper with bread to absorb moisture.

Bacon. In the microwave oven, bacon turns crisp and brown without curling.

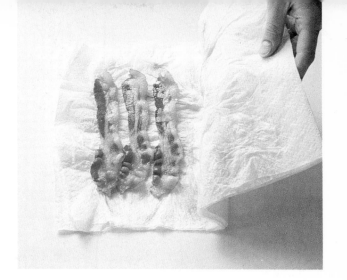

Arrange 3 slices of bacon on three layers of paper towels. Cover with paper towel and press down to prevent spattering and reduce shrinkage. MICROWAVE 2 to 3 MINUTES on HIGH, depending on thickness of bacon and desired doneness. Slight discoloration of paper towel is normal.

Foods with high fat content become very hot. Allow bacon to cool slightly or remove with tongs. If there is grease on the oven floor after bacon is cooked, wipe up with dry paper towels. Bacon can also be cooked on roasting rack (see meat chapter).

Demonstrates: cooking on paper, covering to prevent spatters, heating properties of fats and easy clean-up.

Scrambled Eggs. Eggs scrambled in a microwave oven give greater volume per egg, and you don't have a crusty frying pan to clean. If you are on a low cholesterol diet, egg substitutes work well in the microwave oven.

Place 1 to 2 teaspoons butter in a 2-cup measure, (optional). MICROWAVE on HIGH until butter is melted. Break 2 eggs into cup. Add 2 tablespoons milk. Mix with fork to scramble eggs. MICROWAVE 40 SECONDS on HIGH.

The eggs will have begun to set around the outside of the cup, demonstrating the microwave cooking pattern clearly. With fork, break up cooked portions and stir them to the center. In microwave cooking, stirring is always done from outside in.

MICROWAVE 30 to 40 SECONDS on HIGH. Stir. The eggs will not be completely set. Let stand 1 to 3 minutes to complete cooking. Do not overcook, eggs will toughen.

Demonstrates: stirring and standing.

Tea Ring. Refrigerated rolls make a quick homemade breakfast ring with a minimum of fuss.

Cut refrigerated biscuits (one can) in quarters. Place 4 tablespoons butter in round cake dish and MICROWAVE 1 MINUTE, 30 SECONDS on HIGH, or until butter is melted. Immediately stir ¼-cup firmly packed brown sugar and ½-teaspoon cinnamon into melted butter. Add biscuit quarters, ¼ at a time and stir to coat with mixture. Arrange biscuit quarters evenly in dish. MICROWAVE 4 to 5 MINUTES on HIGH, or until biscuits are slightly firm to the touch.

Demonstrates: using convenience foods for homemade touch.

Let's Get Started *continued*

No clean-up Instant Lunch. Mix canned soup in glass or plastic storage container. Any left-over soup can be refrigerated for a fresh-tasting cup the next day. Place one serving of soup in foam cup or coffee mug. MICROWAVE 1 to 2 MINUTES on HIGH, or until hot.

Place split bun on paper napkin. Place hot dog on open bun. MICROWAVE 30 SECONDS on HIGH.

Demonstrates: convenience and no clean-up.

Microwave Stack-ups. Microwave heating enhances the flavors of foods. In this delicious appetizer, each food retains its own taste and texture. Heating reduces the onion's sharpness without transferring flavor to meat and cheese.

16 pieces
Plate

  4 *slices bacon cooked and cut in ¾-inch pieces*
16 *¾-inch cubes of thuringer or cervelat*
16 *onion squares*
16 *¾-inch squares cheddar cheese, ⅛ to ¼-inch thick*

To make onion squares, halve a small onion from root to stem, separate a few layers and cut into ½-inch squares.

To assemble: place bacon pieces on thuringer cubes. Top with onion squares and cheddar cheese. Secure with toothpicks. Place on paper plate or serving dish. MICROWAVE 40 to 50 SECONDS on HIGH, or until cheese softens.

Demonstrates: Flavor enhancement and cooking on serving dish.

A Microwave Show-off. Children can watch the marshmallow puff.

Muffins From a Mix. Three paper cupcake liners nested together are sturdy enough to hold batter without pans, or use glass baking cups with paper liners. Prepare batter according to directions on box. Fill cups one-half full. Sprinkle with cinnamon and sugar. Place 3 to 4 at a time in oven. MICROWAVE 20 to 30 SECONDS on HIGH per muffin.

Moist spots may appear on surface of muffins. Disregard these unless they penetrate to interior. Thrust a toothpick into a dry spot near center. If it comes out clean, muffin is done.

Demonstrates: testing baked goods for doneness.

Hot and Creamy Shrimp Dip. With a microwave oven you can mix and cook right in the serving dish. This dip is ready to serve in 3 to 4 minutes.

2½ cups
1-quart bowl

1 *package (8-ounces) cream cheese*
1 *can (10¾-ounces) cream of shrimp soup, undiluted*
4 *green onions, including green tops, finely sliced*

Place cream cheese in bowl. MICROWAVE 30 SECONDS to 1 MINUTE on '8', or until cheese is softened.

Stir in soup and onions. MICROWAVE 2 MINUTES on '6', or until dip is hot. Stir once halfway through cooking time.

Demonstrates: softening, mixing, cooking and serving in one dish.

S'mores. The microwave oven softens or melts butter, cheese or chocolate in seconds. This favorite treat is even more popular when cooked in the microwave oven. Because of its high sugar content, the marshmallow heats first. During standing time, heat from the marshmallow melts the chocolate. If you heat a S'more long enough to melt the chocolate, the marshmallow will have scorched spots on the inside.

Place 4 squares of milk chocolate candy bar on a graham cracker. Top with marshmallow. Place on paper napkin. MICROWAVE 15 to 20 SECONDS on HIGH, or until marshmallow puffs. Top with another graham cracker for ease in eating. Let stand 1 minute.

To heat several at a time, add 15 seconds for each additional S'more.

Demonstrates: softening, standing to complete heating, simple cooking children can do.

Frozen Fruit. For a fresh, cool flavor, remove frozen fruit from oven while there are still a few ice crystals present. Pouches of frozen fruit may be placed directly on oven floor.

It is not necessary to prick the pouch, as there will be no steam. MICROWAVE 30 SECONDS on HIGH. Flex pouch briefly to separate fruit and help distribute heat. MICROWAVE 30 SECONDS on '5'. Flex. Let stand 3 to 5 minutes before serving.

If you use fruit frozen in cartons with metal ends, pry off ends and place carton in serving dish. MICROWAVE 30 SECONDS on HIGH until fruit can be loosened from carton. Break up with fork. MICROWAVE 30 SECONDS on '5'. Stir. Let stand 3 to 5 minutes before serving.

Demonstrates: use of plastic pouch, flexing to distribute heat and removal of metal.

Speedy Baked Potato. Foods continue to cook after they are removed from the oven. If you cook the baked potato until it feels soft, it will be over-cooked by serving time.

Place a paper towel on oven floor. Place one medium baking potato in center of oven. MICROWAVE 4 to 5 MINUTES on HIGH, or until potato yields slightly when pressed. Wrap in aluminum foil and let stand 5 to 10 minutes. When microwaving dinner, do potatoes first, then remainder of the meal. Potatoes, wrapped in foil, hold their heat 20 to 30 minutes.

Demonstrates: standing time and covering to complete cooking.

Defrosting Ground Beef. The meat should be defrosted just to the stage where it still has ice crystals but can be broken up with a fork. At this point, the natural juices are still retained in the meat.

Place 1-lb. block of ground beef in an uncovered dish. MICROWAVE 4½ to 5 MINUTES per lb. at '4'. Remove from oven and let stand approximately 5 minutes.

Demonstrates: defrosting meat for maximum retention of natural juices.

Browning Dish Hamburgers. The browning dish has a special coating on the bottom which absorbs microwave energy. When the empty dish is pre-heated, the bottom becomes hot enough to brown foods. Be careful not to touch the bottom of the dish when removing it from the oven.

Form 1 pound ground beef into 4 patties, ½-inch thick. Place empty browning dish in oven. MICRO-WAVE 5 MINUTES on HIGH. Without removing dish from oven, place hamburgers in browner. MI-CROWAVE ½ to 1 MINUTE on HIGH. Turn hamburgers over. MICROWAVE ½ to 1 MINUTE on HIGH, depending on doneness preferred.

Demonstrates: use of browning dish.

Pork Chop Bake. Proper arrangement of foods as-sures even cooking and eliminates turning. The Pork Chop Bake was photographed before cooking to illustrate placement. Soup will be spooned over chops, and will turn golden brown during cooking.

4 servings
12 x 8-inch utility dish

1 *can (16-ounces) sauerkraut, drained*
    small onion, chopped
2 *tablespoons brown sugar*
4 *pork chops*
    Salt and pepper
1 *can (10¾-ounces) condensed cream of chicken*
    soup, undiluted

Combine sauerkraut, onion and brown sugar in (12 x 8-inch) utility dish. Toss lightly with fork. Sprinkle chops with salt and pepper. Arrange over sauerkraut with meaty portions toward outside of dish. Top with soup. MICROWAVE 18 MINUTES on '8', or until pork chops are fork tender.

Demonstrates: arranging foods, heat control.

Fresh Vegetables. Ideal for the microwave, fresh vegetables retain their bright color and delicious crunch when cooked just tender-crisp.

Clean and trim 1-lb. fresh broccoli and cut into spears. Arrange the broccoli in a dish with the stems to the outside and the tender flowerettes to the center. Do not add liquid. Cover the dish with a lid or with plastic wrap, turning back a tiny corner of the wrap to allow excess steam to escape. MICROWAVE 6 to 8 MINUTES on HIGH. Let stand 3 minutes, covered.

If desired, the cooking dish can double as a serving dish. Keep the dish tightly covered until meal time.

Demonstrates: vegetables steamed in their own juices; ideal for broccoli, cauliflower, carrots, summer squash and many other vegetables.

Frozen Peas and Onions Cooked in Serving Dish. Place vegetables in serving dish. Add 1 tablespoon butter, if desired. Cover tightly with plastic wrap. MICROWAVE 3 to 4 MINUTES on HIGH, or until vegetables are tender-crisp, shaking dish after 2 minutes. Remove cover with care because of steam.

Demonstrates: cooking in serving dish and shaking to stir.

Reheating Roast Beef. Fully cooked roasts can be reheated in the microwave to taste as fresh and juicy as the first time around.

Place roast beef on plate or in a baking dish. If available, spoon sauce over the meat surface to prevent drying. Loosely cover with waxed paper. MICROWAVE on '6' just until meat is heated through. Meat reheats very quickly and gets tough if over-heated. A roast about ¼-lb. reheats in 1 to 1½ MINUTES; 2 to 3 thin slices reheat in 20 to 30 SECONDS.

Demonstrates: reheating roast meat to prevent further cooking and to maintain fresh-cooked flavor and juices.

Frozen Brownies. Frozen brownies can be defrosted right in the foil pan. Frosting will not melt. Timing is for brownies stored in 0° freezer.

Remove lid from pan. Place brownies in center of oven, so that foil pan does not touch oven walls. MICROWAVE 1½ to 2 MINUTES on '5'.

Demonstrates: use of metal in microwave oven.

Shown, top to bottom: Frozen Peas and Onions, Reheating Roast Beef, Frozen Brownies.

Cake from a Mix. Treat family and guests to a deliciously easy dessert, made in minutes with the microwave oven.

Cut a piece of waxed paper to fit in the bottom of an 8 or 9-inch square or round baking dish. Prepare a one layer yellow cake mix according to directions on the package. Pour the batter into the paper-lined dish. Let stand for 5 minutes, and then pull a spatula through the batter to remove air bubbles. MICRO-WAVE 4½ MINUTES on HIGH or until the cake pulls away from the edge of the dish.

Cake mixes today generally can be prepared for the microwave following their own package directions. If directions call for more than 1 cup of liquid, however, the liquid should be reduced to 1¼ cup maximum.

Demonstrates: convenience products made even more convenient with microwave.

Lemon Sauce for Cake. Dress up that fresh-baked cake with this quick sauce.

Prepare Lemon Dessert Sauce according to directions on page 203 of this cookbook. Cut up leftover fruits of your choice; strawberries, grapes, oranges, bananas, peaches, etc. Mix the fruits together and spoon on top of cake servings. Pour half the sauce over the servings of cake and pass the remainder.

Demonstrates: using the microwave to make something "special" without having a lot of microwave experience.

Shown, top to bottom: Cake from a mix, Lemon Sauce.

Microwave Menu. A hearty family meal made with the recipes and techniques you've used in this chapter. Notice the order in which foods are prepared.

After-the-Game Family supper

Microwave Stack-ups, page 14

Pork Chop Bake, page 17

Baked Potatoes, page 194

Peas and Onions, see above, left

Sliced Tomatoes and Onion Rings, Marinated in Italian Dressing

Brownies, see above, left

Early in the day:
Slice tomatoes, scatter onion rings on top. Pour on dressing. Cover. Regrigerate. Assemble stack-ups.

25 to 30 minutes before serving time:
Bake potatoes. Let stand wrapped in foil. Assemble pork chop bake. Heat stack-ups. Start pork chops. Serve and enjoy stack-ups with the family. Cook peas and onions when chops are done. Heat brownies while clearing the table.

Demonstrates: menu planning and order of preparation.

Let's Get Started: Microwaving Vegetables

Photos and information in this section describe basic cooking techniques for some of the most frequently microwaved foods...vegetables, meats and desserts. Once, learned here, the techniques can be applied to the many other foods which also are great for microwave cooking.

Microwaving Vegetables

Vegetables are among the most ideal foods for microwave cooking. Because of the short cooking time, vegetables retain their bright, fresh color, their tender-crisp texture and maximum nutrients.

Covered Dish. Many vegetables can be cooked with little or no water added. The tight cover allows the vegetables to steam in their own juices to just tender-crisp. If you prefer vegetables that are more done, just a little additional cooking time is all it takes. Vegetables will continue to cook a little and hold their heat very well until serving time if left in their covered dish. This type of cooking is ideal for broccoli, cauliflower, carrots, zucchini, cabbage wedges and many other vegetables.

Individual Portions. Accommodate the tastes of many different people with individual portions of vegetables cooked in plastic wrap or in muffin cups. Several different vegetables can be fixed for one meal to accommodate different tastes and they can be cooked to degrees of doneness. Each individual serving takes only a few minutes. You can keep fresh vegetables fresh as only the amount needed is cooked at any one time.

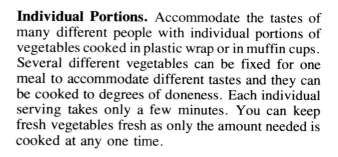

Plastic Wrapped. Odd-shaped vegetables like cauliflower heads and halves of acorn squash can be wrapped in plastic for microwave cooking. Plastic wrap is ideal for vegetable combinations like the one shown here. Be sure, however, that all vegetables in your combination cook in similar times. Check the vegetable cooking timetable later in this cookbook. Plastic wrapped vegetables take minimal space and often can be tucked in alongside other dishes cooking in the microwave. Be sure to allow for the additional cooking time if you do this.

Plastic Covered Dish. Dishes without covers can be tightly covered with plastic wrap. Turn a tiny corner of the wrap back to allow steam to escape. When a dish is completely covered with wrap, the rush of steam upon removing the wrap can cause burns. A dish with plastic wrap cover is ideal for microwaving frozen vegetables. Cook the vegetables in their serving dish and leave them tightly covered until meal time.

Dish with Water Added. With prolonged storage or when left at room temperature too long, certain fresh vegetables begin to loose some of their crispness. These vegetables are best cooked with some water in a dish tightly covered with plastic wrap. Adding water is also important when cooking vegetables like green beans. Heat the water to boiling before adding the vegetables.

Corn on the Cob. There are several easy ways to cook corn on the cob. You can microwave the entire cob including husk and silks. When the ears are cooked, simply pull the husks back until you reach the final layer. Grasp the silks firmly and pull them off the ear. Then remove the final layer of husks. You'll find that if the ears are properly cooked, the silks will slip off easily; if the ear is undercooked, the silks won't come off. If undercooked, simply turn the husks back up around the ear and return to the microwave oven.

Ears of cleaned corn can be individually wrapped in waxed paper or in plastic wrap. After cooking, they can be left wrapped until serving time. They will remain piping hot for 20-30 minutes. Several ears can be cooked in a dish tightly covered with a lid or plastic wrap.

21

Let's Get Started: Microwaving Meats

As in conventional cooking, various types and cuts of meat must be cooked in the microwave oven by different methods for optimum flavor and tender-ness. And while the microwave oven does not cook meats "instantly", the time reduction can be as much as ⅓ to ½ of conventional cooking time.

Dry Roast on Roasting Rack. Use this technique for tender cuts of meat like beef rib roasts, beef tenderloin and pork loin roasts that are best roasted rather than steamed. The automatic thermometer works very well with this method in insure that your meat will be done exactly the way you like it. Remember to allow for standing time for your meat to finish cooking by this method. Roasts 3 pounds and under will rise approximately 15° during stand-ing time. Roasts over 3 pounds raise up to 20°. Juices which collect in the bottom of the rack can be used for gravies and sauces. Salt should be added during the standing period. As in conventional cook-ing salt added during cooking tends to draw juices out and toughen the meat.

Braise in Own Juices. Less tender cuts of meat such as beef pot roast and rump can be covered and cooked in their own juices or a marinade to provide for tenderizing during microwaving. Dry soup mixes sprinkled on top of the meats before cooking enhance both the color and flavor. If the roast has been marinaded add ½-cup of the marinade to the dish during cooking period. The automatic ther-mometer is not advised for this method because these cuts of meat require more time at higher temperature to properly tenderize.

Covered with Sauce. A sauce applied to many cuts of meat during the cooking period keeps them from drying out and provides for lots of tenderizing and added flavor. Ribs, chicken and fish are all good when cooked this way. In some cases you may want to marinade the meat in the sauce for a while before microwaving to allow the flavor to thoroughly pen-etrate. Other times you may just want to cover the meat with sauce just prior to microwaving. A paper towel or waxed paper cover keeps the sauce from splattering.

Shown top to bottom: Dry roasting on rack, Brais-ing, Meat covered with sauce.

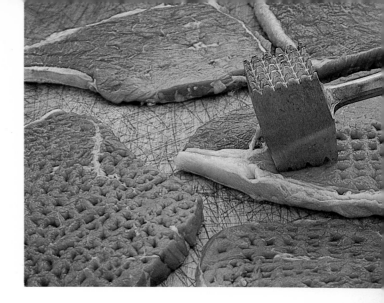

Tenderizers. Tenderizing those less tender chops and steaks is perhaps more important in microwave cooking than when using conventional ovens. With microwave, you don't have the long cooking times which normally break down the tough, more fibrous meats. For cuts like steaks and chops, the most effective method is pounding the meat with a meat mallet or the edge of a saucer. For roasts and larger cuts a sharp prong meat tenderizing utensil or piercing all over with a fork is a good choice. Other good methods are to use a commercial tenderizer or to cook the meat in high acid liquids like tomato juice and wine.

Stewed, Covered Tightly, with Liquid. Use this technique when a dish requires complete blending of flavors and maximum tenderizing. Meats for this method are best cut into smaller pieces and chunks. Most recipes for this type of cooking call for power levels and 50 and 60% to give the time necessary to properly blend the flavors and make the meat tender.

Cooking Bags. Be sure the bag is oven-proof and not the general type of plastic bag used for freezing or storage. Place the bag in a dish to catch drips and substitute string for the standard twist tie. Fasten the string loosely, allowing steam to escape during cooking. Many cuts of meat and most poultry work well with this method. Seasoning may be added as desired and vegetables may be cooked along with the meat or poultry if you wish.

Shown, top to bottom: Tenderizing, Stewing, Cooking in bags.

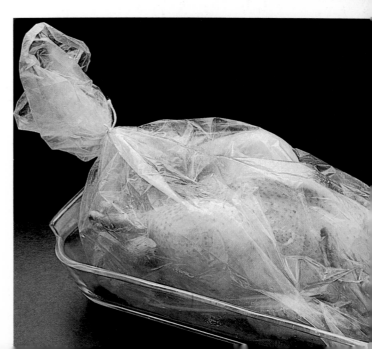

Let's Get Started: Microwaving Desserts

Cakes. A single layer cake can be microwaved, cooled and frosted in less time than it takes to just bake the same cake in a conventional oven. And the end product will be moist and have greater volume than the same cake cooked conventionally. Bundt cakes microwave well using the new Bundt baking dishes. Cupcakes, loaf-style, square and round cakes also cook well in the microwave. Chocolate cakes bake best at a setting lower than other cake varieties. Generally, sponge and angel food cakes don't microwave well. Complete directions for cooking many styles of cakes can be found later in this cookbook.

Fill containers only half full of batter, as cakes rise 20% higher in the microwave. Use extra batter to make cupcakes, or store in the refrigerator and bake a fresh cake several days later.

Always remember to line the bottom of the baking dish with waxed paper. Before baking, allow the cake batter to stand about 5 minutes in the baking dish. Then pull a spatula through the batter to eliminate air bubbles.

Doneness tests are much the same as for conventionally cooked cakes. A toothpick inserted in the center should come out clean; the cake should pull away from the edges of the dish.

Remove cake from the oven while there are still moisture beads on the top of the cake. If all the moisture beads are cooked away, the cake is likely to be tough. If desired, blot the moisture beads away with a paper towel after the toothpick test indicates doneness.

The tops of microwaved cakes will be somewhat uneven, so you may want to add frosting or topping. Refrigerating cakes, especially layer cakes, makes for easier frosting.

Custards and Puddings. Pie and cake fillings, puddings and sauces -- made from scratch or from a convenience mix -- cook quickly in the microwave for a really easy dessert. They can be mixed and cooked in the same dish; even a large glass measuring cup will do the job. Cook until the pudding coats a spoon, just as you would if preparing it by conventional methods.

Some custard recipes for microwave ovens require cooking the classic way in a pan of water. The cooking time, however, is ⅓ to ½ less than for regular oven-baked custard. As with conventionally cooked custard, a knife inserted in the center should come out clean.

Baked Fruit. Compotes are so easy to prepare using a variety of canned or fresh fruits. When cooked in a microwave, fruits hold their shape and fresh color. Hot fruit dessert also requires less water for cooking so juices have a more distinct fruit flavor. Whole fresh fruits can be baked in a matter of minutes. Just stand cored fruits such as pears or apples in individual baking dishes; stuff the center if desired and cover with waxed paper or plastic wrap to avoid splattering. Many baked fruit recipes can be served in their own cooking dishes.

Pies. Pastry cooked by microwave is espically tender and flaky. While there is no browning, the color can be made more attractive by adding vanilla or yellow food coloring or by using solid shortening when mixing up the pastry dough.

For fruit and soft pies, the crust should always be pre-baked before filling is added. To prevent sogginess, brush the crust with egg white before baking. Crumb toppings or lattice-style pastry can be added later. For a quick pastry crust, transfer an unbaked frozen crust to a glass dish. MICROWAVE 1 MINUTE on HIGH to thaw. Re-shape the crust to fit the dish. Prick crust with fork and MICROWAVE 6 to 8 MINUTES on '8', turning once during cooking. Try crumb crusts for more variety in your pies.

Defrosting

The microwave oven is a unique appliance for its rapid defrost capability. All types of food from small vegetables like peas to large roasts and even turkeys can be successfully defrosted in the microwave oven.

Generally foods should be defrosted at low settings so that they thaw evenly. For large quantities

Beef

ITEM	CONTAINER	SETTING	MINUTES PER POUND	TURN OR REARRANGE	STANDING TIME
Chuck arm pot roast	Original package	4	3 - 5	Turn	10 min.
Corned beef	Original package	4	3 - 5	Turn	10 min.
Ground beef	Original package	4	3½ - 5½		5 min.
Hamburger pattie (4 oz.)	Glass plate or plastic wrap	4	45 sec. - 1 min.		3 min.
Liver, sliced	Original package	4	4 - 6	Separate and rinse in cold water	10 min.
Round steak	Original package	4	3½ - 5½		10 min.
Rump roast (boneless)	Original package	4	4 - 6	Turn once	10 min.
Sirloin steak (½-inch thick)	Original package	4	3½ - 5½		10 min.

Pork

Chops (four ½-inch thick)	Original package	4	3½ - 5½	Separate last third of time	5 min.
Sirloin roast	Original package	4	3½ - 5½	Turn once	10 min.
Spareribs	Original package	4	3 - 5		10 min.

Veal

					1½ - 3½
Roast	Original package	4	5 - 7	Turn once	
Sliced	Original package	4	4 - 6	Turn and separate	10 min.

Poultry

Chicken (cut up fryer)	Original package	4	4½ - 6½	Turn once, rinse in cold water	10 min.
Duckling, chicken (whole)	Original package	4	3 - 5	Turn once, rinse in cold water	10 min.

of food, defrost initially at higher settings; then reduce the setting. This will provide for faster, more uniform defrosting.

For best results, defrost until foods are still cool to the touch and contain some ice crystals. They will continue to defrost as they are prepared for cooking. Foods defrosted too long will begin to cook on the edges and also will lose their natural juices.

ITEM	CONTAINER	SETTING	MINUTES PER POUND	TURN OR REARRANGE	STANDING TIME
Rock cornish game hens	Original package	4	4 - 6	Turn once, rinse with water	5-10 min.
Turkey (10-14 pounds)	Original package	4	3½ - 5½	Start breast up. Turn; rest 5 minutes halfway through defrost period. Rinse with water.	15-20 min.

Seafood

ITEM	CONTAINER	SETTING	MINUTES PER POUND	TURN OR REARRANGE	STANDING TIME
Fish fillets	Original package	4	3½ - 5	Separate last half of time.	5 min.
Lobster tail	Original package	4	4 - 6		5 min.
Shrimp or scallops	Original package	2	4 - 5	Separate last half of time.	5 min.

Breads

ITEM	CONTAINER	SETTING	MINUTES PER POUND	TURN OR REARRANGE	STANDING TIME
Loaf, sliced	Original package	4	1½ - 3½		5 min.
Dinner rolls (1 dozen)	Original package	4	1½ - 3½		5 min.
Hamburger buns (½ dozen)	Original package	4	1 - 3		1-2 min.

Desserts

ITEM	CONTAINER	SETTING	MINUTES PER POUND	TURN OR REARRANGE	STANDING TIME
Apple pie, 9-inch, baked	Glass or aluminum pie plate	4	8 - 12	Warm individual slices if desired	10 min.
Cake	Pan	4	4 - 6		5 min.
Fruit	Covered casserole	High	2 - 3		5 min.

Microwave Cooking Techniques

You don't have to learn to cook all over again with microwave, but like any appliance, a microwave oven has special features that make it different. Things cook much faster; you can use utensils you never used before. You still test meat for doneness the same way you always have, by sight and touch. Grandmother's broom straw still tells you when a cake is cooked in the center. Cooking times are approximate because food preferences and portion sizes differ. A vegetable which is "just right" for one person may taste undercooked to another. The materials or shapes of cooking dishes can make a difference, too. A large, shallow casserole heats faster than a deep one of the same capacity. Some microwave cooking "tips" are just as good in conventional cooking: you notice the difference faster with microwave because microwave cooks faster.

Food Shapes. When cooking a stew on a conventional range, large chunks of meat, carrots or potatoes take longer to cook. Small size foods like peas are added at the end. Oriental cooks, who are experts at instant cooking, cut everything up into small pieces which cook quickly and uniformly. Microwave cooking is just the same; large or thick pieces take longer to defrost or cook than small or thin ones. When several foods are cooked together, they should be similar in size and shape so that everything is done at the same time.

Starting Temperature. In both conventional and microwave cooking, the starting temperature of food affects cooking time. Frozen dishes take longer than refrigerated. Refrigerated food takes longer than food at room temperature. Warm foods need only a few seconds by microwave to make them piping hot.

Stirring. Microwave cooking requires less stirring than conventional cooking. When a recipe directs you to stir once, do so about halfway through the cooking period. Two or more stirrings should be done at approximately even intervals, but it is not necessary to be precise.

Foods which cannot be stirred are turned over, rearranged or repositioned by turning the dish. Since the oven shuts off when the door is opened, stirring does not affect cooking time.

When cooking on a conventional range top, you stir things up from the bottom to redistribute the heated parts. In microwave cooking, you stir from the outside in, for the same reason. Sauces and puddings which call for "constant stirring" in conventional recipes need only occasional stirring in microwave.

Some foods cannot be stirred. In microwave cooking two techniques are used to achieve the same result.

1. *Rearranging*. Roasts and whole birds are turned over during cooking. Smaller items, such as chicken parts or ribs can be turned over and repositioned in the dish.

2. *Turning Dish*. With cakes, quiches and souffles, which can neither be stirred nor rearranged, the cooking dish is rotated for even heating. Turn the side of the dish which is near the oven door until it is near the back of the oven. This technique is also used when foods which cook best at a lower setting must be cooked on High.

Small pieces cook faster than large ones.

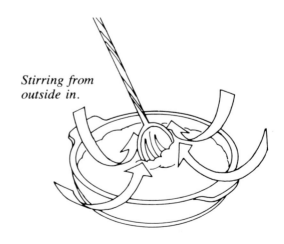

Stirring from outside in.

Standing Time. No matter how you cook them, all foods continue to cook after they are removed from the heat source. With small items, such as vegetables, this may be no longer than the time it takes to serve them. For large items such as roasts, conventional cookbooks recommend a standing time to finish cooking, retain juices and facilitate carving. The same principle is true for microwave. If, after standing time, the food is not cooked to your liking, with microwave, you can always add a few moments more. Overcooking can never be corrected, no matter how you cook.

Shielding. Here's one place where foil can be used in the microwave oven. Wrap small pieces or strips of foil around delicate parts, such as the tips of chicken wings and legs, to retard cooking until the bulky parts are almost done. When foil is removed, all parts finish cooking together. This is comparable to conventional cooking when a turkey breast or a pie crust may be covered to prevent over-browning before the interior is cooked.

Heat Control. In conventional cooking, you control the temperature of your range burner or oven. If you are cooking a pudding, you bring it to a boil, then reduce to simmer. You select an oven temperature to suit the food you are cooking. Microwave ovens with heat control work the same way. You're completely in control, with less time and fuss than ever before. The recipes in this cookbook suggest settings, but feel free to adjust them to suit your cooking style.

Roasting. The microwave roasting rack serves the same purpose as the metal rack in a conventional roasting pan, but is designed for use in the microwave oven. Use it under meats, to keep them from steaming in their juices, under bacon and other foods which need to drain, under breads to allow steam to escape. If you do not have a microwave roasting rack, use inverted saucers.

Covering. When you cook conventionally, you cover pans and casseroles to retain moisture and speed cooking. You do the same in microwave cooking, but the covers may be different. When our recipes direct you to cover, you may use plastic wrap which does not touch the food, an inverted plate, or a microwave-safe casserole cover. Be careful when removing these covers, as steam may burn your hand. If the recipe does not direct you to cover, the dish should be cooked uncovered.

''Cover loosely'' in our recipes is comparable to ''partially cover'' in conventional recipes. The cover helps retain heat, but excess steam escapes. Lay a sheet of waxed paper over a casserole, or form a waxed paper ''tent'' over a roast.

Some recipes call for covering with paper towels or napkins. These allow steam to escape, absorb excess moisture and prevent spatters.

Browning. Here is one area where microwave techniques differ from conventional cooking. In conventional cooking, browning occurs because of a high outside heat source which sears the surface before the center cooks. In microwave cooking the only heat is inside the food itself. Roasts and whole chickens will brown but smaller cuts such as steak, chops or chicken parts cook so quickly they do not have time to brown. If browning is desired, it can be achieved in three ways; by pre-searing meat in a fry pan conventionally and finishing quickly with microwave; by brushing meat with bottled browning sauce (Kitchen Bouquet) or by sprinkling with dry browning powders or gravy mix; by using a microwave browning dish.

Testing for doneness. Line voltage is higher in some parts of the country. Your house power may fluctuate during the day, or vary from summer to winter. To reduce the possibility of overcooking, the recipes give minimum times, with directions for checking doneness and further cooking if needed. It's easy to add more time, but nothing can be done for foods that are overcooked.

Meat. Special meat thermometers identified ''for microwave oven use'' offer the best means for testing doneness of large roasts. Do not use meat thermometers without this designation. The thermometer should be inserted during the last third of the estimated cooking time. Place it in the thickest part of the meat without touching any bone. In ovens with a temperature probe, follow the manufacturer's directions for use.

Poultry. Cooked poultry will pull away from the bone. On a whole bird, the leg should be easy to move, indicating tenderness and doneness. You also can test doneness using a microwave meat thermometer.

Vegetables. As in conventional cooking, vegetables can be tested for tenderness using a fork. The more easily the fork pierces the vegetables, the more tender they are.

Fish. As with conventional cooking, over-cooked fish will become dry and tasteless. When fish is done, the flesh is opaque and it flakes easily with a fork. Shellfish flesh becomes opaque and firm.

DONENESS TESTS YOU ALREADY KNOW

Meat thermometer

Vegetables are ''fork tender''

Meat is firm when pressed with fingers.

Fish flakes easily

Covering. When a recipe directs you to cover, you may use a casserole lid or plastic wrap. If a cover is not mentioned, the food is to be cooked uncovered. Some dishes are cooked covered at one time and uncovered at another.

Quantities. In conventional cooking, a chicken takes longer than a game hen. Even three TV dinners takes longer than two. Microwave is just the same, except you notice the difference faster because microwave heats the food, not the oven. In Microwave cooking it is sometimes faster to cook two three-portion servings than one six-portion serving. In doubling a recipe add approximately two-thirds of the original cooking time.

Heat Control Setting. The recipes in this cookbook have been developed around ovens with heat control. And many include a change of setting during cooking.

Heat control settings are like a conventional range's settings, such as simmer, medium and high. In both conventional and microwave cooking, you can cook foods faster or slower than a recipe directs. For example, when cooking small portions of a recipe, a lower setting or shorter time will provide the same results as a higher setting or longer time for a large portion of the same recipe. Changing a setting or a time is determined by the type and quantity of food being cooked. In microwave cooking, changing the setting rather than the time usually is more effective. For example, a reduced setting for a smaller portion still allows time for flavors to blend and develop. This is true for foods like desserts, meats and sauces. Vegetables are an exception in that a short cooking time provide for maximum retention of flavor and crispness.

While many microwave recipes call for a change of setting, it is possible to simply adjust the oven once at a lower setting and allow the food to cook for a longer time. Some ovens can be programmed so that all settings can be determined at once, thus requiring minimal extra attention. In short, microwave heat control settings allow you to select the cooking technique – timing and temperature – that best suits your needs.

Baking. In the Baking, Desserts, and Candy and Cookie chapters, you'll find sections on "Basics," which tell you what recipes are best for converting to microwave baking, how to use mixes, and more. Keep in mind that baked goods rise more in a microwave oven, so reduce leavening by one-fourth and fill pans only half full. And for best results, choose cakes made with whole eggs.

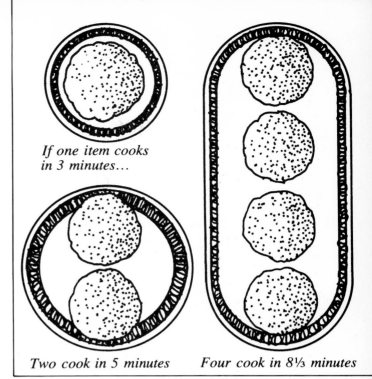

If one item cooks in 3 minutes...

Two cook in 5 minutes   *Four cook in 8⅓ minutes*

Microwaving Quantities

How to Convert Your Favorite Recipes To Microwave Recipes

Many of your favorite dishes can be cooked in the microwave oven with few, if any, changes. Use a similar recipe from this cookbook, or the cooking charts as a guide to method, time and heat control setting.

Fish, Meats, Poultry, Casseroles, Soups. Any recipes which call for steaming, covering or cooking in liquid will work well in the microwave oven. Pot roasts, stews and other foods which call for long cooking can be prepared in one-third to one-half the time, using a lower heat control setting.

Your microwave oven cooks so quickly that seasonings aren't cooked away, so reduce the amount of seasonings. Add salt *after* you cook meats. Presoak dried ingredients such as dry beans. Otherwise, quick cooking won't allow them time to soften.

Cut up meat for stews into pieces of uniform size and shape. If your recipe calls for flouring and browning the meat, coat it-the flour is still needed to thicken the gravy-but skip the browning.

When you prepare foods for the freezer, don't use cornstarch, because it breaks down when frozen.

For maximum microwave efficiency, choose recipes which serve four to six. Because cooking time depends on volume, very large quantities take almost as long to cook by microwave as they do conventionally.

How to Cook by Temperature with the Automatic Thermometer

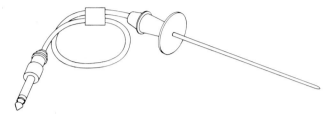

The automatic thermometer aids you in cooking foods to the exact doneness you desire and then turns the microwave oven off. If you wish to know how long your food will take to cook, consult the time charts for that particular food to get a general idea.

All you have to do is insert the Automatic Thermometer into the center of the food. To insure you are placing the tip of the thermometer at the exact center, examine the outside of the food and/or dish, locating the exact center of the food. Line up the thermometer with this point. Place your finger on the thermometer where it meets the outside of the food and/or dish. Hold that place. Then press the

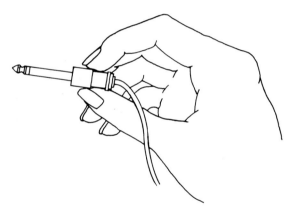

Plug Automatic Thermometer into recepticle in oven wall.

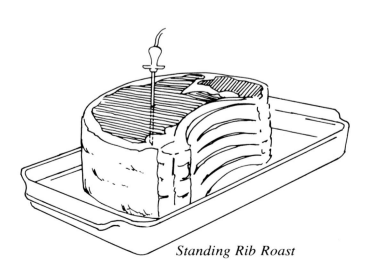

Rolled Rib Roast

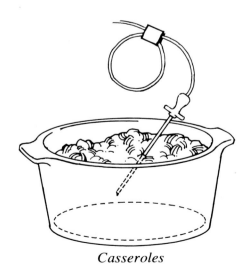

Casseroles

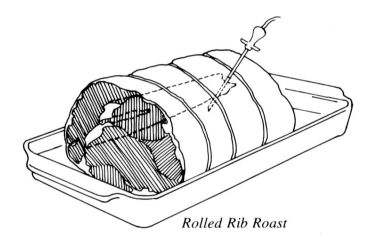

Standing Rib Roast

thermometer into the food until there is no more space between the food and the spot on the thermometer you're holding. Remember that at least one half of the thermometer should be inserted into the food. Insert the thermometer as horizontally as possible so that the maximum amount of the probe is covered by the food.

After you have positioned the thermometer in the food, place the food in the oven and plug the Automatic Thermometer into the oven. When properly positioned in the food, the Automatic Thermometer will turn the microwave oven off when the exact doneness you have selected has been reached. It is important to position the thermometer carefully. If the thermometer is too near bone or resting in fat it can turn the oven off too early, or overcook your food. Study the illustrations below and compare them to the food you are cooking to help you position the thermometer as accurately as possible. When cooking casseroles or liquids to temperature, use the clip on the cord of the thermometer to hold it in place. Position the thermometer in the center of the dish.

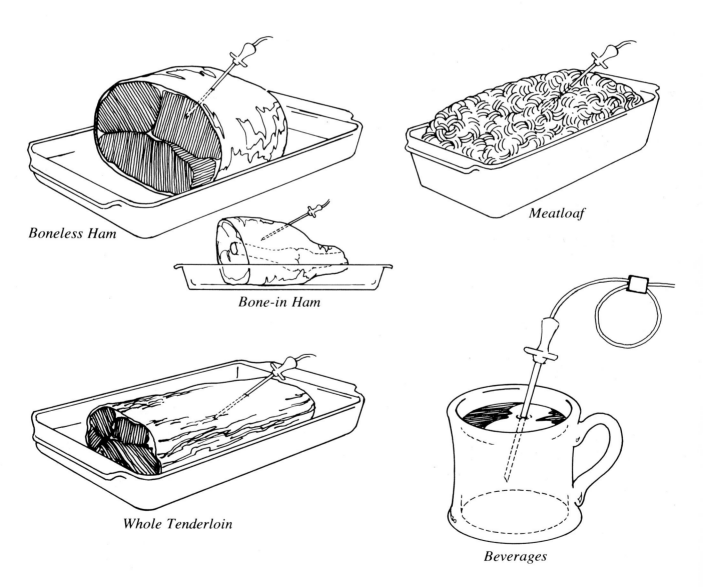

Boneless Ham

Bone-in Ham

Meatloaf

Whole Tenderloin

Beverages

Cooking With The Automatic Thermometer

MEATS

FOOD	MINUTES/LB.	HEAT SETTING	TEMPERATURE	FINISH ON HEAT SETTING # 2 TO TEMPERATURE
Beef				
Boneless Rib Roast	Rare 5-7	6	120°-125°	135°-140°
	Med. 7-9	6	125°-130°	140°-150°
	Well 9-12	6	135°-140°	150°-155°
Standing Rib Roast	Rare 7-8	6	105° turn 120°-125°	135°-140°
	Med. 9-10	6	110° turn 125°-130°	140°-150°
	Well 10-12	6	110° turn 135°-140°	150°-155°
Rolled Rib Roast (over 4 lbs.)	Rare 7-8	6	105° turn 120°-125°	135°-140°
	Med. 9-10	6	110° turn 125°-130°	140°-150°
	Well 10-12	6	110° turn 135°-140°	150°-155°
Tenderloin	Rare 8-9	6	120°-125°	135°-140°
	Med. 10-11	6	125°-130°	140°-150°
	Well 12-13	6	135°-140°	150°-155°
Sirloin Tip	Rare 8-9	6	120°-125°	135°-140°
	Med. 9-10	6	125°-130°	140°-150°
	Well 12-13	6	135°-140°	150°-155°
Eye of Round	Rare 10-11	4	120°-125°	135°-140°
	Med. 12-13	4	125°-130°	140°-150°
	Well 14-15	4	135°-140°	150°-155°
Boneless Rump	Rare 10-11	4	120°-125°	135°-140°
	Med. 12-13	4	125°-130°	140°-150°
	Well 14-15	4	135°-140°	150°-155°
Pork				
Loin Roast (bone in)	11-12	6	140°-145°	160°-170°
Loin Roast (boneless)	12-13	6	140°-145°	160°-170°
Crown Roast	17-18	6	110° turn 140°-145°	160°-170°
Ham				
Canned	9-11	6	120°	140°
Boneless	11-13	6	120°	140°
Shank	9-10	6	120°	140°

Note: All temperatures are in Fahrenheit. See Meat Section for turning instructions.

FOOD	MINUTES/LB.	HEAT SETTING	TEMPERATURE	FINISH ON HEAT SETTING # 2 TO TEMPERATURE
Lamb				
Rack of Lamb	Med. Rare 5-6	6	140°-145°	155°-160°
	Med. Well 7-8	6	150°-155°	165°-170°
Leg of Lamb	Med. Rare 10-11	6	140°-145°	155°-160°
	Med. Well 11-13	6	150°-155°	165°-170°
Boneless Rolled Shoulder	9-10	6	150°-155°	165°-170°

HEATING OTHER FOODS

FOOD	MINUTES/LB.	HEAT SETTING	TEMPERATURE	
Soups (Broth base) (Cream base)		High 8	160° 150°	
Casseroles (precooked)		8	140°-160°	
Thick Meat Sandwiches		8	115°-120°	
Baked Products		6	110°	
Syrup		3	150°	
Coffee & Tea		High	160°-180°	
Cocoa		8	150°-160°	

Note: All temperatures are in Fahrenheit.

IMPORTANT THINGS TO REMEMBER WHEN USING YOUR AUTOMATIC THERMOMETER

Try not to let the tip of the Automatic Thermometer touch the cooking container. The temperature reading will not be as accurate.

Do not use metal or foil containers, such as TV dinner trays.

Do not use plastic wraps or plastic containers. However, you can use oven cooking bags.

For best results, we do not recommend using the Automatic Thermometer with poultry. Test doneness with a regular thermometer outside the oven or use a microwave thermometer or follow one of the other doneness tests for poultry as recommended elsewhere in the book.

If you use the Automatic Thermometer when heating baby food, set the oven for 10° less than the desired temperature. Stir before serving.

When the chart shows a setting of 2 at the end of cooking, this takes care of the standing time of the meat or casserole. If desired, you can remove the meat or casserole from the oven, tent it with foil, shiny side in, and let stand for 15 to 20 minutes to complete cooking. If your oven has a keep warm feature, you can program it and allow the food to remain in the oven for 15 to 20 minutes.

Do not force the probe into frozen food.

When cooking foods that should be turned over or rearranged, remove the probe before doing this step and then reposition the probe again.

Be sure to disconnect the Automatic Thermometer when you're finished cooking with it. Leaving the thermometer connected may damage the thermometer or the oven.

Complete Meal Magic

Cook a complete meal-roast, baked potatoes and another vegetable or dessert and have the entire meal finished piping hot from the oven all at once. It's easy to do. In this case, we took a 5-pound rolled beef roast, 4 medium baking potatoes and started them together, microwaved them on high for 32 minutes, turned the meat, added the frozen brussel sprouts and microwaved another 32 minutes on high.

To get the approximate cooking time, add the time of the meat and the starch items together. In our example, we figured the roast at 10 minutes per pound, or a total of 50 minutes, and 14 minutes total for the potatoes. We did not add any extra time for the vegetables.

Depending on your desired doneness of the meat (rare, medium, or well done) and depending on the size and weight of the potatoes, the total cooking time may vary a little. One of the items may require a little additional microwave time to finish cooking.

Do not be afraid to try other combinations using this general pattern. Start the meat and the heavy starch item, such as potatoes, rice, or winter squash, together. Add the remaining dish when you turn the meat.

The following pages will get you started on other complete meal combinations. Each of these meals is designed to served four people.

20 Minute One Step Meals

Barbecued Chicken, English Peas, Apple Crisp.

Place dishes as shown. The chicken and the peas were covered before microwaving.

One Step Meals

Select one from each column. Prepare these items following recipe directions but do not use the cooking times given. Instead, MICROWAVE all 3 items 20 to 25 MINUTES on HIGH. Items in columns 1 and 3 can be placed in either the left rear or front of the oven. Items in column 2 should be placed in the right rear. All of these foods except desserts should be covered before cooking. You may have to add time for an item or remove a food early if it is cooking too fast.

1½-quart utility dish (6½ x 10½)	1-quart utility dish (5½ x 9)	1-quart utility dish (5½ x 9)
Meatloaf (p. 110-112)	Asparagus Casserole (p. 178)	Corn on the Cob (p. 193)
Veal Chops Parmigiana (pg. 117)	Baked Beans (p. 178)	Buttered Potatoes (p. 194)
Ham slice (p. 126) (or use 2 lb. canned ham)	Green Bean and Bacon Casserole (p. 178)	Lemon Potato Wedges (p. 188)
Barbecued Pork Chops (p. 122)	Broccoli, frozen (p. 192)	Sweet Potato Marsharole (p. 187)
Pork Chops Creole (p. 123)	Carrots (p. 192)	Stuffed Peppers (p. 115)
Barbecued Chicken (p. 143) (1½ to 2 pounds - chicken breasts)	Cauliflower (p. 192)	Apple Crisp (p. 221) (8x8-in. baking dish)
Easy Bake Chicken (p. 142) (1½ to 2 pounds - chicken breasts)	English Pea Casserole (p. 184)	Fruit Cocktail Torte (p. 214) (8x8-in. baking dish)
	Matterhorn Vegetable Bake (p. 189)	Pecan Pie (p. 219) (9-in. pie plate)

One step meals allow you to prepare and microwave your entire dinner at once. Both preparation and microwave cooking time are quick. After selecting your meal components, look up the recipes and follow the instructions as precisely as possible.

These directions are based on weight, ingredients and amounts as stated in the recipe. If standing time is called for in the recipe, it is also important here. If you vary the quantities called for in the recipe, it can alter the cooking time slightly.

50 Minute Two Step Meals

Finished meal: Pork Roast, Potatoes with Butter and Parsley, and Brussel Sprouts.

Place meat in dish using an inverted saucer as a trivet.

Turn meat over. Place other dish in oven as above.

Two Step Cooking

Select one from each column. Place meat in recommended dish. MICROWAVE 25 MINUTES on '6'. Add remaining dishes. MICROWAVE 25 MINUTES on HIGH.

1-quart mixing bowl or baking dish (8 x 8)	1-quart utility dish (5½ x 9)	1-quart utility dish (5½ x 9)
Beef Bourguignonne (p. 109)	Quick rice (p. 199)	Fresh limas (p. 191)
Lamb Stew (p. 131)	Buttered potatoes (p. 194)	Frozen brussel sprouts (p. 192)
Pork roast (p.121) (2½ to 3 pounds	Escalloped Corn (p. 184)	Asparagus (p. 190)
Chicken Parisienne (p. 138) (1½ to 2 pounds chicken breasts)	Frozen whole kernel corn (p. 193)	Summer vegetable casserole (p. 161)
Rolled rib roast (p. 100) (3 pounds)	Pears in red wine (p. 223)	Spicy carrots (p. 183)
Smothered Pork Tenderloins (p. 121)	Curried fruit (1½-qt. dish) (p. 223)	Braised celery (p. 183)

After selecting one item from each column, look up the recipe in the book and follow it as precisely as possible. These times are based on the weights, amounts, and ingredients as stated in the recipe. If you vary the quantities in the recipes, it could vary the cooking slightly and you may have to add additional time to one item or remove an item early that may be cooking faster.

The meat items should always be placed in the left rear corner of the oven. Place the foods from the second column in the right rear corner. Place the foods from the third column in the front. Always cover vegetables and other foods as directed in the recipe.

If the recipe you are using calls for standing time, it's still important when using two-step meal cooking techniques.

One-Dish Meals

Cook an entire meal at once-all in one dish. The only trick is placing the slowest cooking foods at the ends of the dish and the quicker cooking foods in the center. Cover with a tight-fitting cover or plastic wrap before microwaving. Note that the roast is halved with one half placed at each end.

BARBECUE BEEF SHORT RIBS AND CORN ON THE COB

4 servings
12 x 8-inch baking dish

2 -2½ pounds beef short ribs
8 mini ears of corn on the cob, (frozen)
1 -1½ cups barbecue sauce

Arrange ribs in each end of baking dish and place corn in center of dish. Pour barbecue sauce over ribs. Cover with plastic wrap. MICROWAVE 30 to 40 MINUTES on HIGH.

CORNISH HENS AND RICE

4 servings
12 x 8-inch baking dish

4 -1 pound cornish hens
½ cup butter or margarine
1 teaspoon seasoned salt
1 package (8-ounces) chicken flavored rice mix

Place rice mix in bottom of (12 x 8-inch) baking dish. Add 1 cup water. Combine butter and salt in a 1 cup measure. Brush the cavity and the outside of cornish hens with butter and salt mixture. Arrange cornish hens on top of rice mixture MICROWAVE 40 MINUTES on HIGH.

ROAST WITH POTATOES AND CARROTS

4 servings
12 x 8-inch baking dish

3 *pounds chuck roast*
3 *to 4 potatoes, cut into 1½-inch chunks*
6 *carrots, peeled and sliced*
1 *package (1¼-ounces) onion soup mix*

Place roast in baking dish. Arrange potatoes and carrots around roast. Sprinkle with onion soup mix. Cover with plastic wrap. MICROWAVE 25 to 35 MINUTES on HIGH.

STUFFED ROLLED CHICKEN BREASTS WITH BROCCOLI AND LEMON POTATOES

4 servings
12 x 8-inch baking dish

Stuffed rolled chicken breasts, page 146
Lemon Potato Wedges, page 188

1 *pound fresh broccoli*

Place chicken breasts in one end of baking dish, potato wedges in the other end, and broccoli in the center. Cover dish with plastic wrap. MICRO-WAVE 20 to 25 MINUTES on HIGH. Let stand 5 minutes, covered.

Simmer Cooking

Slow simmer cooking techniques bring you old-fashioned goodness and the convenience of starting dinner early and forgetting it until it is time to serve. These delicious and carefree meals can be yours by simply following the recipes in this chapter. With simmer cooking, exact cooking times are not important as with most microwave cooking. In fact, most of the following recipes can stand up to an hour before serving.

For best results when simmer cooking use a 5-quart covered casserole dish that is recommended for microwave cooking. Place the lid on the casserole dish tightly to hold as much heat and steam as possible.

POT SIMMERED CHICKEN

6 servings
5-quart covered casserole dish

1 (2½-3 pound) whole fryer
6 carrots, peeled and sliced
1 cup sliced celery
2 medium onions, quartered
1 tablespoon tarragon

Remove giblets. Wash chicken well with cold water. Pat dry. Place carrots, celery and onions in bottom of 5-quart casserole dish. Place chicken (breast-side down) on top of vegetables. Sprinkle with tarragon. Add water to cover vegetables. Cover. MICROWAVE 10 MINUTES on HIGH, then 60 MINUTES on '5'.

TEXAS CHILI

10 to 12 servings
5-quart covered casserole dish

2 pounds stew meat cut into ½-inch pieces*
2 cans (16-ounces each) kidney beans
2 cans (16-ounces each) whole tomatoes, cut up
3 cans (8-ounces each) tomato sauce
2 medium green bell peppers, chopped
2 large onions, chopped
3 jalapeno peppers, chopped
1½ teaspoons cumin
1 teaspoon pepper
½ teaspoon oregano

In a 5-quart casserole dish combine ingredients. Cover. MICROWAVE 15 MINUTES on HIGH, then 90 MINUTES on '5'.

* 2 pounds ground beef, cooked and drained may be substituted for stew beef, if desired.

SPAGHETTI SAUCE

Approximately 4-quarts sauce
5-quart covered casserole dish

3 pounds lean ground beef
3 tablespoons olive oil or salad oil
2 medium onions, chopped
2 green peppers, chopped
3 cloves garlic, pressed or finely chopped
2 cans (16-ounces) tomatoes, cut up
4 cans (8-ounces) tomato sauce
2 cans (12-ounces) tomato paste
2 cans (12-ounces) water
½ cup finely chopped fresh parsley or ¼ cup
    dried parsley
3 teaspoons oregano
2 teaspoons thyme
4 bay leaves
1 teaspoon fennel seed, crushed
    Salt and pepper, to taste

Crumble beef into 5-quart casserole dish. Add oil, onion, peppers and garlic. MICROWAVE 8 MINUTES on HIGH, or until beef is set. Drain fat. Add remaining ingredients. Cover. MICROWAVE 15 MINUTES on HIGH, then 90 MINUTES on '5'.

PINTO BEANS

10 to 12 servings
5-quart covered casserole dish

2 packages (1-pound each) pinto beans
½ pound fatback
2 tablespoons salt

In a 5-quart casserole dish, cover beans with water and soak overnight. Add additional 5 cups water, fatback and salt. Cover. MICROWAVE 15 MINUTES on HIGH, then 180 MINUTES on '5' (two 90 MINUTE periods).

BARBECUE BEEF SHORT RIBS

4 servings
5-quart covered casserole dish

3 pounds beef short ribs
1½ to 2 cups barbecue sauce

Place ribs in a 5-quart casserole dish. Pour sauce over ribs. Cover. MICROWAVE 15 MINUTES on HIGH, then 90 MINUTES on '5'.

BEEF STEW

6 servings
5-quart covered casserole dish

2 pounds beef stew, cut into 1-inch cubes
½ cup flour
2 bay leaves
1 tablespoon Worcestershire sauce
2 onions, chopped
2 teaspoons instant beef bouillon
½ teaspoon pepper
2 teaspoons salt
1 teaspoon sugar
6 carrots, sliced into 1-inch pieces
1 cup sliced celery
4 potatoes, peeled and cut into 1-inch cubes
4 cups water
¼ cup flour
½ cup water

Coat meat with flour. Place in a 5-quart casserole dish. Add bay leaves, Worcestershire sauce, onions, bouillon, pepper, salt, sugar and vegetables. Pour water over all. Cover. MICROWAVE 15 MINUTES on HIGH, then 120 MINUTES on '5' (two 60 MINUTE periods). Combine flour and water in a small bowl and stir until smooth. Stir into beef stew. MICROWAVE 10 MINUTES or until thickened.

BLACKEYED PEAS

6 servings
5-quart covered casserole dish

2-pound package blackeyed peas
½ pound ham hocks
3 teaspoons salt

In a 5-quart casserole dish, cover peas with water and soak overnight. Add additional 5 cups water, ham hocks and salt. Cover. MICROWAVE 15 MINUTES on HIGH, then 150 MINUTES on '5' (one 90 MINUTE period, one 60 MINUTE period).

POT ROAST

6 servings
5-quart covered casserole dish

3 *to 3½ pound chuck or 2 to 3 inch thick rump roast*
3 *potatoes, quartered lengthwise*
6 *carrots, sliced into 1-inch pieces*
3 *to 4 cups water*
1 *package (1¼-ounces) onion soup mix*

Slice roast in half. Place potatoes and carrots in bottom of a 5-quart casserole dish. Place roast on top of vegetables. Add water. Sprinkle onion soup mix on top of roast. Cover. MICROWAVE 10 MINUTES on HIGH, then 60 MINUTES on '5'.

BLACK BEAN SOUP

8 servings
5-quart covered casserole dish

1 *pound (2½ cups) dried black beans*
4 *slices bacon, sliced*
2 *medium onions, chopped*
3 *stalks celery, chopped*
¼ *cup parsley flakes*
2 *quarts water*
1 *ham hock or bone*
1 *bay leaf*
¼ *teaspoon thyme, crushed*
2 *cloves garlic, pressed or finely chopped*
1 *teaspoon dry mustard*
¼ *cup dry sherry, optional*
  Salt and pepper, to taste
8 *lemon slices*

Place bacon, onion, celery and parsley in 5-quart casserole dish. Cover. MICROWAVE 6 MINUTES on HIGH, or until vegetables are tender. Add beans and remaining ingredients except sherry, salt and pepper. Cover. MICROWAVE 15 MINUTES on HIGH, then 180 MINUTES on '5' (two 90 MINUTE periods). Remove meat from bone. Discard bone. Place meat in soup. In small batches blend in soup in a blender or food processor. Return to casserole. Add sherry, salt and pepper. Garnish with lemon slices.

VEGETABLE SOUP

8 to 12 servings
5-quart covered casserole dish

1 *cup celery*
4 *carrots, diced*
3 *potatoes, peeled and cut into ½-inch cubes*
2 *medium onions, cut into eighths*
2 *cans (16-ounces each) tomatoes*
1 *package (10-ounces) frozen corn*
1 *package (10-ounces) frozen lima beans*
1 *package (10-ounces) frozen okra*
2 *teaspoons whole peppercorns*
1 *tablespoon parsley flakes*
1 *bay leaf*
3 *beef bouillon cubes*
2 *quarts water*
  Salt and pepper, to taste

Place all ingredients in a 5-quart casserole dish. Stir. Cover. MICROWAVE 15 MINUTES on HIGH, then 180 MINUTES on '5' (two 90 MINUTE periods).

NOTE: Fresh vegetables may be substituted for frozen vegetables. Use 1 cup corn, 1 cup lima beans and 1 cup sliced okra.

CORN BEEF BRISKET

6 servings
5-quart covered casserole dish

3½ *pound corned beef brisket*
4 *medium onions, halved*
4 *potatoes, quartered*
2 *quarts water*
1 *large cabbage*

Arrange onions and potatoes in bottom of a 5-quart casserole dish. Place corned beef on top of vegetables. Cover. MICROWAVE 15 MINUTES on HIGH, then 150 MINUTES on '5' (one 90 MINUTE period, one 60 MINUTE period). Remove corned beef, potatoes and onions to a covered dish. Cut cabbage in six pieces and place in the 5-quart casserole dish. Cover. MICROWAVE 12 to 16 MINUTES on HIGH.

*The corned beef should be covered with the liquid during the cooking period. If necessary, an inverted saucer can be placed on top of the corned beef brisket to keep it in the liquid.

Reheating Foods

The microwave oven will reheat most foods and make them taste like freshly cooked foods without a warmed over taste. Be careful when reheating not to over do. Many foods will start to cook again if reheated too long and they will become tough. Times given are for reheating foods from a refrigerated state. Room temperature foods will reheat faster.

MEATS

Most meat will reheat very well. Care must be taken not to reheat beyond its original doneness temperature or it will start to cook again. If desired, the Automatic Thermometer can be positioned in the meat to insure correct temperature. Times will vary with the weight and size of the portion of meat to be reheated. Several thin slices of meat are easier to reheat than one thick one. Meats should be reheated in their own juices if available or covered with wax paper to retain moisture.

FOOD	QUANTITY	HEAT SETTING	TIME
Pork chops	1	6	1½-2 min.
	2	6	2-3 min.
Chicken	¼	8	1½-2 min.
	½	8	2-3 min.
Sliced beef, pork, ham or turkey	2 oz.	6	1-1½ min.
	4 oz.	6	2-3 min.
Prime rib or steak	6 oz.	rare 6	1-1½ min.
		med. or well 6	1½-2 min.
Prime rib or steak	8 oz.	rare 6	1½-1¾ min.
		med. or well 6	2-2½ min.

MAIN DISHES AND CASSEROLES

Main dishes and casseroles can be reheated in their original containers. Many seem to improve in flavor when they are prepared ahead of time and reheated later. Dishes should be covered during heating and, if possible, stirred or rearranged once or twice during the reheating period to insure even distribution of heat.

Chili	8 oz.	8	3-3½ min.
	16 oz.	8	4-5 min.
Beef stew	8 oz.	8	3-3½ min.
	16 oz.	8	4-5 min.
Meat and vegetable casseroles	8 oz.	8	3-3½ min.
	16 oz.	8	4-5 min.
Noodle casseroles	8 oz.	8	3-3½ min.
	16 oz.	8	4-5 min.
Spaghetti sauce	8 oz.	8	3½-4 min.
	16 oz.	8	5-6 min.

SIDE DISHES/VEGETABLES

Single portions of most vegetable side dishes reheat very well. Saucy dishes such as scalloped potatoes and au gratin dishes do extremely well. Some vegetables such as broccoli and asparagus lose color and texture while they have been standing or stored and although they taste good when reheated they do not regain their fresh, just cooked color or texture. If reheating a whole casserole, stir if possible during the reheating time or rearrange the dish.

Peas, beans or corn	4 oz.	H	1-1½ min.
	8 oz.	H	1½-2 min.
	16 oz.	H	4-5 min.
Asparagus spears, broccoli or corn on the cob	4 oz. (1 serving)	H	2-2½ min.
	8 oz.	H	3-3½ min.
	16 oz.	H	4-5 min.
Potatoes or squash	4 oz.	H	1-2 min.
	8 oz.	H	2-3 min.
	16 oz.	H	3-4 min.

SOUP

Soups reheat quickly and easily, and are often better when reheated giving additional time for flavors to blend. They can be reheated right in the individual soup bowl or cup, or in a measuring cup or mixing bowl.

Clear liquid base	6 oz.	H	1½-2½ min.
	12 oz.	H	3-4 min.
	16 oz.	H	4-6 min.
Cream or milk base	6 oz.	6	2-3 min.
	12 oz.	6	4-6 min.
	16 oz.	6	6-8 min.

DESSERTS

You can have hot pie in seconds, hot sauces and toppings for ice cream and hot fruit dishes with all of the goodness and freshness of the first time around. Be careful when reheating things with sugary fruit fillings and toppings. They become very hot very quickly even though the pastry surrounding them may remain cool.

Dessert sauces: hot fudge, caramel or butterscotch	2 oz.	8	½-1 min.
	4 oz.	8	1-1½ min.
	8 oz.	8	2-3 min.
Pie	1 slice	H	¾-1⅓ min.
	2 slices	H	1½-2 min.
	4 slices	8	3-4 min.
	whole pie	8	4-6 min.
Baked fruit; apples or pear	1	H	1-1½ min.
	2	H	1½-2 min.

BAKERY GOODS

Bread products reheat very quickly in the microwave and care must be taken not to overheat them or they will become tough and hard. When heating bread and rolls it is best to wrap them in paper napkins or towels to absorb moisture and keep them from getting soggy. Never reheat bread products tightly covered.

Sweet rolls doughnuts	1	6	30 sec.
	2	6	30-45 sec.
	4	6	1 min.
Dinner rolls	1	6	10-15 sec.
	2	6	15-20 sec.
	4	6	30-45 sec.
	6	6	¾-1 min.
Muffins	1	6	20-25 sec.
	2	6	25-30 sec.
	4	6	¾-1 min.
	6	6	1-1⅓ min.

BEVERAGES

Beverages can be warmed up to piping hot in just seconds. If you wish to have your coffee, tea or cocoa the exact temperature you desire, use the Automatic Thermometer. 170° to 180° is a good place to start. If the beverage has just cooled off, it will only take a few seconds to reheat. If it had been chilled in the refrigerator, use the following times.

Coffee or tea	1 cup	H	1½-2½ min.
	2 cups	H	3-4 min.
	4 cups	H	4½-6 min.
Cocoa	1 cup	8	2-3 min.
	2 cups	8	3-4½ min.
	4 cups	8	5-7 min.

REHEATING PLATED FOODS

Individual plates of leftovers can be prepared and heated all at once. Place heavier foods such as meats and potatoes toward the outside of the dish and delicate, easier to heat foods, such as peas or kernel corn, to the center of the dish. Cover dish with a piece of wax paper or paper towel.

Meats plus 2 vegetables	1 plate	8	2-3 min.

Microwave Menus

Planning a microwave menu is similar to planning a conventional menu. Nutritional balance, contrast of color and texture and compatible flavors are all important factors As with any meal, cooking in an orderly manner will minimize last-minute fuss.

Since foods reheated by microwave maintain their fresh look and taste, part of the meal may be cooked in advance. Other foods may be partially cooked and finished just before serving.

Especially in the new, large size microwave ovens, several dishes can be cooked simultaneously. When cooking complete meals in the microwave, cook the foods which require the longest times first. Then cook those dishes with the next longest times, etc. Take advantage of standing times to assure all dishes will be ready for the table at once. If necessary, reheat to serving temperature in one or two minutes.

"How to Cook the Dinner on the Cover", page 40 shows the order in which foods are prepared to take advantage of partial cooking, standing and heating. The menu below illustrates a dramatic presentation for a gala dinner, made easy by microwave.

Italian Supper for 6 to 8

Antipasto Relish, page 236

Spaghetti and Meat Sauce,
page 114

Broccoli Italian Style (double
recipe), page 181

Garlic Bread, page 206

Fantastic Chocolate Fondue,
page, 221

A day or two before:
Make Anitpasto Relish. Refrigerate.

Early in the day:
Prepare fruits. Dip banana slices in lemon juice to prevent darkening. Refrigerate berries and pineapple. Prepare Garlic Bread. Set aside.

40 *minutes before serving, or earlier:*
Prepare fondue sauce. Set aside to reheat. Cook and drain spaghetti. Make meat sauce. Cook two packages broccoli, page 181, for 12 to 14 minutes. Set broccoli aside, covered. Place Antipasto Relish in serving dish. Finish and warm broccoli, if necessary. Heat Garlic Bread. After dinner, reheat Fondue Sauce while clearing the table.

Leftover Lamb Dinner

Lamb Pilaf, page 131

Zucchini Parmesan, page 189

Tossed Green Salad with Tomato
Wedges, Pitted Black Olives

Fruit Cocktail Torte, page 222

35 *to* 45 *minutes before serving time:*
Cook rice conventionally. While rice is cooking, bake Torte. Cook lamb mixture. Prepare zucchini for cooking. While zucchini is cooking, layer lamb casserole. Heat casserole. Prepare salad. Reheat zucchini, if necessary.

Italian Supper

Thanksgiving Dinner

Carrot Curls, Celery Sticks,
* Green Onions*

Pickles & Olives

Rolls

Roast Turkey with Gravy

Yellow Rice Stuffing, page 198

Cranberry-Orange Relish, page 236

Sweet Potato Marsharole

Asparanuts, page 178

Perfection Salad

Pumpkin Pie, page 219

Day before:
Prepare Cranberry-Orange Relish. Make and refrigerate salad.

Early in the day:
Defrost turkey if necessary. Prepare and cool Yellow Cake Stuffing. Stuff turkey just before roasting. Roast conventionally. Prepare carrots, celery and onions. Refrigerate in ice water to crisp. Prepare and bake pastry shell.

45 minutes before serving time:
Fill and bake Pumpkin Pie. Remove turkey from oven. Let stand, tented with foil. Make gravy. Heat Sweet Potatoes. Let stand, covered. Cook Asparanuts. Reheat gravy and Sweet Potatoes if necessary. Warm rolls.

Company Chicken Dinner

Zippy Madrilene (double recipe),
* page* 83

Chicken Saltimbocca, page 145

Stuffed Mushrooms, page 68

Endive, Orange & Onion Salad
* with Oil & Vinegar Dressing*

Assorted Dinner Rolls

Mocha Torte, page 216

Early in the day:
Bake and refrigerate Moca Torte. Prepare and refrigerate salad ingredients.

45 minutes to 1 hour before guests arrive:
Prepare mushroom stuffing. Bake Chicken Breasts. While chicken is cooking, stuff mushrooms. Combine soup ingredients. Assemble chicken for final heating.

At serving time:
Heat and serve Zippy Madrilene. Heat Chicken Saltimbocca. Toss salad while chicken is heating. Bake mushrooms. Warm rolls while serving chicken, mushrooms and salad.

Family Style Meatloaf Dinner

Meatloaf, page 110

Sour Cream Mashed Potato Puff,
* page* 186

Spicy Carrots, page 183

Lettuce Wedges

Ireland's Fudge Pie, page 214

Early in the day:
Bake Ireland's Fudge Pie

About 1 hour before serving time:
Mix and bake meatloaf. While meatloaf is baking, prepare Sour Cream Mashed Potato Puff. Prepare carrots for cooking. Cut lettuce wedges. While carrots are cooking, slice meatloaf. Arrange on plate. Cover with waxed paper.

Reheat meatloaf, if necessary.

"Souper Lunch"

*New England Clam Chowder,
page 82*

Onion Herb Bread, page 206

*Mixed Green Salad with
Tomato Wedges, Radish Slices,
French Dressing*

Raspberry Swirl, page 215

Early in the day:
Bake cake. Prepare and refrigerate salad ingredients. Melt butter for Herb Butter.

20 minutes before serving:
Cook chowder. Prepare Herb Bread while chowder is cooking. Toss salad during final heating of chowder.

No Time To Cook For Company Dinner

Ham Roll Ups, page 69

*Salmon Piquante with
Cucumber Sauce, page 94*

Peas, page 194

*Small Potatoes (canned) in
Dill-butter Sauce*

*Bananas Foster with Ice Cream,
page 223*

30 minutes before guests arrive:
Prepare Ham Roll Ups. Prepare Salmon Piquante for cooking. Make cucumber sauce. Refrigerate. Prepare Bananas Foster for cooking. Drain and rinse canned potatoes. Combine with butter. Sprinkle with dill.

When guests arrive:
Heat and serve Ham Roll Ups.

20 to 30 minutes before serving time:
Bake salmon. Let stand, covered. Heat potatoes. Cook peas. After dinner, bake Bananas Foster while dishing ice cream. Ignite at table.

Get Together Buffet

Quick & Easy Clam Dip, page 60

Crackers and Chips

Baked Ham, page 127

Chicken Barbecue, page 143

German Potato Salad, page 186

*Cole Slaw with Old-Fashioned
Cooked Dressing, page 202*

Onion Cheese Sticks, page 207

Harvey Wallbanger Cake, page 212

Early in the day:
Make salad dressing. Cool and refrigerate. Bake Harvey Wallbanger Cake. Prepare relishes. Refrigerate. Make Cole Slaw. Refrigerate. Make Chicken Barbecue. Cool and refrigerate. Prepare German Potato Salad. Cool. Refrigerate. Make Quick & Easy Clam Dip. Prepare Onion Cheese Sticks.

When guests arrive:
Serve dip. Bake ham. Halfway through the cooking time, turn ham and return to guests. While ham is standing, reheat chicken. Set aside, covered. Reheat potato salad. Carve ham.

Beef Bouquetiere Dinner

Italian Shrimp, page 69

Beef, see chart, page 100

Broccoli and Carrots, page 192

Watercress and Cherry Tomato Salad with Vinaigrette Dressing

Onion Cheese Sticks, page 207

Corn Muffins, page 206

Pears in Red Wine, page 223

Early in the day:
Prepare vegetables. *Under* cook them slightly. Plunge broccoli into cold water to stop cooking. Slice lemons and refrigerate.

Wash and dry watercress and tomatoes. Refrigerate. Make vinaigrette dressing.

Arrange cooled vegetables in "bouquets" around a microwave-safe platter. Leave center open. Cover with plastic wrap. Refrigerate.

Bake bread sticks. Prepare muffin batter and refrigerate until baking time.

Arrange pears in serving dish. Pour boiling syrup over. Cover with plastic wrap. Let stand on kitchen counter.

When guests arrive:
Cook shrimp. Start roast and serve shrimp. After half the cooking time, turn roast and return to guests.

While roast is standing, bake muffins. Toss salad. Let stand in refrigerator to blend.

Reheat vegetables while carving meat. Arrange slices in center of platter. If roast has cooled during carving, return platter to oven to warm briefly on '5'. Garnish with lemon.

After dinner, cook pears while clearing the table.

Children's Luncheon

Chili, page 154

Peanut Butter Kidwiches, page 73

S'Mores, page 15

20 minutes before serving:
Prepare Chili. While chili is cooking, assemble Kidwiches and S'Mores. Ladle chili into bowls. Heat sandwiches. After lunch, let children heat S'Mores and watch them puff.

Veal Paprika Dinner

Creamy Velvet Veal, page 117

Poppy Seed Noodles

Stuffed Tomatoes, page 189

Spinach Salad

Pumpkin Bars, page 231

Early in the day:
Make Pumpkin Bars. Prepare spinach leaves for salad. Refrigerate.

About 30 minutes before serving:
Cook noodles conventionally. While water is coming to a boil, brown veal. Cook tomato stuffing. Mix veal sauce. Cook veal. Stuff tomatoes while veal is cooking. Bake tomatoes. While tomatoes are cooking, toss salad and dress noodles with butter and 2 teaspoons poppy seed.

Busy Day Supper

Orangeberry-glazed Luncheon Meat, page 133

Instant Mashed Potatoes with Parmesan Cheese

Canned Green Bean Salad with Italian Dressing

Hot Fudge Sundae with Bottled Ice Cream Topping

Early in the day:
Place can of green beans in refrigerator to chill.

About 10 minutes before serving time:
Slice and fill luncheon meat with cranberry relish. In 1-quart measure prepare mashed potatoes as directed on package. Stir in 2 tablespoons parmesan cheese. Let stand, covered, while heating meat.
While meat is cooking, drain beans and toss salad. After dinner, heat fudge topping while dishing ice cream.
NOTE: Children can help spread relish on luncheon meat. An older child could prepare the entire dinner.

Ladies' Luncheon

Luncheon Shrimp, page 90

Grapefruit & Avocado Salad

Assorted Relishes

Buttermilk Bran Muffins, page 206

Lemon Butter Dessert Squares, page 231

Early in the day:
Prepare grapefruit sections. Refrigerate. Bake Lemon Butter Dessert Squares. Prepare and Refrigerate muffin batter.

25 minutes before serving:
Prepare and bake Luncheon Shrimp. While shrimp is cooking, arrange relish plate. Spoon muffin batter onto paper baking cups. Peel and slice avocado. Assemble salad. Bake muffins while shrimp is standing.

Family Breakfast

Orange Juice

Bacon, page 132

Scrambled Eggs, page 173

Muffins, page 209

Fresh Strawberry Jam, page 235

Day before:
Make Strawberry Jam

About 15 minutes before serving:
Cook bacon. Mix muffins while bacon is cooking. Bake muffins. Scramble eggs. Reheat bacon, if desired.

Sunday Brunch

Beautiful Baked Apples, page 222

Eggs Benedict, page 172

Asparagus Spears, page 190

Down Home Streusel Coffeecake, page 208

Day before:
Bake coffeecake.
Prepare apples for baking.

25 minutes before serving:
Bake apples. Make Mock Hollandaise Sauce. Cook asparagus spears. Toast English Muffins. While asparagus is standing, poach eggs. Arrange ham on muffins. Assemble Eggs Benedict. Heat.

Holiday Brunch Buffet

Holiday Fruit Pudding, page 222

Mushroom Quiche, page 170

Link Sausage, page 133

Chilled Salmon Loaf Scandinavian with Cucumber Sauce, page 95

Bacon Wands, page 66

Date Nut Bread with Cream Cheese, page 209

Parisian Mocha, page 86

Day before:
Prepare Holiday Fruit Pudding. Cool. Refrigerate. Bake Salmon Loaf. Cool. Refrigerate. Mix and refrigerate quiche shell. Bake Date Nut Bread. Mix ingredients for Parisian Mocha.

Morning of the Brunch:
Bake quiche shell. Slice Date Nut Bread and spread with softened cream cheese. Arrange on plate. Cover with plastic wrap. Wrap bread sticks with bacon. Refrigerate.

20 minutes before serving:
Make quiche filling. Bake quiche. While quiche is baking, garnish salmon loaf with cucumber sauce. Do not warm sauce. Cook Bacon Wands. Fry sausages conventionally while Bacon Wands are cooking. Make Parisian Mocha while guests are at buffet.

"I Forgot to Defrost the Meat" Dinner

Freezer to Table Swiss Steak, page 103

Cheese Stuffed Potatoes (half recipe), page 186

Cole Slaw

Apple Crisp, page 221

About 40 minutes before serving time:
Bake two potatoes, page 194. Wrap in foil and let stand. Cook Swiss Steak. While Swiss Steak is cooking, make cole slaw. Stuff potatoes. Prepare ingredients for Apple Crisp, but do not sprinkle topping on apples. While Swiss steak is standing, heat potatoes. Top apples. Bake Apple Crisp while eating dinner.

Elegant Beef Dinner

Party Appetizer Pie, page 64

Beef Rib Roast, page 58

Peas in Onion Cups, page 58

Honey Glazed Carrots, page 58

Spiral Cut Mushrooms, page 59

First Prize Cake, page 214

Early in the day:
Bake First Prize Cake. Frost and Refrigerate. Wash and "flute" mushrooms.

1½ hours before serving time:
Peel and microwave onions. Let cool. Defrost peas. Prepare glaze for carrots. Bake Party Appetizer Pie.

45 minutes before serving time: Start roast.

15 minutes before serving:
Glaze and microwave carrots. Stuff onions while carrots cook. Cook onions. Heat mushrooms 1 to 2 minutes.

1 Peel white onions. Arrange in baking dish. Cover with plastic wrap. MICROWAVE 4 to 5 MINUTES on HIGH, or until onions have softened, but are not cooked. Set aside to cool.

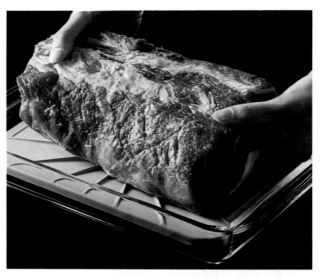

2 Place roast fat side down on microwave roasting rack in 12 x 8-inch utility dish. MICROWAVE 5 MINUTES on HIGH. *Reduce setting.* MICROWAVE ON '6' or '5' for half the estimated roasting time. The initial 5 minutes on high is counted as part of the total time. (See chart on page 100.)

5 When meat has reached the proper temperature, tent with aluminum foil, shiny side in. Leave the ends open; if meat is tightly sealed it will acquire a slight steamed taste. Let roast stand 10 minutes.

6 While meat is standing, defrost, but do not cook peas. Set them aside. Melt 2 tablespoons of butter or margarine and 1 tablespoon of honey in measuring cup. Pour over frozen carrots. Cover. MICROWAVE 4 to 6 MINUTES on HIGH, or until carrots are tender.

3 While meat is roasting, prepare mushrooms. Wash mushrooms, dry with paper towel, trim the base of the stems. Using a sharp paring knife, flute mushrooms by making a V-shaped cut and lifting out wedge. Rotate mushroom against the knife for a spiraled cut.

4 Before the end of the estimated cooking time, check internal temperature of roast by inserting a meat thermometer into thickest part. Refer to chart for temperature meat should be on removal from the oven, in order to reach your desired doneness after standing. If meat needs more cooking, remove thermometer (unless you have a special microwave thermometer) and return roast to oven.

7 While carrots are cooking, remove centers from softened onions. Fill hollows with peas. Set aside cooked carrots, covered. Place onions and peas in oven. MICROWAVE 3 to 4 MINUTES on HIGH, or until peas are hot.

8 Mushrooms in the picture were not cooked. If you wish to serve them hot, brush with butter and MICROWAVE 1 MINUTE, 30 SECONDS to 2 MINUTES on '6', or until hot. Mushrooms will lose their shape and design if overcooked. When cooking on '5', add 20 seconds more time.

Appetizers

Hot appetizers add excitement to a party, and microwave cooking makes them quick and easy. Many can be assembled in advance for a brief last-minute heating, while others can be made on the spur of the moment from ingredients kept on hand in the pantry.

The recipes in this section cover three categories: Bite-sized morsels served on cocktail picks, Canapes and Dips. They heat so quickly you can serve an assortment, perhaps one or more of each type.

PATIO DIP

1½ cups
1-quart casserole or bowl

½ cup orange marmalade
2 tablespoons firmly packed brown sugar
1 tablespoon vinegar
½ teaspoon Worcestershire sauce
½ teaspoon salt
¼ teaspoon curry powder
1 cup dairy sour cream
  Assorted raw fruits and vegetables, cut in bite-size pieces: oranges, apples, pears, raw beans, broccoli, cauliflower

Combine marmalade, brown sugar, vinegar, Worcestershire sauce, salt and curry powder in 1-quart casserole. MICROWAVE 1 to 2 MINUTES on HIGH, or until mixture boils. Stir. MICROWAVE 2 MINUTES on HIGH, or until sugar is dissolved. Stir to blend.

Refrigerate 10 minutes. Blend in sour cream. Serve with fruit and vegetables for dipping.

QUICK AND EASY CLAM DIP

2 cups
1-quart casserole or bowl

1 package (8-ounces) cream cheese
2 cans (6½-ounces each) minced clams, drained. Reserve liquid
  from 1 can
1 teaspoon horseradish
1 small onion, finely chopped
  Salt and pepper to taste

Place cheese in 1-quart casserole or bowl. MICROWAVE 1 to 2 MINUTES on '6', or until softened. Drain clam liquid in casserole. Add clams, horseradish and onion, mix thoroughly. MICROWAVE 1 to 2 MINUTES on HIGH, or until hot.

Dips, from top: Patio Dip, Chili Cheese Dip, Quick and Easy Clam Dip

RAREBIT DIP ⊞

2 cups

1 jar (16-ounces) pasteurized process cheese spread
¼ cup beer (substitutes: wine, ginger ale
   or taco sauce)

Remove cap from jar. MICROWAVE 3 MINUTES
on '5', or until cheese melts. Pour into serving bowl.
Stir. MICROWAVE 1 to 2 MINUTES on '5', or
until hot. Add beer and stir until foam subsides.
Serve with pretzels.

CHILI CHEESE DIP

Approximately 3 cups
1-quart casserole

½ pound pasteurized processed cheese
1 can (16-ounces) chili without beans
   Taco chips

Cut cheese into 2-inch squares.

In 1-quart casserole, MICROWAVE cheese 2 MIN-
UTES, 30 SECONDS to 3 MINUTES, 30
SECONDS on '8', or until melted. Stir once or twice
during cooking time.

Add chili, stir until blended. MICROWAVE 1
MINUTE, 30 SECONDS to 2 MINUTES, 30 SEC-
ONDS on '8', or until heated through, stirring once.

Serve with taco chips.

Can be reheated as necessary.

CHICKEN 'N BACON BITS

1 cup
Plate lined with paper towel

8 slices bacon, cooked crisp and crumbled
1 can (5-ounces) boned chicken, or 1 cup finely
   chopped leftover chicken
1 tablespoon finely chopped pimiento
¼ cup mayonnaise
   Salt and pepper to taste
   Crisp crackers or Melba toast

In a 1-quart bowl, combine crumbled bacon, chick-
en, pimiento, mayonnaise, salt and pepper. Spread
on crackers or Melba toast. Place 10 at a time on a
paper towel-lined plate. MICROWAVE 1 MINUTE
on HIGH, or until hot.

HOT CHEESE DIP WITH FRUIT

3 to 4 cups
1-quart glass bowl

1 can (5.33-ounces) evaporated milk
1 cup shredded sharp American cheese
1 cup shredded Swiss cheese
1 tablespoon prepared mustard
1 teaspoon Worcestershire sauce
   Dash bottled hot pepper sauce
¼ cup finely chopped pimiento
6 to 8 firm fresh apples or pears, cut in wedges

Combine milk, cheese, mustard, Worcestershire
sauce and pepper sauce in bowl. MICROWAVE 6
MINUTES on '6', or until cheese melts. Stir once
half way through, and again when removed from
oven. Stir in pimiento and serve hot, as a dip for
apple or pear wedges. Can be reheated.

SEA SALAD CANAPES

20 pieces
Plate lined with paper towel

1 can (6½-ounces) tuna, salmon or crab, drained
   and broken up with fork
¼ cup mayonnaise
2 tablespoons catsup
2 teaspoons finely chopped onion
2 teaspoons horseradish
1 teaspoon Worcestershire sauce
½ teaspoon dry mustard
½ teaspoon lemon juice
   Toast squares or crisp crackers
   Parsley flakes

Combine tuna, mayonnaise, catsup, onion, horseradish, Worcestershire sauce, mustard and lemon
juice in 1-quart mixing bowl. Mix well. Spoon 2
teaspoons mixture on each toast square. Sprinkle
with parsley flakes. Place on paper towel-lined
plate.

8 canapes: MICROWAVE 30 SECONDS to 1 MIN-
UTE on HIGH, or until hot.
12 canapes: MICROWAVE 45 SECONDS to 1
MINUTE, 30 SECONDS on HIGH, or until hot.

ARTICHOKE NIBBLES

60 crackers
Small plate

2 jars (6-ounces each) marinated artichoke hearts,
   chopped
1 small onion, finely chopped
1 clove garlic, pressed or finely chopped
4 eggs, slightly beaten
½ pound sharp Cheddar cheese, shredded
   (about 2 cups)
¼ teaspoon salt
⅛ teaspoon pepper
⅛ teaspoon liquid hot pepper seasoning
¼ teaspoon oregano leaves
¼ cup fine dry bread crumbs
2 tablespoons finely chopped parsley

Combine onions, garlic, and the liquid from 1 jar of
artichokes in a 2-cup measure. MICROWAVE on
HIGH for 4 MINUTES. (Discard liquid from second
jar.)

In medium mixing bowl, combine onions and garlic
with remaining ingredients. Mix well.

Put a spoonful of mixture on each of 9-10 wheat
crackers. Place on small plate covered with paper
towel. PROGRAM TO MICROWAVE on HIGH for
1 MINUTE to 1 MINUTE and 30 SECONDS.

BUTTERFLIED WIENERS

2½ cups sauce
1½-quart casserole

1 pound wieners
¼ cup honey
1 bottle (18-ounces) barbecue sauce

Cut wieners crosswise in 3 pieces. Cut each piece in
half lengthwise to make 6 pieces. Slit each piece
through ends, leaving a ¼-inch join in center. Set
aside.

Mix honey and barbecue sauce in 1½-quart
casserole. Cover lightly with plastic wrap or waxed
paper. MICROWAVE 1 MINUTE on HIGH. Stir.
Add wieners. Cover lightly. MICROWAVE 3
MINUTES on HIGH, or until ends of wieners curl.
Serve with cocktail picks.

BACON-BLEU CHEESE HORS D'OEURVES

16 to 20 pieces
Small bowl
Plate lined with paper towel

1 package (3-ounces) cream cheese
3 tablespoons crumbled bleu cheese
3 slices bacon, cooked crisp and crumbled
½ teaspoon Worcestershire sauce
   Dash hot pepper sauce
   Crisp crackers or Melba toast

Place cream cheese and bleu cheese in small bowl.
MICROWAVE 1 MINUTE on '5'. Blend in remaining ingredients. Spread mixture on crackers or Melba
toast, using 1 teaspoon per cracker.

Place 10 at a time on paper towel-lined plate. MI-
CROWAVE 1 to 2 MINUTES on '6', or until cheese
begins to bubble.

Butterflied Wieners

ESCARGOT

4 to 6 servings
Ceramic escargot dish or small plate

½ cup butter or margarine
½ teaspoon garlic powder
1 teaspoon parsley flakes
1 tablespoon finely chopped shallots or onion
1 can (4½-ounces) snails with shells

Soften butter slightly in measuring cup or small bowl. Add garlic powder, parsley flakes and shallots and cream well.

Wash and drain snails. Place ¼ teaspoon butter mixture in each shell. Place snails in shells. Pack remaining butter mixture in shells to seal.

Place six at a time in escargot dish or on small plate. MICROWAVE 3 MINUTES on '5', or until butter begins to bubble.

Serve with crusty bread.

NOTE: Make ahead and refrigerate until needed.

HERBED SCALLOPS

6 servings
1-quart casserole

½ pound scallops, washed and drained
¼ cup butter or margarine
¼ teaspoon chopped chives
¼ teaspoon tarragon, crumbled
½ teaspoon chopped parsley
    Dash pepper

Cut scallops in half, if large. Place butter in 1-quart casserole. MICROWAVE 1 to 2 MINUTES on HIGH, or until melted and hot. Stir in scallops and remaining ingredients. Cover. MICROWAVE 3 to 5 MINUTES on '6', or until scallops are tender, stirring after 2 minutes. Be careful not to overcook. Serve on cocktail picks.

GARLIC CHEESE SPREAD

1½ cups
1-quart mixing bowl

1 cup processed cheese spread
1 stick butter or margarine
4 to 6 cloves garlic, pressed or finely chopped
1 package (4-ounces) grated Cheddar cheese

In a 1-quart bowl place cheese spread, butter and garlic. MICROWAVE 3 to 4 MINUTES on HIGH, or until soft. Stir. MICROWAVE 4 MINUTES on '8' until hot and bubbly. Stir in grated Cheddar. Allow to cool. Serve on crackers.

PARTY APPETIZER PIE

2 cups
8-inch pie plate

1 package (8-ounces) cream cheese, softened
2 tablespoons milk
1 jar (2½-ounces) diced dried beef, finely chopped
2 tablespoons instant minced onion
2 tablespoons finely chopped green pepper
⅛ teaspoon pepper
½ cup dairy sour cream
¼ cup coarsely chopped walnuts

Blend cream cheese and milk in 1-quart mixing bowl. Add dried beef, onion, green pepper and pepper. Mix well. Stir in sour cream. Spread evenly in 8-inch pie plate. Cover with waxed paper. MICROWAVE 2 MINUTES, 15 SECONDS on HIGH, or until entire mixture is hot.

Let stand 2 minutes to firm slightly. Sprinkle with walnuts. Serve with assorted crackers.

Variation:
Substitute five slices bacon, cooked crisp and crumbled, for dried beef.

COCKTAIL NIBBLES

8 cups
3 to 4-quart casserole

¾ cup butter or margarine
3 tablespoons Worcestershire sauce
1½ teaspoons onion salt
1¼ teaspoons garlic salt
1 teaspoon celery salt
1 can (6¾-ounces) cocktail peanuts
1 package (9 to 10-ounces) thin pretzel sticks
2 cups bite-size shredded wheat cereal
2 cups bite-size shredded rice cereal
2 cups puffed oat cereal

Combine butter, Worcestershire sauce and salts in 3-quart casserole. MICROWAVE on HIGH until butter is melted. Add remaining ingredients, tossing thoroughly until well coated. MICROWAVE 8 MINUTES on HIGH, tossing every 2 minutes to distribute seasoned butter. Cool and store in air-tight container.

Left to right: Liverwurst Pâté, Cheese Nachos, Seafood Tantalizers, Easy-Does-It Canapés

LIVERWURST PÂTÉ ON TOAST

30 pieces
1-quart bowl
Plate lined with paper towel

3 *ounces liverwurst*
1 *package (3-ounces) cream cheese*
1 *tablespoon dairy sour cream*
¼ *teaspoon salt*
⅛ *teaspoon pepper*
  Melba toast rounds or soda crackers

Place liverwurst and cream cheese in 1-quart bowl. MICROWAVE 1 to 2 MINUTES on '5', or until softened. Mix together with a fork until well combined. Mix in sour cream, salt and pepper.

Mound pate on Melba toast. Place 8 at a time on paper towel-lined plate. MICROWAVE 30 SECONDS to 1 MINUTE on HIGH, or until bubbly. Can be garnished with parsley before heating, if desired.

CHEESE NACHOS

30 pieces
Paper plate

1 *can (3⅛-ounces) jalapeno bean dip*
1 *bag (5½-ounces) Taco chips*
1 *bag (6-ounces) shredded Cheddar cheese*

Spread bean dip lightly on taco chips. Top with cheese. Place 8 to 10 chips at a time on paper plate. MICROWAVE 30 SECONDS on '5', or until cheese begins to melt.

NOTE: Filling for cracker canapés can be made ahead and spread on at time of serving. Crackers will get soft if spread with filling ahead of time.

SEAFOOD TANTALIZERS

16 pieces
Plate lined with paper towel

1 *can (6½-ounces) crab, shrimp or tuna, drained,*
  broken up with a fork
½ *cup finely chopped celery*
2 *teaspoons prepared mustard*
4 *teaspoons chopped sweet pickle*
½ *cup mayonnaise*
  Crisp crackers or Melba toast

In a 1-quart bowl, combine seafood, celery, mustard, pickle and mayonnaise well.

Spread on crackers or Melba toast. Place 10 to 12 at a time on a plate lined with a paper towel.

MICROWAVE 30 SECONDS to 1 MINUTE on HIGH, or until hot.

EASY-DOES-IT CANAPÉS

Plate lined with paper towel

Crispy crackers
Luncheon meat cut in quarters or squares
Triangles of cheese or generous pinches
  grated cheese

Place a piece of meat on each crisp cracker. Top with cheese. Garnish with any of the following: parsley, chives, crumbled bacon bits, sliced olives or pickles.

Place 10 at a time on paper towel-lined plate, MICROWAVE 30 SECONDS to 1 MINUTE on HIGH, or until cheese begins to melt.

NOTE: One piece of sliced luncheon meat makes 4 canapés.

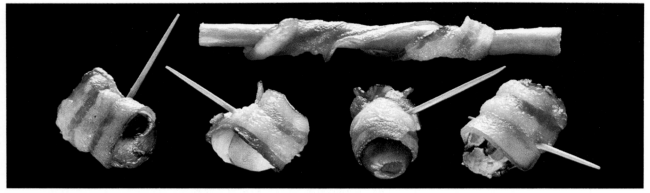

Left to right: Rumaki, Shrimp in Bacon, Olives in Bacon Blankets, Bacon Oysters, Rear: Bacon Wands

RUMAKI

3 dozen
Plate lined with paper towels

1 *can (6-ounces) water chestnuts, drained*
8 *ounces chicken livers, fresh or frozen and*
  defrosted
  Soy sauce
12 *slices bacon, cut in thirds*

Slice drained water chestnuts in thirds. Cut chicken livers in 1-inch pieces. Dip in soy sauce. Place 1 slice water chestnut and 1 piece chicken liver on 1 piece bacon. Roll up and secure with wooden pick. Place 10 at a time on paper towel-lined plate. Cover with paper towel. MICROWAVE 6 to 7 MINUTES on HIGH, or until bacon is crisp.

NOTE: Bacon right from refrigerator is easier to handle.

NOTE: Rumaki and variations can be cooked on a microwave roasting rack, covered loosely with a paper towel.

SHRIMP IN BACON

18 pieces
Plate lined with paper towel

18 *large shrimp, fresh or frozen, defrosted*
 6 *slices bacon, cut in thirds*

Wrap shrimp as in Rumaki. Place on paper towel-lined plate. MICROWAVE 5 to 6 MINUTES on HIGH, or until bacon is crisp and shrimp pink.

OLIVES IN BACON BLANKETS

18 pieces
Plate lined with paper towel

18 *large stuffed olives, drained*
 6 *slices bacon, cut in thirds*

Wrap olives as in Rumaki. Place on paper towel-lined plate. MICROWAVE 5 to 6 MINUTES on HIGH, or until bacon is crisp.

BACON OYSTERS

24 pieces
Plate lined with paper towel

1 *can (8-ounces) oysters, drained*
12 *slices bacon, cut in half*

Wrap oysters as in Rumaki. Place 8 at a time on paper towel-lined plate. MICROWAVE 4 MINUTES on HIGH, or until bacon is crisp.

BACON WANDS

12 pieces
Plate lined with paper towels

12 very thin bread sticks
12 slices bacon

Wrap each bread stick with a bacon slice, in a spiral. Place 6 at a time on paper towel-lined plate. Cover with paper towel. MICROWAVE 6 MINUTES on HIGH, or until bacon is crisp, turning once.

SWEET & SOUR BACON STICKS

Makes 20 breadsticks
Roasting rack and dish

 2 *tablespoons brown sugar*
 1 *teaspoon dried mustard*
10 *slices bacon*
20 *bread sticks*

Mix brown sugar and mustard in a small bowl. Cut bacon slices in half. Sprinkle with sugar mixture. Wrap bacon, with sugar mixture against bread sticks, in a spiral around the sticks. Place on roasting rack 10 at a time. MICROWAVE 3 to 5 MINUTES on HIGH, or until bacon is crisp. Rotate dish once during cooking time. Serve immediately.

MINI MEATBALLS

About 40 pieces
Plate lined with paper towels

1 *pound lean ground beef*
1 *tablespoon instant minced onion*
1 *tablespoon parsley flakes*
1½ *teaspoons salt*
⅛ *teaspoon allspice*
  Pinch of cloves
¼ *teaspoon garlic salt*
½ *cup dry bread crumbs*
1 *egg*
2 *tablespoons milk*

Combine all ingredients in a large mixing bowl. Form into one-inch meatballs. Place 8 to 10 on a paper towel-lined plate. Cover with paper towel to prevent spatters. Meatballs may be refrigerated and cooked just before serving.

To cook: MICROWAVE 3 MINUTES on HIGH. Serve hot with cocktail picks.

NOTE: Meatballs may be frozen on baking sheets, then stored in freezer containers. To cook, arrange meatballs on plate, as above, and MICROWAVE 5 MINUTES on HIGH, or until meatballs are no longer pink, turning over once.

MUSHROOM KABOBS

15 to 20 pieces
Custard cup
Plate lined with paper towel

8 *ounces fresh mushrooms, 1-inch diameter*
2 *tablespoons butter or margarine*
2 *medium green peppers, cut in 1-inch squares*

Remove mushroom stems. (Save for casseroles.) Place butter in custard cup. MICROWAVE on HIGH until butter melts. Dip mushrooms in butter. Place on wooden pick between two pieces of green pepper. Arrange on paper towel-lined plate. MICROWAVE 1 MINUTE, 30 SECONDS to 2 MINUTES on HIGH, or until hot.

NOTE: Remove paper towel, serve on same plate which is already warm.

Variation:
Add cubes of pineapple or water chestnuts.

HAM AND PINEAPPLE KABOBS

24 pieces
2-cup measure
Plate lined with paper towel

¼ *cup honey*
¼ *cup firmly packed brown sugar*
¼ *cup barbecue sauce*
24 *1-inch cubes cooked ham*
1 *can (8-ounces) pineapple chunks, drained*

Combine honey and brown sugar in 2-cup measure. Stir to soften sugar. MICROWAVE 1 MINUTE on HIGH, or until boiling. Add barbecue sauce. MICROWAVE 30 SECONDS on HIGH, or until boiling.

Alternate ham cubes and pinneapple chunks on wooden picks. Dip in sauce. Arrange on paper towel-lined plate. MICROWAVE 1 MINUTE on HIGH, or until hot.

NOTE: Leftover sauce may be used later.

MARINATED CHICKEN WINGS

16 to 20 pieces
2-cup measure
10 × 8-inch utility dish

8 *to 10 chicken wings*
2 *tablespoons firmly packed brown sugar*
2 *tablespoons soy sauce*
1 *tablespoon Worcestershire sauce*
1 *tablespoon white vinegar*
1 *teaspoon sliced crystallized ginger or ½ teaspoon ground ginger*
2 *teaspoons lemon juice*
½ *cup water*

Disjoint chicken wings, discarding tips. Arrange chicken wings in a single layer in (10 x 8-inch) utility dish. Set aside.

Combine sugar, soy sauce, Worcestershire sauce, vinegar, ginger, lemon juice and water in 2-cup measure. MICROWAVE 2 MINUTES on HIGH. Pour hot marinade over chicken wings. Cover. Marinate at least 3 to 4 hours at room temperature, preferably overnight in refrigerator.

10 minutes before serving time, drain marinade. Cover tightly. MICROWAVE 3 to 4 MINUTES on HIGH, or until fork tender. Let stand 3 minutes.

11 Ways
To Stuff A Mushroom

Clockwise from spoon: Mexican, Polynesian, Florentine, Chestnut-Celery, Crab, Bacon, Bleu Cheese. Center: Italian.

BASIC RECIPE

6 to 8 servings
Small bowl
Plate

8 *ounces fresh, uniform size mushrooms, cleaned*
1 *small onion, finely chopped*
2 *tablespoons butter or margarine*
¼ *cup seasoned bread crumbs*

Remove stems from mushrooms. Chop stems finely. Combine butter, chopped stems and onions in small bowl. MICROWAVE 1 to 2 MINUTES on HIGH, or until onions are transparent and mixture is hot, stirring once. Stir in bread crumbs.

Spoon mixture into caps with teaspoon. Place 10 to 12 on plate. Depending on size of mushrooms, MICROWAVE 1 MINUTE 30 SECONDS to 3 MINUTES on '8', or until mushrooms and filling are hot.

Variations:
ITALIAN

½ *pound ground sausage, cooked and drained*
2 *tablespoons catsup*
⅛ *teaspoon oregano*
 Dash garlic powder
2 *tablespoons fresh parsley, torn in small pieces*
 Grated mozzarella cheese

Mix cooked sausage, catsup, oregano and garlic powder in measure or small bowl. MICROWAVE 1 MINUTE on HIGH. Fill caps. Sprinkle parsley on filling. Top with grated cheese. Heat as in Basic Recipe, or until mushrooms are hot and cheese melts.

SHRIMP

1 *can (6-ounces) shrimp*
1 *teaspoon cream*
 Basic filling

Finely chop enough shrimp to make 1 tablespoon. Add chopped shrimp and cream to basic filling with crumbs. Fill caps, top with additional shrimp. Heat as in Basic Recipe.

MEXICAN

¼ *pound crumbled ground beef, cooked and drained*
1 *tablespoon taco sauce*
1 *small tomato, chopped*
 Grated cheese

Combine hamburger and taco sauce. Fill mushroom caps. Spread chopped tomatoes on filling, top with grated cheese. Heat as in Basic Recipe, or until mushrooms are hot and cheese melts.

CHESTNUT-CELERY

½ *teaspoon cream sherry*
 Basic filling
16 *slices celery, ⅛-inch thick*
5 *chestnuts, cut in triangles*

Add sherry to basic filling after heating. Fill caps. Garnish with celery slices and chestnut triangles. Heat as in Basic Recipe.

BLEU CHEESE

¼ *cup crumbled bleu cheese*
 Basic filling

Mix 1 tablespoon cheese into basic filling. Fill caps. Top with remaining cheese. Heat as in Basic Recipe.

CRAB OR LOBSTER

1 *can (6½-ounces) crab or lobster, drained and flaked*
1 *tablespoon mayonnaise*
1 *package (3-ounces) cream cheese, softened*
½ *teaspoon lemon juice*
  Dash prepared mustard

Mix above ingredients well. Fill caps. Garnish with parsley. Heat as in Basic Recipe.

POLYNESIAN

1 *can (8-ounces) pineapple chunks, drained*
1 *can (5-ounces) chicken*
2 *tablespoons mayonnaise*
½ *teaspoon lemon juice*
16 *walnut halves*

Combine pineapple, chicken, mayonnaise and lemon juice. Fill caps. Garnish with walnut halves. Heat as in Basic Recipe.

FLORENTINE

1 *package (3-ounces) cream cheese*
1 *can (8-ounces) spinach, drained and chopped*
2 *slices bacon, cooked and crumbled*

Soften cream cheese. Mix in spinach. Fill mushroom caps. Garnish with small bacon pieces. Heat as in Basic Recipe.

BACON

1 *package (3-ounces) cream cheese*
½ *teaspoon finely chopped onion*
6 *slices bacon, cooked and crumbled*

Soften cream cheese. Cream in onion. Form in balls. Roll balls in crumbled bacon. Fill caps. Heat as in Basic Recipe.

STROGANOFF

¼ *pound crumbled ground beef, cooked and drained*
1 *packet (.18-ounces) single serving instant beef broth, diluted with 1½ teaspoons water*
2 *tablespoons dairy sour cream*

Combine ground beef and beef broth in small bowl. MICROWAVE 1 MINUTE on HIGH. Stir in sour cream. Fill caps. Heat as above.

NOTE: Stuffed mushrooms also make a good vegetable side dish.

LOW-CAL STUFFED MUSHROOMS

6 to 8 servings
Large pie pan

8 *ounces large mushrooms*
3 *medium green onions*
1 *teaspoon sour cream*
½ *teaspoon seasoned garlic salt*

Remove stems from mushrooms and chop finely. Thinly slice green onions including tops. Combine with mushroom stems. MICROWAVE 2 MINUTES on High.

Add sour cream and garlic salt to chopped stems and green onions. Spoon filling into mushroom caps. Place 10 to 12 filled caps on pie pan. MICROWAVE 2 to 3 MINUTES on '8'. Allow to cool slightly before serving.

ITALIAN SHRIMP

6 servings
8-inch cake dish

½ *cup butter or margarine*
12 *ounces frozen, uncooked, peeled and deveined shrimp, defrosted*
  Garlic salt
  Paprika
  Parsley

Place butter in (8-inch) cake dish. MICROWAVE on HIGH, until butter melts.

Add remaining ingredients. Stir to coat shrimp. Cover with plastic wrap. MICROWAVE 3 to 5 MINUTES on HIGH, or until shrimp are pink, stirring once. Serve on cocktail picks.

NOTE: Small shrimp cook faster than large ones. Overcooking will toughen the shrimp.

HAM ROLL-UPS

16 pieces
Plate

4 *slices Danish ham*
16 *strips Swiss cheese, ¼ x ¼ x 1-inch*
  Cranberry-orange relish

Cut each ham slice in 4 pieces. Place 1 strip Swiss cheese and ½ teaspoon cranberry-orange relish on each piece and roll up. Secure with wooden pick. Arrange on plate. MICROWAVE 30 SECONDS to 1 MINUTE on HIGH, or until cheese begins to melt. Serve hot.

Sandwiches

Hot sandwiches are just seconds away by microwave. Most of them cook on a napkin, so there's no clean-up. Be creative. A touch of microwave magic and a new ingredient transform the common sandwich into a taste sensation.

BEEF HOAGIE

4 servings
paper towel

1 loaf French bread split in half
¼ cup mayonnaise or salad dressing
1 tablespoon prepared horseradish
2 tablespoons catsup
¼ pound roast beef, thinly sliced
¼ pound corned beef, thinly sliced
   Assorted sliced sandwich meat
4 slices American cheese, cut in triangles

Mix together salad dressing, horseradish and catsup. Spread on cut sides of bread. Layer meat loosely. Top with cheese triangles. Garnish with tomato and green pepper slices. Place sandwich on paper towel. MICROWAVE 2 MINUTES on '6', or until cheese melts.

SEAFOOD HOAGIE

4 servings
paper towel

1 loaf French bread, split in half
¼ cup mayonnaise or salad dressing
1 teaspoon lemon juice
3 tablespoons softened butter or margarine
2 tablespoons chopped pickles or capers
1 can (6 to 8-ounces) light chunk tuna, drained
1 can crab meat leg sections
1 can (6 to 8-ounces) salmon
2 large dill pickles sliced lengthwise
2 slices Swiss cheese cut in 1-inch strips

Mix salad dressing, lemon juice, softened butter and pickles together. Spread mix over open sides of sliced bread. Arrange seafood over dressing. Top with pickles and cheese. Place sandwich on paper towel. MICROWAVE 2 MINUTES on '6', or until cheese just starts to melt.

SANDWICH BASICS

Sandwiches heat very quickly. Be careful not to overcook. Heat bread until warm, not hot, cheese just begins to melt.

The best sandwiches are made with day-old or toasted bread; breads rich in eggs or shortening; full-bodied breads such as rye or whole wheat.

Several thin slices of meat heat better than one thick slice.

Always heat sandwiches on paper napkins or towels to absorb steam which can make the bread soggy, except when grilling cheese or Reuben sandwiches in the browning dish.

FRENCH RIVIERAS

6 sandwiches
Paper napkin

¼ cup butter or margarine, softened
1 tablespoon prepared mustard
6 large hard rolls, split
6 slices bologna
6 slices cooked ham
6 slices salami
6 slices Swiss cheese, Cheddar or American process cheese

Blend butter with mustard in small bowl. Spread inside rolls. For each sandwich layer 1 slice bologna, 1 slice ham, 1 slice salami and 1 slice cheese on half of roll and cover with other half. Secure top with toothpick and place on paper napkin. MICROWAVE 45 SECONDS on '8', or until cheese melts.

NOTE: Long loaf sandwiches are easy for entertaining. Cut French bread in half lengthwise, layer with your favorite cold cuts and cheese. Garnish with fresh tomatoes and cucumbers. Follow above directions for heating.

All-American Cheeseburger

HAMBURGERS

3 to 4 hamburgers
Microwave roasting rack

1 *pound lean ground beef*
½ *teaspoon Kitchen Bouquet, mixed with 2*
   tablespoons water
   Salt and pepper to taste

Combine all ingredients in medium bowl. Mix well. Form into 3 to 4 patties. Place on roasting rack. MICROWAVE 2 MINUTES, 30 SECONDS to 4 MINUTES on HIGH, or until desired doneness, turning once.

NOTE: Hamburger is medium-rare when juice begins to ooze to surface, medium when surface appears juicy, and well done when no pink remains.

Variations:

Mix one or more of the following with meat before forming patties:
Chopped onion
Chopped olives
Chopped mushrooms
1 teaspoon horseradish
1 tablespoon steak sauce
1 tablespoon chili sauce
Finely diced cheese
Crumbled bleu cheese

NOTE: Above variations may be used for the browning-dish hamburgers.

ALL-AMERICAN CHEESEBURGERS

4 servings
2-cup measure
Paper towel

1 *tablespoon butter or margarine*
1 *medium onion, sliced and separated into rings*
4 *hamburger patties, cooked*
4 *sesame buns, split*
4 *slices American process cheese*

Place butter in 2-cup measure. MICROWAVE on HIGH, until melted. Stir onion rings into hot butter until coated.

Place hamburger patties on bottom half of buns. Top with cheese slices and onion rings. Arrange on paper towel. MICROWAVE 30 SECONDS to 1 MINUTE on HIGH, or until cheese starts to melt. Cover with tops of buns.

GRILLED CHEESE SANDWICH

1 serving
Browning dish

2 *slices American process cheese*
2 *slices bread*
   Butter or margarine

Place cheese slices between bread slices. Spread butter on outsides of sandwich. To preheat browning dish, MICROWAVE 4 MINUTES on HIGH. With oven door open, place sandwich in browning dish for 30 seconds. Turn to brown other side 30 seconds. MICROWAVE 30 SECONDS on HIGH, if necessary, to melt cheese.

HOT DOGS

2 to 4 servings
Paper towel or napkin

4 *wieners*
4 *wiener buns, split*

Place wieners on open buns. Arrange on paper towel. For 1 wiener on bun, MICROWAVE 30 SECONDS on '8'. For 4 wieners on buns, MICROWAVE 1 MINUTE, 30 SECONDS, or until wiener feels warm. Let stand 1 minute.

GROUND BEEF GUMBOS

4 servings
1-quart casserole

½ *pound lean ground beef*
1 *medium onion, chopped*
1 *can (10¾-ounces) condensed chicken gumbo*
   soup, drained of excess liquid
2 *tablespoons catsup*
2 *tablespoons prepared mustard*
½ *teaspoon salt*
4 *English muffins, split and toasted*

Crumble ground beef into 1-quart casserole. Add onion. Cover with paper towel. MICROWAVE 2 MINUTES on HIGH, or until meat is set.
Stir in soup, catsup, mustard and salt. Mix well. MICROWAVE 4 MINUTES on '8', or until bubbly hot. Spoon over muffins.
NOTE: Hamburger buns may be substituted for muffins.

PEANUT BUTTER KIDWICHES

1 serving
Paper napkin

The children's favorite sandwich filling forms the base for hot and bubbly sandwiches they can microwave themselves.

1 *slice toast*
   Peanut butter

Spread toast with peanut butter. Top with one of the following combinations:

Jelly
Marshmallow
Cheese
Bacon bits
Tomato slice
Cheese

Place sandwich on napkin. MICROWAVE 15 SECONDS to 30 SECONDS on HIGH, or until melty.

BARBECUES

4 servings
1-quart casserole

½ *pound lean ground beef*
½ *cup chopped onion*
½ *cup catsup*
2 *tablespoons vinegar*
1 *tablespoon brown sugar*
½ *teaspoon salt*
¼ *teaspoon dry mustard*
4 *split hamburger buns*

Combine ground beef and onion in 1-quart casserole. Cover. MICROWAVE 2 to 3 MINUTES on HIGH. Add catsup, vinegar, brown sugar, salt and mustard. Cover.
MICROWAVE 5 MINUTES on '8', or until bubbly. Serve on hamburger buns.

DENVER SANDWICH

1 serving
1-cup measure
Small plate

1 *egg*
1 *tablespoon chopped green pepper*
2 *tablespoons chopped onion*
3 *tablespoons diced ham*
   Toasted bun

Beat all ingredients together with fork in 1-cup measure. Pour onto small plate. MICROWAVE 45 SECONDS to 1 MINUTE on '8', or until egg is set. Place on toasted bun and serve.

SWISS HAM SANDWICHES

3 to 6 servings
Paper napkins

¼ *cup butter or margarine, softened*
2 *tablespoons finely chopped onion*
1 *teaspoon prepared mustard*
1 *teaspoon poppy seed*
6 *large hard rolls, split*
6 *thin slices cooked ham*
6 *slices Swiss cheese*

Combine butter, onion, mustard and poppy seed in small bowl. Spread seasoned butter inside each roll. Top with 1 slice each ham and cheese. Cover with other half of roll. Place three buns on paper napkins. MICROWAVE 1 MINUTE to 1 MINUTE 30 SECONDS on '8', or until cheese melts.

Hot Meat and Gravy Sandwiches

HOT MEAT AND GRAVY SANDWICHES

4 servings
2-cup measure
Paper towel

4 *slices bread or toast*
8 *slices meat or meat loaf*
1½ *cups gravy, leftover or prepared from mix or
    sauce*

Choose meat and topping from the following
suggestions:

Roast beef
Gravy or canned mushroom sauce

Roast pork
Gravy or barbecue sauce or applesauce

Roast lamb
*Gravy or canned mushroom sauce or curry sauce or
    mint sauce*

Roast chicken or turkey
*Giblet gravy or chicken gravy or canned mushroom
    sauce*

Meat loaf
*Gravy or tomato sauce or cheese sauce or cranberry
    sauce*

Measure leftover gravy or sauces into 2-cup
measure. MICROWAVE 3 to 4 MINUTES on
HIGH, or until hot. Set aside.

If using gravy mix, prepare according to package
directions in 2-cup measure. MICROWAVE 3
MINUTES, 30 SECONDS to 4 MINUTES, 30
SECONDS on HIGH, or until thickened. Set aside.

Line oven shelf with paper towel. Top bread slices
with 2 slices meat each. Arrange sandwiches on
paper towel. MICROWAVE 3 to 4 MINUTES on
HIGH, or until meat is hot.

Place sandwiches on plates. Pour hot sauce or gravy
over meat. Serve immediately.

TURKEY DIVAN SANDWICHES

4 to 6 servings
1-quart mixing bowl

1½ *cups chopped, cooked turkey*
  1 *jar (8-ounces) American process cheese spread*
  1 *package (10-ounces) frozen broccoli spears,
     cooked and drained, (page 192)*
  4 *English muffins, split, toasted and buttered*

Blend turkey and cheese spread in 1-quart bowl until
smooth. MICROWAVE 3 to 5 MINUTES on '6', or
until hot.

Place cooked broccoli spears on English muffins.
Top with hot turkey sauce. If necessary,
MICROWAVE 30 SECONDS on HIGH to reheat.

FISHBURGER

1 serving
Paper towel

1 *frozen fish patty*
1 *tablespoon mayonnaise*
1 *sweet pickle, sliced*
1 *hamburger bun, split*

Place frozen fish patty on paper towel. Top with
mayonnaise and sliced pickle. MICROWAVE 1
MINUTE, 30 SECONDS on HIGH, or until hot.

Serve on bun. Garnish with tartar or chili sauce.

CHEESE 'N TUNA BUNS

8 to 12 servings
Paper napkins

1 *can (6½-ounces) tuna, drained and flaked*
1 *cup grated sharp cheddar cheese*
½ *cup mayonnaise*
3 *hard cooked eggs, finely chopped*
¼ *cup finely chopped onion*
¼ *cup finely chopped stuffed green olives*
¼ *cup sweet pickle relish*
8 *hamburger buns, split*

Combine tuna, cheese, mayonnaise, eggs, onion, olives and relish in medium bowl. Mix well. Spoon mixture into buns. Wrap each bun in paper napkin. Place 2 at a time in oven. MICROWAVE 1 to 2 MINUTES on '8', or until cheese has softened into mixture.

NOTE: Tuna mixture can be made ahead and refrigerated. Allow extra time for cooking from refrigerated temperature.

OPEN-FACE BEANS AND WIENER SANDWICHES

4 servings
Paper towel

1 *can (12-ounces) baked beans*
4 *slices bread, toasted*
4 *wieners, split in half lengthwise*
½ *cup catsup*
¼ *cup chopped onion*

Spread ¼ cup beans on each toast slice. Arrange on paper towel. Cover with paper towel to prevent spatters. MICROWAVE 4 MINUTES on '6', or until beans are hot.

Place wieners on beans. Top with catsup and onion. MICROWAVE 2 to 3 MINUTES on '6', or until wiener is hot and sauce is bubbly.

SOUTH-OF-THE-BORDER-BUNS

8 sandwiches
2-quart casserole

1 *pound lean ground beef*
1 *medium onion, chopped*
1 *small green pepper, chopped*
1 *clove garlic, pressed or finely chopped*
1 *can (8-ounces) tomato sauce*
1 *teaspoon Worcestershire sauce*
½ *teaspoon salt*
¼ *teaspoon chili powder*
  Dash hot pepper sauce
8 *hamburger buns, split*
  Tomato slices
  Shredded lettuce
  Grated cheddar cheese

Crumble ground beef into 2-quart casserole. Add onion, pepper and garlic. MICROWAVE 4 to 5 MINUTES on HIGH, or until beef loses its pink color.

Stir in tomato sauce, Worcestershire sauce, salt, chili powder and pepper sauce. Cover. MICROWAVE 5 to 6 MINUTES on HIGH, or until sauce is thickened and very hot. Serve in hamburger buns. Garnish with tomato slices, shredded lettuce and grated cheese.

CONEY ISLANDS

10 to 12 servings
1-quart casserole
Paper towel

1 *can (15-ounces) chili without beans*
1 *package (1-pound) wieners*
6 *wiener buns, split*
½ *cup chopped·onion*
  Grated cheddar cheese

Place chili in 1-quart casserole. MICROWAVE 2 MINUTES on HIGH, or until hot and bubbly, stirring once. Set aside.

Place wieners on open buns. Arrange on paper towel. MICROWAVE 2 to 3 MINUTES on '8', or until wiener feels warm.

Spoon chili over wieners. Sprinkle with raw onion. Top with grated cheddar cheese. MICROWAVE 10 SECONDS on HIGH, or until cheese begins to melt.

Magic Meltwiches

A microwave show-off, Magic Meltwiches are easy to assemble, quick to heat and delicious to eat. They team up two appliances, the toaster and the microwave oven. Make them for lunch, a snack or a party, to serve one person or fifty. Follow the suggestions below, or invent your own combinations.

Ingredients are listed in order used. Start with a piece of toast, add meat or fish, a vegetable or fruit garnish, sauces or cheese. MICROWAVE 15 to 30 SECONDS. Watch through the oven door for melting or bubbling since timing varies with the amount and type of filling used. Sandwiches topped with cheese heat rapidly.

Magic Meltwiches are a great idea for an informal party, easy on the hostess and entertaining for the guests. Arrange a buffet on a counter near your microwave oven. Start with a selection of toasted breads: white, dark and light rye, whole wheat, and English muffins. Add assorted sliced meats, cheese, and seafood.

Bowls of sandwich filling: crab and cream cheese or tuna salad
Garnishes: onion and green pepper rings, fresh tomato slices, sliced or chopped canned mushrooms, avocado wedges, orange segments, sliced ripe or stuffed green olives, chopped pickle. Condiments: tomato sauce, catsup, mustard, mayonnaise.

Let each guest assemble a sandwich on a paper napkin and heat it in the microwave oven. For a complete supper, add cole slaw, potato salad, or a tossed green salad.
NOTE: Breads may be toasted in advance, cooled and covered tightly with plastic wrap.

15-SECOND PIZZA

Half toasted English muffin
Pepperoni slices
Canned pizza sauce
Grated mozzarella cheese
Oregano leaves
Chopped onions
Garnish with ripe olives or chopped mushrooms, if
desired

15-Second Pizza, Instant Cheeseburger, Roast Beef Special, Wide Open Reuben

INSTANT CHEESEBURGER

Toasted whole wheat bread
Pre-cooked ground beef
Salt and pepper
Onion rings
Sliced American process cheese

ROAST BEEF SPECIAL

Toasted pumpernickel bread
Lettuce
Thinly sliced roast beef
Sliced Swiss process cheese
Green pepper ring

WIDE-OPEN REUBEN

Toasted pumpernickel bread
Shaved corned beef
Sauerkraut
Mustard
Swiss cheese triangles

SOUTH-OF-THE-BORDER

Toasted corn bread
Avocado slices
Thin tomato slices
Taco sauce
Crumbled cooked bacon
Chopped ripe olives
Grated Monterey Jack cheese

ORIENTAL BEEF OR PORK

Toasted white bread
Pinch of dry mustard
Thin slices of rare roast beef or roast pork
Marmalade mixed with softened cream cheese

HOT LOX AND BAGEL

Half toasted bagel
Cream cheese
Thinly sliced smoked salmon
Onion rings
Garnish with chopped or sliced ripe olives

BOLOGNESE

Toasted French or Italian bread
Sliced chicken or turkey
Thin slice ham or turkey
Sliced mozzarella cheese

HANS CHRISTIAN ANDERSEN

Toasted white bread
Liver pate
2 slices crisp cooked bacon
Thin tomato slices
Sprinkle with fresh parsley after heating

REUBEN SANDWICH

1 serving
Browning dish

1 *tablespoon mayonnaise or salad dressing*
1 *teaspoon prepared mustard*
2 *slices pumpernickel or other dark bread*
3 *to 4 thin slices corned beef*
2 *teaspoons drained sauerkraut*
1 *slice Swiss cheese*
 Butter or margarine

Mix mayonnaise and mustard together. Spread on bread slices. Layer corned beef, sauerkraut and Swiss Cheese between bread slices. Butter both sides of sandwich.

Place browning dish in oven. MICROWAVE 4 MINUTES on HIGH.

Add sandwich. MICROWAVE 2 MINUTES on HIGH, or until cheese starts to melt, turning sandwich over after 1 minute.

BARBECUED CRAB SANDWICHES

6 servings
1-quart casserole

 3 *tablespoons butter or margarine*
½ *cup finely chopped celery*
¼ *cup finely chopped onion*
 1 *teaspoon instant chicken bouillon*
½ *cup tomato sauce*
 2 *teaspoons Worcestershire sauce*
 2 *teaspoons soy sauce*
 2 *whole cloves*
 2 *bay leaves*
¼ *teaspoon salt*
⅛ *teaspoon pepper*
 1 *can (6½-ounces) crab meat, broken up with fork*
 1 *teaspoon parsley flakes*
 6 *large rolls, split and buttered*

Combine butter, celery and onion, in 1-quart casserole. MICROWAVE 3 MINUTES on HIGH, or until onion is transparent.

Add instant bouillon, tomato sauce, Worcestershire sauce, soy sauce, cloves, bay leaves, salt and pepper. Mix well. MICROWAVE 2 MINUTES on HIGH, or until bubbly. Remove bay leaves and cloves.

Stir in crab meat and parsley. MICROWAVE 2 MINUTES on '6' to heat crab meat. Spoon hot mixture on warm biscuits. Garnish with stuffed olives.

Soups & Beverages

Versatile soups can be a quick pick-me-up or a hearty meal. Microwave a mug full of water for an instant cup of soup. Canned soups can be heated right in the bowl to eliminate clean-up. Prepare dehydrated soups in a 4-cup measure for easy pouring.

Made-from-scratch soups take more time, but with heat control, soup meat cooks tender and flavors blend in less time than it takes conventionally. If you have favorite "short-cut" recipes for old favorites, such as chowder, French onion, or borscht, try them in the microwave oven. The time will be cut shorter than ever.

Microwave works wonders with 2 to 3 quarts of soup. For more than that, cook soup conventionally and microwave the rest of the meal.

BOUILLABAISSE

5-quart casserole
12 servings

      3 *cans (10¾ ounces each) chicken broth*
      1 *soup can water*
      2 *onions, diced in ½ to ¾-inch pieces*
      1 *cup chopped celery*
    15 *to 16 clams, in shell*
      2 *pounds red snapper, cut in 1 to 1½-inch chunks*
      2 *dozen large shrimp, in shell*
      7 *to 8 king crab legs*
    1½ *cups white wine*
      2 *tablespoons chopped fresh parsley*
      2 *teaspoons seasoned salt*
    1½ *teaspoons basil*
      1 *teaspoon thyme*
      3 *bay leaves*
      3 *fresh tomatoes, peeled and quartered*
      8 *ounces fresh mushrooms, sliced*

In 5-quart casserole place broth, water, onions and celery; MICROWAVE 3 MINUTES on HIGH.

Add clams, fish, shrimp, crab, wine, parsley, seasoned salt, basil, thyme and bay leaves. Mix well. Cover. MICROWAVE 12 to 15 MINUTES on HIGH, or until mixture boils. MICROWAVE 25 to 35 MINUTES on '6', or until all seafood is cooked. Stir once or twice during cooking time.

Add tomatoes and mushrooms. MICROWAVE 5 to 10 MINUTES on '6', or until mushrooms and tomatoes are tender.

SPLIT PEA SOUP

8 to 10 servings
4-quart mixing bowl

2 *quarts boiling water*
1 *pound split dried peas*
  Ham bone
1 *small onion, sliced*
5 *peppercorns*
1 *cup diced cooked ham*
½ *cup diced potato*
⅓ *cup sliced carrot*
  Salt and pepper to taste

Combine water, peas, ham bone, onion and peppercorns in 4-quart mixing bowl. Cover tightly. MICROWAVE 25 MINUTES on HIGH, or until peas are tender, stirring after 15 minutes.

Remove ham bone. Cut away any meat and add to soup. Add diced ham, potatoes and carrots. Cover. MICROWAVE 15 to 20 MINUTES on HIGH, or until vegetables are tender-crisp. Taste for seasoning and correct.

CREAMY TOMATO SOUP

4 to 6 servings
2-quart casserole

¼ *cup butter or margarine*
1 *tablespoon finely chopped onion*
3 *tablespoons flour*
2 *tablespoons sugar*
1 *teaspoon salt*
  Pepper to taste
1 *can (16 to 18-ounces) tomato juice*
2 *cups milk*

Combine butter and onion in 2-quart casserole. MICROWAVE 2 MINUTES on HIGH, or until butter is melted. Blend in flour, sugar, salt and pepper. Gradually stir in tomato juice. MICROWAVE 4 MINUTES on HIGH, or until hot, stirring after 2 minutes.

Gradually stir in milk. MICROWAVE 8 to 10 MINUTES on '8', or until mixture is about to boil, stirring every 2 minutes. Serve hot garnished with croutons or oyster crackers, if desired.

CHEESE SOUP CANADIENNE

5 to 6 servings
2-quart casserole

1 *cup hot tap water*
1 *cup finely chopped onion*
1 *cup finely chopped potatoes*
¼ *cup finely chopped carrots*
¼ *cup finely chopped celery*
1 *can (10¾-ounces) chicken broth, diluted with ¾*
  cup water or 2 tablespoons instant bouillon
  dissolved in 2 cups water
1 *cup grated sharp Cheddar cheese*
½ *cup whipping cream*
3 *peppercorns*
2 *tablespoons snipped fresh parsley*

Combine water and vegetables in 2-quart casserole. Cover. MICROWAVE 7 to 8 MINUTES on HIGH, or until vegetables are tender-crisp.

Stir in broth, cheese, cream and peppercorns. Cover. MICROWAVE 5 MINUTES on '8', or until hot. Remove peppercorns and stir. Garnish with parsley.

CHILI CON QUESO SOUP

4 to 6 servings
1½-quart bowl or casserole

3 *tablespoons butter or margarine*
1 *cup finely chopped onion*
1 *can (14½-ounces) stewed tomatoes*
1 *can (4-ounces) chopped green chilies, rinsed*
  of seeds
1 *jar (2-ounces) chopped pimiento*
1 *teaspoon salt*
½ *teaspoon pepper*
½ *pound Monterey Jack or Cheddar cheese,*
  finely diced
  Beer

Combine butter and onion in 1½-quart bowl, MICROWAVE 3 MINUTES on HIGH, or until onion is transparent.

Stir in tomatoes, chilies, pimiento, salt and pepper. MICROWAVE 3 MINUTES on HIGH, or until very hot. Gradually add cheese, stirring after each addition until melted. After last addition, MICROWAVE 1 MINUTE on '5', if necessary to complete melting. If soup is too thick, thin with beer to desired consistency.

QUICKIE CORN CHOWDER

4 to 6 servings
3-quart casserole

1 tablespoon butter or margarine
1 small onion, finely chopped
1 can (10¾-ounces) condensed cream of
    mushroom soup, undiluted
4 cups milk
1 can (16-ounces) whole kernel corn, drained
½ teaspoon salt
    Pepper

Combine butter and onion in 3-quart casserole.
MICROWAVE on HIGH until onion is transparent.

Add soup, milk, corn, salt and pepper. Stir until
well blended. MICROWAVE 7 to 8 MINUTES on
HIGH, or until hot.

CHICKEN SOUP WITH LITLE DUMPLINGS

4 servings
2-quart casserole

3½ cups chicken stock or 2 cans (10¾-ounces each)
    chicken broth
1 small onion, quartered
1 stem celery, cut in 4 pieces
¼ teaspoon thyme
1½ teaspoons dried parsley flakes
½ teaspoon salt
1 egg
¼ cup all-purpose flour
⅛ teaspoon salt

Combine chicken broth, onions, celery, thyme, parsley and salt in 2-quart casserole. Cover. MICRO-
WAVE 8 to 10 MINUTES on HIGH, or until mixture
begins to boil.

Reduce setting. MICROWAVE 5 MINUTES on '6',
or until celery and onion are soft. Remove vegetables
with slotted spoon, discard.

While soup is cooking, combine egg, flour and salt in
1-quart mixing bowl. Beat until batter is smooth.

After removing vegetables, drop batter into soup by
rounded half-teaspoonfuls. Do not cover. MICRO-
WAVE 2 MINUTES, 25 SECONDS to 3 MIN-
UTES, 35 SECONDS on '5'.

Variation:
For a hearty soup, add 1 can (6-ounces) boned chick-
en and broth to stock ingredients before first cooking
period.

FRENCH ONION SOUP

6 to 8 servings
3-quart bowl or casserole

2 tablespoons butter or margarine
3 medium onions, thinly sliced
3 cans (10½-ounces) condensed beef broth, diluted
    with 2⅓ cups water, or 2 tablespoons instant beef
    bouillon dissolved in 6 cups water
    Salt to taste
    French bread slices, toasted
    Grated Parmesan cheese

Combine butter and onions in 3-quart bowl or casserole. Cover. MICROWAVE 8 MINUTES on HIGH,
or until onions are transparent, stirring once.

Stir in broth. Cover. MICROWAVE 8 to 10 MIN-
UTES on HIGH, or until onions are tender and soup
is hot. Salt to taste.

Top each serving with slice of toasted French bread.
Sprinkle generously with Parmesan cheese.

SPICED MEATBALL SOUP

6 to 8 servings
12 x 8-inch utility dish
2-quart casserole

1 pound lean ground beef
1 egg, slightly beaten
1 teaspoon basil
1 teaspoon salt
    Dash pepper
1 medium onion, finely chopped
1 clove garlic, pressed or minced
3 teaspoons instant beef bouillon dissolved in
    3 cups hot water
1 can (6-ounces) tomato paste
1 teaspoon ground cumin

Mix together ground beef, egg, basil, salt and pepper
in medium mixing bowl. Drop by rounded teaspoonfuls into (12 x 8-inch) utility dish. MICROWAVE 3
to 4 MINUTES on HIGH, or until meat is set. Drain
fat, set meatballs aside.

Combine onions, garlic, beef broth, tomato paste
and cumin in 2-quart casserole. Mix well. MICRO-
WAVE 6 MINUTES on HIGH, or until mixture
begins to boil.

Reduce setting. Cover. MICROWAVE 6 MIN-
UTES on '6'. Add meatballs to simmering stock,
cover. MICROWAVE 2 to 3 MINUTES on '6', or
until meatballs are heated through.

SEAFOOD GUMBO

6 to 8 servings
3-quart casserole

2 *tablespoons butter or margarine*
⅔ *cup chopped green onions and tops*
½ *cup chopped celery*
2 *cloves garlic, pressed or finely chopped*
1 *package (10 ounces) frozen okra, defrosted*
   and sliced
1½ *teaspoons salt*
½ *teaspoon pepper*
¼ *teaspoon sugar*
¼ *teaspoon crushed thyme*
1 *whole bay leaf*
6 *drops liquid hot pepper sauce*
1 *pound raw, cleaned shrimp, fresh or frozen*
½ *pound crab meat, fresh, frozen or canned*
2 *cans (1 pound each) stewed tomatoes*

Thaw frozen seafood.

In 3-quart casserole, combine butter, onions, celery, garlic, okra and seasonings. Cover. MICROWAVE 2 to 4 MINUTES on HIGH, or until celery is tender, stir once or twice.

Add shrimp, crab meat and tomatoes. Cover. MICROWAVE 8 to 12 MINUTES on HIGH, or until shrimp is cooked. Stir once or twice during cooking time. Let stand 5 minutes before serving. Remove bay leaf. Serve with rice, if desired.

SURFSIDE SOUP

6 servings
3-quart casserole

½ *cup chopped celery*
½ *cup chopped onion*
2 *tablespoons butter or margarine*
1 *can (24-ounce) V-8 juice*
1 *package (9-ounce) frozen green beans*
1 *tablespoon lemon juice*
⅛ *teaspoon dill seed*
1 *pound fresh white fish fillets, cut in 2-inch pieces*
½ *cup white wine*

In a 3-quart casserole, MICROWAVE celery and onion in butter on HIGH for 2 to 3 MINUTES or until onions are transparent. Add remaining ingredients except fish and wine. Cover and MICROWAVE on HIGH for 8 MINUTES. Stir to separate beans. MICROWAVE on '6' for 5 MINUTES. Add fish and wine. Cover and MICROWAVE on '6' for 5 to 7 MINUTES or until fish is done.

NEW ENGLAND CLAM CHOWDER

6 servings
2-quart casserole

3 *slices bacon, chopped*
3 *cans (6½-ounces each) minced clams*
2 *cups peeled and diced potatoes*
1 *medium onion, chopped*
¼ *cup flour*
2 *cups milk*
¾ *cup light cream*
1 *teaspoon salt*
⅛ *teaspoon pepper*

Place chopped bacon in 2-quart casserole. MICROWAVE 2 MINUTES on HIGH. Drain clam liquid into bacon and drippings. Set clams aside.

Stir in potatoes and onion. Cover. MICROWAVE 8 MINUTES on HIGH, or until vegetables are tender.

Blend in flour until smooth. Stir in milk. Cover. MICROWAVE 3 MINUTES on '8'.

Stir in clams, cream, salt and pepper. Do not cover. MICROWAVE 3 MINUTES on '8', or until piping hot.

MANHATTAN CLAM CHOWDER

8 servings
3-quart casserole

3 *slices bacon, chopped*
3 *cans (6½-ounces each) minced clams*
1 *can (1¾ pounds) tomatoes*
1 *cup sliced onions*
1 *cup diced carrots*
1 *cup diced celery*
3½ *cups peeled and diced potatoes*
1 *tablespoon snipped parsley*
2 *teaspoons salt*
1½ *teaspoons thyme*

Place chopped bacon in 3-quart casserole. MICROWAVE 2 MINUTES on HIGH. Drain clam liquid into bacon and drippings. Set clams aside.

Stir in tomatoes, onions, carrots, celery, potatoes, parsley, salt and thyme. Cover. MICROWAVE 10 to 12 MINUTES on HIGH, or until vegetables are tender.

Stir in clams. MICROWAVE 2 MINUTES on HIGH, or until hot.

BORSCHT

4 to 6 servings
3-quart casserole

½ pound beef stew meat, cut in ½-inch cubes
1 onion, thinly sliced
1 clove garlic, pressed or finely chopped
7 cups water
1 bay leaf
1 teaspoon dried thyme
½ teaspoon pepper
2 cups finely shredded cabbage
1 carrot, thinly sliced
1 turnip, thinly sliced
2 medium tomatoes, peeled and chopped
1 tablespoon salt
2 large beets, cooked, peeled, cut in julienne strips
1 carton (8-ounces) dairy sour cream

Combine meat, onion, garlic, water, bay leaf, thyme and pepper in 3-quart casserole. Cover. MICRO-WAVE 10 MINUTES on HIGH.

Reduce setting. MICROWAVE 30 MINUTES on '6'.

Stir in cabbage, carrot, turnip, tomatoes and salt. Cover. MICROWAVE 10 MINUTES on '6'.

Add beets. Cover. MICROWAVE 5 MINUTES on '6', or until beets are heated through and vegetables tender-crisp. Let stand 5 minutes, covered.

Remove bay leaf before serving. Top each serving with sour cream.

NOTE: Beets lose their color if allowed to stand in soup. To make ahead, remove soup from oven before adding beets. Cool and refrigerate. Before serving, reheat, add beets and finish cooking.

Borscht

ZIPPY MADRILENE

2 servings
1-quart measure

1 can (13-ounces) consomme madrilene
1 dash hot pepper sauce
2 tablespoons sherry

Combine consomme and pepper sauce in 1-quart measure. MICROWAVE 3 to 4 MINUTES on HIGH, or until just beginning to bubble. Stir in sherry and serve immediately. Garnish with lemon slices, if desired.

INSTANT VICHYSSOISE

4 servings
2-quart batter bowl

4 servings prepared instant mashed potatoes
1 teaspoon instant chicken bouillon
1 cup hot water
1 cup light cream or milk
1½ teaspoons Worcestershire sauce
1 teaspoon onion powder
⅛ teaspoon white pepper
½ to 1 teaspoon chopped chives

Prepare potatoes according to package directions using 2-quart batter bowl. Add instant bouillon to hot water and blend with cream, Worcestershire sauce, onion powder and pepper. Blend into instant mashed potatoes with wire whip to make a smooth soup. MICROWAVE 4 to 5 MINUTES on HIGH, or until bubbly, stirring once. Garnish with chives. Serve hot or cold.

OYSTER STEW

6 servings
2-quart casserole

1 *quart light cream*
1 *pint fresh oysters, drained, reserve liquor*
½ *teaspoon onion salt*
½ *teaspoon Worcestershire sauce*
⅛ *teaspoon pepper*
6 *tablespoons butter or margarine*

Combine light cream and reserved oyster liquid in 2-quart casserole. Cover. MICROWAVE 10 to 12 MINUTES on '8', or until mixture is almost boiling.

Add oysters, salt, Worcestershire sauce and pepper. Do not cover.

MICROWAVE 2 MINUTES on '8', or until oysters swell and edges begin to curl.

Place 1 tablespoon butter in each soup bowl. Ladle stew into bowls. Serve at once.

HEARTY SAUSAGE SOUP

4 to 8 servings
4-quart casserole

1 *medium onion, chopped*
4 *cups hot water*
3 *medium carrots, thinly sliced*
2 *medium stalks celery (with leaves), thinly sliced*
2 *teaspoons salt*
½ *teaspoon dried basil leaves*
½ *teaspoon dried chervil leaves*
½ *teaspoon dried thyme leaves*
¼ *teaspoon cracked pepper*
2 *medium zucchini, cut lengthwise in half, then into ¼-inch slices*
1 *pint cherry tomatoes, cut in half*
1 *Polish sausage, cut into ¼-inch slices*
1 *can (15-ounces) white beans*

In a 4-quart casserole combine water, onion, carrots, celery, and seasonings. Stir. Cover. MICROWAVE 8 to 10 MINUTES on HIGH, or until mixture boils.

Reduce setting. MICROWAVE 6 MINUTES on '6'. Stir in zucchini, tomatoes, sausage, and beans. Cover. MICROWAVE 12 MINUTES on '6'.

CREAMY CHICKEN 'N HAM SOUP

4 servings
3-quart casserole

1 *can (10½-ounces) condensed cream of celery soup, undiluted*
1 *can (10½-ounces) condensed chicken vegetable soup, undiluted*
1½ *soup cans milk or water*
1 *cup chopped cooked ham*
2 *teaspoons parsley flakes*
¼ *teaspoon crushed rosemary*
 Salt and pepper to taste

Combine all ingredients in 3-quart casserole. Stir until well blended. Cover. MICROWAVE 7 to 8 MINUTES on HIGH, or until hot.

CREAM OF TURKEY SOUP

6 servings
3-quart casserole

3 *cups turkey stock*
1 *cup finely chopped potatoes*
2 *teaspoons finely chopped onion*
1 *can (10¾-ounces) condensed cream of celery soup, undiluted*
½ *cup diced, cooked turkey*
6 *slices bacon, cooked crisp and crumbled*
2 *tablespoons snipped parsley*
½ *teaspoon salt*
 Pepper

Combine turkey stock, potatoes and onion in 3-quart casserole. Cover. MICROWAVE 14 MINUTES on HIGH, or until potatoes are tender.

Add remaining ingredients. Mix well. MICROWAVE 6 MINUTES on HIGH, or until hot.

TOMATO SOUP EXCEPTIONAL

2 to 4 servings
3-quart casserole

2 *tablespoons butter or margarine*
2 *tablespoons chopped green onions, including tops*
1 *can (10¾-ounces) condensed tomato soup, undiluted*
1 *soup can milk or water*
¼ *teaspoon Worcestershire sauce*

Combine butter and onion in 3-quart casserole. MICROWAVE on HIGH until onion is transparent.

Add soup, milk and Worcestershire sauce. Stir until well blended. Cover. MICROWAVE 7 to 8 MINUTES on HIGH, or until hot.

VEGETABLE SOUP ❄

8 to 10 servings
4-quart casserole

1 *pound extra lean ground beef*
1 *medium onion, finely chopped*
1 *cup sliced celery*
1 *cup thinly sliced carrots*
1 *cup diced potatoes*
1 *bay leaf*
½ *teaspoon basil*
2 *teaspoons salt*
1 *cup shredded cabbage*
1 *can (16-ounces) tomatoes, including liquid*
3 *cups hot water*

Crumble ground beef into 4-quart casserole. MICROWAVE 4 MINUTES on HIGH, or until set. Drain fat.

Add onion, celery, carrots, potatoes, bay leaf, basil, salt, cabbage, tomatoes and water. Mix thoroughly. Cover. MICROWAVE 10 MINUTES on HIGH. Stir.

Reduce setting. MICROWAVE 20 to 30 MINUTES on '8', or until vegetables are tender crisp. Let stand 5 to 10 minutes.

TURKEY SOUP

8 servings
4-quart casserole

1 *turkey carcass*
3 *quarts hot water*
1 *large onion, finely chopped*
½ *cup finely chopped celery*
1 *teaspoon salt*
½ *teaspoon pepper*
2 *cups chopped carrots*
1 *cup uncooked rice*

Combine turkey water, onion, celery, salt and pepper. Cover. MICROWAVE 30 to 40 MINUTES on HIGH. Remove turkey carcass. De-bone turkey, discard carcass and return turkey meat to soup.

Add carrots. MICROWAVE 10 MINUTES on HIGH.

Add rice. MICROWAVE 10 MINUTES on HIGH. Let stand 10 minutes, covered.

CREAM OF PUMPKIN SOUP

4 to 6 servings
3-quart casserole

2 *tablespoons butter or margarine*
1 *large onion, finely chopped or pureéd*
1½ *teaspoons flour*
1 *can (10½-ounces) undiluted chicken broth*
1 *can (16-ounces) packed pumpkin*
2 *cups milk*
1 *cup light cream*
1 *teaspoon salt*
¼ *teaspoon ginger*
⅛ *teaspoon pepper*
⅛ *teaspoon cinnamon*

In 3-quart casserole, combine butter and onion. MICROWAVE 3 to 4 MINUTES on HIGH. Add flour, stir until blended. Add chicken broth, stir until smooth. MICROWAVE 4 to 5 MINUTES on HIGH and 10 MINUTES on '6'. Blend in remaining ingredients. Stir until smooth. MICROWAVE 3 MINUTES on '8' and 8 to 10 MINUTES on '6', or until hot. Stir once or twice during cooking time.

MINESTRONE SOUP

6 servings
3-quart casserole dish

2½ *cups hot water*
1 *pound stew meat cut in ½-inch squares*
1 *small onion*
¼ *teaspoon cracked pepper*
1 *teaspoon basil*
½ *cup thinly sliced carrots*
1 *can (16-ounces) Italian tomatoes*
½ *cup uncooked spaghetti broken into 1-inch pieces*
2 *cups zucchini sliced in ¼-inch pieces*
1 *can (16-ounces) kidney beans drained*
1 *cup shredded cabbage*
1 *teaspoon salt*

Combine all ingredients in a 3-quart casserole dish. Cover. MICROWAVE 10 MINUTES on HIGH. Stir, cover. MICROWAVE 40 MINUTES on '6'.

Parisian Mocha, Left; Hot Mulled Wine, Right

PARISIAN MOCHA

2 servings
1-quart measure

2 *cups water*
3 *packages (1-ounce each) instant cocoa mix*
2 *tablespoons instant coffee*
½ *teaspoon cinnamon*
  Whipped cream
  Shaved chocolate curls
2 *cinnamon sticks*

Measure water into 1-quart measure. MICRO-WAVE 4 to 5 MINUTES on HIGH, or until almost boiling.

Combine cocoa mix, instant coffee and cinnamon. Add to water. Stir. Pour into cups. Garnish with whipped cream and chocolate curls.

Add cinnamon sticks. Serve immediately.

COFFEE HOUSE VARIETIES

Experiment with your own coffee house varieties.

Suggestions:

CAFÉ AU LAIT
Equal parts coffee and milk

ESPRESSO ROYALE
1 *teaspoon cognac*
  Sugar cube to each cup

HOT MULLED WINE

2 servings
1-quart measure

2 *cups red wine*
4 *whole cloves*
2 *sticks cinnamon*
1 *teaspoon lemon juice*
1 *slice lemon, halved and studded with 8*
  whole cloves

Combine wine, cloves, cinnamon sticks and lemon juice in 1-quart measure. MICROWAVE 3 to 4 MINUTES on HIGH, or until steaming hot. Pour into mugs. Garnish with lemon slice studded with cloves.

HOT TODDY

1 serving
Mug

1 *tablespoon sugar*
¾ *cup water*
¼ *teaspoon lemon juice*
1 *jigger (1½-ounces) light rum*
1 *teaspoon butter*
  Nutmeg

Dissolve sugar in water and lemon juice in coffee mug or cup. MICROWAVE 1 to 2 MINUTES on HIGH, or until piping hot. Add rum. Float butter on top. Sprinkle with nutmeg.

HOT CHOCOLATE

4 to 6 servings
2-quart bowl or pitcher

1 *cup water*
2 *ounces unsweetened chocolate*
¼ *cup sugar*
¼ *teaspoon salt*
3 *cups milk*

Measure water into 2-quart bowl. Add chocolate. MICROWAVE 5 MINUTES on HIGH, or until chocolate melts. Blend well.

Mix in sugar and salt. Gradually stir in milk. MICROWAVE 4 to 6 MINUTES on HIGH, or until mixture begins to boil. Beat with rotary beater until frothy.

ELEGANT EGG NOG

8 to 12 servings
2-quart batter bowl or casserole

4 *eggs, separated*
3 *tablespoons sugar*
½ *cup sugar*
¼ *teaspoon salt*
3 *cups milk*
1 *teaspoon rum or vanilla extract*

Beat egg whites until foamy in 1-quart bowl. Beat in 3 tablespoons sugar, 1 tablespoon at a time. Continue beating until stiff and glossy. Set aside.

Combine egg yolks, ½ cup sugar and salt in a 2-quart bowl. Beat until thick and lemon-colored. Stir in milk and rum or vanilla. MICROWAVE 4 MINUTES on HIGH, or until mixture is hot but not boiling.

Carefully fold egg whites into milk mixture until well blended. Fill serving cups ½ to ¾ full. Top with grated chocolate or nutmeg.

NOTE: To serve cold, cool to room temperature and then refrigerate. Egg nog cannot be reheated, as egg white will cook.

QUICK COCOA

1 serving
Mug

1 *tablespoon cocoa*
1 *tablespoon sugar*
   Milk

Combine cocoa and sugar in mug. Add enough milk to make a thin paste. Mix until smooth. Add milk to fill cup. MICROWAVE 1 MINUTE, 20 SECONDS on HIGH, or until steaming.

SPICED CIDER

6 to 8 servings
2-cup measure
1½-quart bowl or pitcher

1 *cup water*
¼ *cup firmly packed brown sugar*
2 *sticks cinnamon*
1 *teaspoon whole cloves*
½ *teaspoon mace*
¼ *teaspoon nutmeg*
1 *quart cider*

Combine water, sugar and spices in 2-cup measure. MICROWAVE 10 to 12 MINUTES on HIGH, until mixture is reduced to ½ cup. Strain into 1½-quart bowl or pitcher. Stir in cider. MICROWAVE 4 to 5 MINUTES on HIGH, or until cider is hot.

CAFE BRULOT

8 servings
2-quart casserole

2 *cinnamon sticks, broken*
6 *whole cloves*
   Rind of 1 medium orange, cut in thin slivers
   Rind of ½ lemon, cut in thin slivers
8 *lumps sugar*
¾ *cup cognac or brandy*
4 *cups strong, hot coffee*

Combine cinnamon, cloves, orange, lemon rinds and sugar in 2-quart casserole. Pour in cognac. MICROWAVE 1 MINUTE, 30 SECONDS to 2 MINUTES on HIGH, or until hot. Stir in hot coffee. Serve in demitasse or brulot cups.

KILLARNEY COFFEE

1 serving
Coffee mug or Irish coffee goblet

1 *teaspoon firmly packed brown sugar*
4 *to 6 ounces strong black coffee*
1 *jigger (1½-ounces) Irish whiskey*
1 *rounded tablespoon whipped cream*

Dissolve sugar in black coffee in coffee mug or Irish coffee goblet. MICROWAVE 1 to 2 MINUTES on HIGH, or until hot. Add Irish whiskey.

Top with whipped cream.

Fish & Seafood

The classic methods of cooking seafood have always been poaching and steaming. A microwave oven achieves the same delicate flavor and flaky-firm texture without elaborate procedures. No need to tie fish in cheese cloth or use a special fish-poacher. Shellfish steam tender with very little water.

STUFFED JUMBO SHRIMP

4 servings
1-quart casserole
8-inch cake dish

1 *pound large shrimp in the shell*
2 *tablespoons butter or margarine*
¼ *cup finely chopped celery*
1 *small onion, finely chopped*
3 *tablespoons melted butter or margarine*
½ *cup bread crumbs*
¼ *teaspoon basil*
½ *teaspoon chopped fresh parsley*
¼ *teaspoon garlic salt*

Peel shrimp, leaving shell on tail section. Lay on back. With a sharp knife split almost through, ½-inch below tail. Devein. Wash under running water.

Combine celery, onion, and butter in 1-quart casserole. MICROWAVE 3 MINUTES on HIGH, or until onion is transparent. Stir in remaining ingredients.

Brush shrimp with melted butter.

Spoon 1 tablespoon of mixture into butterflied area of shrimp.

Place in 8-inch round cake dish with tails resting straight up on the sides of dish.

MICROWAVE 3 to 6 MINUTES on '8', or until shrimp are opaque. Do not overcook. Time varies slightly with size of shrimp.

SHRIMP CREOLE

5 to 6 servings
1½-quart casserole

1 *clove garlic, pressed or finely chopped*
1 *cup chopped onion*
1 *green pepper, chopped*
½ *cup chopped celery*
3 *tablespoons butter or margarine*
1 *can (12-ounces) tomato sauce*
½ *cup dry red wine, or water*
2 *small, whole bay leaves*
2 *tablespoons snipped parsley*
¼ *teaspoon thyme*
½ *teaspoon salt*
   Dash cayenne pepper
1 *package (12-ounces) frozen, uncooked cleaned shrimp, defrosted*
3 *cups hot cooked rice*

Combine garlic, onion, green pepper, celery and butter in a 1½-quart casserole. MICROWAVE 3 MINUTES on HIGH, or until onion is transparent.

Stir in tomato sauce, wine, bay leaves, parsley, thyme, salt and pepper. Cover with waxed paper. MICROWAVE 5 MINUTES, covered, to finish cooking. Remove bay leaf.

Add shrimp; stir. Cover with waxed paper. MICROWAVE 4 MINUTES on HIGH. Let stand 5 minutes. Serve over rice.

FISH AND SEAFOOD BASICS

Microwaved fish should be covered unless coated with crumbs to seal in juices. Avoid overcooking which dries and toughens fish and seafood. Fish is so delicate that, once it is hot, it almost cooks itself. Fish is done when flesh becomes opaque and flakes easily with a fork. When shellfish is done, the flesh is opaque and firm. Cook fish for the minimum time. Let stand. If necessary microwave a few moments more before serving.

Most fillets cook well on a high setting. Lower heat control settings give thick steaks, whole fish and most seafood the gentle treatment they deserve.

LUNCHEON SHRIMP

6 servings
1½-quart casserole

12 ounces cooked shrimp
 3 tablespoons butter or margarine
 ¼ cup finely chopped onion
 1 green pepper, finely chopped
 1 clove garlic, pressed or finely chopped
 1 cup uncooked converted rice
 8 ounces fresh mushrooms, sliced
 1 jar (2-ounces) chopped pimiento, drained
 1 bay leaf
1½ cups hot tap water
 1 teaspoon salt

Cut shrimp in half, if large. Combine butter, onion, green pepper and garlic in 1½-quart casserole. MICROWAVE 3 to 5 MINUTES on HIGH, or until onion is transparent.

Add shrimp, rice, mushrooms, pimiento, bay leaf and water. Mix well. Cover. MICROWAVE 10 MINUTES on '8', or until rice is almost tender. Stir in salt. Let stand 5 minutes, covered, to finish cooking.

NOTE: If using frozen shrimp, defrost partially.

CANTONESE SHRIMP AND PEA PODS

6 servings
3-quart casserole

 1 small onion, thinly sliced
 1 clove garlic, pressed or finely chopped
 1 tablespoon salad oil
1½ teaspoon instant chicken bouillon, dissolved in
    1 cup boiling water
1½ pounds fresh or frozen defrosted shrimp, un-
    cooked and cleaned (or frozen pre-cooked, see
    note)
 ½ teaspoon ginger
    Dash pepper
 2 tablespoons corn starch
 2 tablespoons cold water
 1 package (9-ounces) frozen pea pods or cut
    green beans, defrosted
 1 teaspoon salt

Combine onion, garlic and oil in 3-quart casserole. MICROWAVE 3 MINUTES on HIGH, or until onion is transparent.

Add chicken broth, shrimp, ginger and pepper. Cover. MICROWAVE 3 MINUTES on '7'.

Blend corn starch and water. Stir into shrimp mixture. Cover. MICROWAVE 5 MINUTES on '7'.

Add pea pods and MICROWAVE 6 to 8 MINUTES on '7', or until pea pods are cooked and sauce is thick. Add salt during last 2 minutes of cooking.

NOTE: When using pre-cooked shrimp, stir in after adding corn starch to prevent over-cooking.

SEAFOOD NEWBURG

4 servings
1½ quart casserole

2 cups (12-ounces) cooked lobster, crab or shrimp
¼ cup butter or margarine, melted
3 egg yolks, beaten
1 cup whipping cream
1 teaspoon paprika
  Salt to taste

Combine seafood and butter in 1½-quart casserole. MICROWAVE 2 MINUTES on '7'.

Add beaten egg yolks to cream. Combine with lobster. Add paprika. MICROWAVE 5 MINUTES on '7', or until sauce is heated but not boiling, stirring after every 2 minutes. Add salt. Serve over rice or buttered toast points.

Coquilles Saint Jacques

CRAB MORNAY

5 to 6 servings
8x8-inch baking dish

2 cups (12-ounces) cooked crab meat
2 cups white sauce, (page 201)
½ pound Swiss or Cheddar cheese, grated

Layer half of crab meat, half of sauce and half of cheese in (8x8-inch) baking dish. Repeat with second layers. MICROWAVE 10 MINUTES on '7'. Garnish with parsley and paprika, if desired.

NOTE: 2 cans (6½-ounces) each crab meat or 12-ounces cooked langouste may be substituted for crab.

COQUILLES SAINT JACQUES

6 to 8 servings
2-quart casserole
1-cup measure
2-cup measure
6 to 8 shells or individual ramkins

1 pound scallops, fresh or frozen, defrosted
2 tablespoons butter or margarine
1 small onion, finely chopped
1 package (8-ounces) fresh mushrooms, sliced
2 tablespoons lemon juice
1 cup dry white wine
1 bay leaf
¼ teaspoon savory
½ teaspoon salt
⅛ teaspoon pepper
3 tablespoons butter or margarine
3 tablespoons flour
1 cup light cream
½ cup dried bread crumbs
  Lemon wedges
  Parsley sprigs

Cut scallops in half. Spread on bottom of 2-quart casserole. Set aside.

Combine butter and onions in 1-cup measure. MICROWAVE 3 MINUTES on HIGH, or until onions are transparent. Stir in mushrooms and lemon juice. Pour over scallops. Add wine, bay leaf, savory, salt and pepper. Cover. MICROWAVE 4 to 6 MINUTES on '8', or until scallops are tender. Remove bay leaf. Drain and reserve liquid.

Place 3 tablespoons butter in 2-cup measure. MICROWAVE on HIGH until melted. Blend in flour to make a smooth paste. Stir in reserved liquid and cream. Pour over scallops. MICROWAVE 3 to 4 MINUTES on '8', or until sauce thickens.

Spoon mixture into serving shells or individual ramkins. Sprinkle with bread crumbs. Place 3 to 4 shells at a time in oven. MICROWAVE 1 to 2 MINUTES on '8', per serving, or until piping hot. Garnish with lemon wedges and parsley sprigs.

NOTE: Watch carefully during final heating. Shells and ramkins differ in size and shape, which affects heating time.

QUICK PAELLA 🔲

4 servings
2-quart casserole

Spanish Sauce, (see below)
½ pound medium shrimp, fresh or frozen and defrosted
1 cup cubed, cooked chicken (large chunks)
1 can (6½-ounces) clams, drained
2 cups hot cooked rice

Prepare Spanish Sauce in 2-quart casserole. Add shrimp, chicken and clams to sauce when adding tomatoes, mushrooms and seasonings before final cooking period. If necessary, microwave a little longer to finish cooking shrimp. Serve over rice. Garnish with lemon wedge, if desired.

Variations:

For more elaborate Paella, add one or more of the following:

Cut-up lobster meat	*Cooked cubed beef*
Cooked cubed ham	*Cooked cubed pork*
Cooked cubed veal	*Cooked sliced sausage*

Any of the above may be substituted for chicken in basic recipe.

SPANISH SAUCE

2 to 3 cups
1-quart casserole

1 large green pepper, chopped
1 medium onion, chopped
½ clove garlic, pressed or finely chopped
2 tablespoons bacon fat or salad oil
1 can (15½-ounces) stewed tomatoes
1½ teaspoons Worcestershire sauce
½ teaspoon dry mustard
Dash cayenne pepper
½ teaspoon salt
1 can (2-ounces) mushroom stems and pieces

Combine peppers, onion, garlic and fat in 1-quart casserole. MICROWAVE 1½ MINUTES to 3 MINUTES on HIGH, or until onions are transparent.

Stir in remaining ingredients. Cover with waxed paper. MICROWAVE 5 to 6 MINUTES on HIGH, or until sauce reaches desired consistency, stirring after 2½ minutes.

Serve as a sauce for Spanish omelet, meat loaf, rice or pasta.

HALIBUT HAWAIIAN

4 to 6 servings
8 x 8-inch baking dish

2 packages (12-ounces each) frozen Halibut steaks defrosted
1 cup Sweet-Sour Sauce, (see below)
1 can (8-ounces) crushed pineapple, drained (reserve juice)
1 cup fine dry bread crumbs
3 tablespoons lemon juice
½ teaspoon curry powder
1 can (8-ounces) pineapple rings, drained (reserve juice)
Tomato wedges
Parsley sprigs

Cut Halibut in serving pieces. Arrange in (8 x 8-inch) baking dish. Set aside.

Prepare Sweet-Sour Sauce, using juice from crushed pineapple and pineapple rings. Reserve ½ cup sauce.

Combine remaining ½ cup Sweet-Sour Sauce, crushed pineapple, bread crumbs, lemon juice and curry powder. Spread mixture on Halibut. Pour reserved sauce evenly over top. Cover with plastic wrap. MICROWAVE 15 to 18 MINUTES on '8', or until fish flakes easily.

Garnish each serving with 1 pineapple ring. Place tomato wedge and parsley sprig in center of ring.

SWEET-SOUR SAUCE

1 cup
1-quart measure

½ cup pineapple juice
¼ cup distilled white vinegar
¼ cup firmly packed brown sugar
2 tablespoons salad oil
2 teaspoons soy sauce
½ teaspoon pepper

Combine all ingredients in 1-quart measure. MICROWAVE 2 MINUTES on HIGH, or until sauce boils.

Serve with eggs, fish, poultry or vegetables.

Whole Lobster

WHOLE LOBSTER

1 to 2 servings
12 x 8-inch baking dish

Live lobster (about 1½-pounds)
¼ cup hot water

On a cutting board, place lobster on its back. To kill, sever the spinal cord by plunging the point of a sharp knife through the back shell, where tail and body cavity are joined together.

With a sharp knife, cut lengthwise through the under shell, leaving the back shell intact. Remove small sack below the head and the intestinal vein which runs from it to the tip of the tail.

To prevent curling, peg the tail by running a wooden skewer through it lengthwise. Place lobster shell side up in (12 x 8-inch) baking dish. Pour in ¼ cup hot water. Cover tightly with plastic wrap. MICRO-WAVE 2 MINUTES on HIGH.

Turn lobster over. Cover. MICROWAVE 2 MINUTES on HIGH.

Turn lobster shell side up. Cover. MICROWAVE 6 to 8 MINUTES on '6', or until shell is bright red. Let stand 5 minutes, covered.

Serve with melted butter and lemon wedges.

LOBSTER TAILS

2 servings
12x8-inch baking dish

2 lobster tails (7 to 8-ounces each), defrosted
2 tablespoons butter or margarine, melted

Split each lobster tail through top shell and release meat, leaving it connected to shell at one end. Pull meat through slit and place on top of shell. Arrange tails in baking dish and brush with butter. Cover with plastic wrap.

MICROWAVE 5 to 6 MINUTES on HIGH, or until meat is opaque and shell turns red. To cook one tail, MICROWAVE 3 MINUTES on HIGH, or until meat is opaque. Let stand to complete cooking if necessary. Overcooking causes meat to toughen.

BAKED FISH

3 to 4 servings
10 x 6 or 8 x 8-inch baking dish

1 *pound fresh or frozen fish fillets, defrosted*
1 *package (2-ounces) seasoned coating mix for fish*

Wash fillets and shake off excess water. Place coating mix in bag provided with mix. Add 1 or 2 fillets at a time and shake to coat with crumbs.

Place fillets in (10 x 6 or 8 x 8-inch) baking dish with thinner parts toward inside of dish. MICROWAVE 7 MINUTES on HIGH, or until fish flakes easily.

BAKED TORSK

4 to 6 servings
12 x 8-inch baking dish

1½ *pounds torsk, cut in serving pieces*
  Salt and pepper
¼ *cup butter or margarine, melted*
¼ *cup green pepper, chopped*
  1 *can (4-ounces) mushroom stems and pieces, drained*

Place torsk in (12 x 8-inch) baking dish. Sprinkle with salt and pepper. Combine butter, green pepper and mushrooms. Pour over fish. Cover. MICROWAVE 4 to 5 MINUTES on HIGH, or until fish flakes easily with a fork.

Garnish with lemon and lime wedges, if desired.

ITALIAN POACHED FISH

4 servings
8 x 8-inch baking dish

2 *tablespoons chopped parsley*
1 *clove garlic, pressed or finely chopped*
1 *to 1½ tablespoons olive oil*
¼ *cup hot water*
1 *pound white fish fillets, fresh or frozen defrosted*
⅛ *teaspoon oregano leaves*
  Salt and pepper to taste

Place parsley, garlic, olive oil and water in baking dish. MICROWAVE 30 SECONDS on HIGH. Arrange fillets with thickest portions to outside of dish. Sprinkle with seasonings. Cover tightly with plastic wrap. MICROWAVE 5 to 6 MINUTES on HIGH, or until fish flakes easily. Let stand 2 minutes, covered. Serve with liquid.

NOTE: Over-cooking toughens fish.

SALMON PIQUANTE

4 to 6 servings
8 x 8 or 12 x 8-inch baking dish

1 *medium onion, thinly sliced*
1 *lemon, thinly sliced*
1 *clove garlic, thinly sliced*
1 *teaspoon mixed pickling spice*
1 *teaspoon salt*
1½ *pounds salmon or steaks*
½ *cup mayonnaise*
½ *cucumber, peeled and finely chopped*

Spread onion, lemon, garlic and spices on bottom of baking dish. Arrange salmon on top, thickest portions toward outside of dish. Cover tightly with plastic wrap. MICROWAVE 14 to 16 MINUTES on '8', or until salmon flakes easily.

Mix mayonnaise and cucumber. Serve as sauce for steaks. Garnish with lemon twists and parsley sprigs.

FISH SURPRISE

3 to 4 servings
2-quart casserole

1 *bay leaf*
6 *whole cloves*
1 *slice lemon*
1 *slice onion*
½ *teaspoon salt*
1 *tablespoon vinegar*
½ *inch red pepper*
1 *pound halibut, cut in serving pieces, fresh or frozen and defrosted*
½ *cup water*
2 *cups medium white sauce*
½ *cup blanched almonds or salted cashews, finely chopped*
½ *cup toasted bread crumbs*

Place bay leaf, cloves, lemon, onion, salt, vinegar, red pepper and fish in 2-quart casserole. Pour in water. Cover. MICROWAVE 3 to 5 MINUTES on HIGH, or until fish flakes easily. Let stand, covered, while preparing white sauce.

Remove fish, drain broth and discard. Break fish into 1-inch pieces. Return to casserole. Stir nuts into white sauce. Pour over fish. Top with bread crumbs. MICROWAVE 3 to 4 MINUTES on '6', or until sauce bubbles.

SALMON LOAF SCANDINAVIAN

4 to 6 servings
9 x 5-inch loaf dish

1 *can (15½-ounces) salmon*
  Milk
2 *eggs*
1 *cup coarsely crushed cracker crumbs*
3 *tablespoons chopped onion*
2 *tablespoons lemon juice*
¼ *teaspoon salt*
¼ *teaspoon pepper*
  Cucumber sauce, below

Drain salmon into 2-cup measure. Add milk to make 1½-cups liquid. Set aside. Remove bones and skin from salmon and flake meat thoroughly.

In 2-quart bowl, beat eggs. Add salmon liquid. Stir in cracker crumbs, onion, lemon juice, salt and pepper. Add salmon and stir lightly until just moistened.

Handling gently, spread mixture in (9 x 5-inch) glass loaf dish. MICROWAVE 15 MINUTES on '7', or until center is set. Serve with cucumber sauce.

CUCUMBER SAUCE

½ *cup dairy sour cream*
½ *cup chopped cucumber*
2 *green onions, finely chopped*
2 *tablespoons light cream*

Combine all ingredients. Mix until blended. Serve over salmon loaf. MICROWAVE 1 MINUTE on '5' to warm.

Salmon Steaks Limone

SALMON STEAKS LIMONE

4 servings
Custard cup
12 x 8-inch baking dish

1 *tablespoon butter or margarine*
1 *teaspoon lemon juice*
4 *salmon steaks, cut 1-inch thick (about 2-pounds)*
  fresh, or frozen and defrosted

Combine butter and lemon juice in custard cup. MICROWAVE on HIGH until butter melts.

Arrange salmon steaks in (12 x 8-inch) baking dish with meatiest portions to outside of dish. Brush with lemon butter. Cover with plastic wrap. MICRO-WAVE 14 to 16 MINUTES on '8', or until fish flakes easily. Let stand 5 minutes, covered. Garnish with lemon twists and parsley sprigs, if desired.

BAKED SALMON WITH MUSHROOMS

4 to 5 servings
8x8-inch or,
12x8-inch baking dish

2 *pounds fresh or frozen salmon steaks, defrosted*
¼ *cup butter or margarine, melted*
1 *can (4-ounces) mushroom stems and pieces,*
  drained
2 *tablespoons lemon juice*
1 *teaspoon onion, grated*
  Salt and pepper to taste

Arrange salmon in baking dish with thin ends toward center. Combine butter, mushrooms, lemon juice and onion. Spoon over salmon. Cover with plastic wrap. MICROWAVE 12 MINUTES on HIGH, or until fish flakes easily. Let stand 5 minutes, covered. Season with salt and pepper.

FABULOUS BAKED FISH

3 to 4 servings
2-cup measure
12 x 8-inch baking dish

1 *pound whole fish (trout, pike, perch, haddock or flounder)*
4 *tablespoons butter or margarine*
2 *tablespoons finely chopped onion*
1 *cup dry bread crumbs*
1 *teaspoon salt*

Dry fish thoroughly. Rub inside with two tablespoons butter. Set aside.

Combine 2 tablespoons butter and onion in 2-cup measure. MICROWAVE on HIGH until butter is melted. Add bread crumbs and salt. Mix well. Stuff fish with bread crumb mixture. Secure with string, wooden picks or poultry skewers. Place in (12 x 8-inch) baking dish. Spread any remaining stuffing over fish. Cover with plastic wrap. MICROWAVE 8 MINUTES on '7'. Garnish with lemon slices and parsley, if desired.

NOTE: If fish is too large for dish, wrap gently in plastic wrap and place on floor of oven.

SEAFOOD AU GRATIN

4 servings
4 individual casseroles

1 *medium onion, chopped*
1 *stem celery, chopped*
⅓ *cup chopped green pepper*
2 *tablespoons fresh parsley, chopped*
1 *clove garlic, pressed or finely chopped*
2 *tablespoons butter or margarine*
2 *tablespoons flour*
¼ *teaspoon chicken bouillon, dissolved in ½ cup hot water*
½ *pound lump crab meat, fresh, frozen or canned*
½ *pound cleaned, raw shrimp, fresh, frozen or canned*
½ *pound lobster meat, fresh, frozen or canned*
⅓ *cup grated Cheddar cheese*
⅓ *cup grated Swiss cheese*

Defrost any frozen seafood. Flake or cut lobster into chunks. Set aside.

In 1-quart bowl, combine onion, celery, green pepper, parsley, garlic and butter. MICROWAVE 3 to 4 MINUTES on HIGH, or until vegetables are tender. Add flour, stir until smooth. Add bouillon to water; stir till smooth. MICROWAVE 30 to 45 SECONDS on HIGH, or until thickened. Add seafood; mix well.

Divide mixture evenly among four individual casseroles. MICROWAVE 4 to 5 MINUTES on HIGH, or until seafood turns opaque. Stir once.

Combine cheeses. Sprinkle over the top of each casserole. MICROWAVE 1 MINUTE 30 SECONDS on HIGH, or until cheese is melted.

Top: Savory Fish Fillets, Fillets Almondine
Bottom: White Fish Poached In Wine, Fillets With Shake-On Coating

FILLET OF SOLE CASSEROLE

4 to 6 servings
12 x 8-inch baking dish

1½ to 2 pounds fillet of sole, or other white fish,
    cut in serving pieces, fresh, frozen
    and defrosted
1 can (10¾-ounces) condensed cream of shrimp
    soup, undiluted
½ cup toasted bread crumbs

Arrange fillets in (12 x 8-inch) baking dish, meatiest portions to outside of dish. Spread soup on fish. Sprinkle with crumbs. MICROWAVE 6 to 8 MINUTES on HIGH, or until fish flakes easily with a fork.

SAVORY FISH FILLETS

4 to 5 servings
10 x 8-inch baking dish

1 pound white fish fillets, fresh or defrosted
½ cup French dressing

Place fillets in (10 x 8-inch) baking dish. Pour dressing over, and turn to coat fillets. Cover and marinate at least 2 hours in refrigerator.

Drain. Arrange fish with thickest portions to outside of dish. Cover tightly with plastic wrap. MICROWAVE 5 MINUTES on HIGH, or until fish flakes. Let stand 2 minutes, covered.

WHITE FISH POACHED IN WINE

2 servings
8 x 10 or 9 x 9-inch baking dish

2 tablespoons butter or margarine
½ small onion, chopped
½ teaspoon parsley
¼ teaspoon basil
½ teaspoon lemon juice
    Salt
    Pepper
8 to 10-ounces white fish (2 medium fillets)
¼ cup white wine

Place butter, onion, parsley, basil and lemon juice in (8 x 8-inch) baking dish. MICROWAVE 40 SECONDS on HIGH.

Salt and pepper fillets; arrange in dish, turning to coat with butter. Sprinkle with white wine. Cover with plastic wrap. MICROWAVE 3 MINUTES on HIGH, or until fish flakes easily with a fork.

FILLETS ALMONDINE

4 servings
8 x 8-inch baking dish

¼ cup butter or margarine
¼ cup slivered almonds
1 pound white fish fillets, fresh or defrosted
2 teaspoons lemon juice
¼ teaspoon salt

Place butter and almonds in (8 x 8-inch) baking dish. MICROWAVE 5 MINUTES on HIGH, until almonds are golden, stirring once. Remove and set aside. Arrange fillets in baking dish with thickest portions to outside of dish, turning to coat with butter. Sprinkle with lemon juice and salt. Cover tightly with plastic wrap. MICROWAVE 5 to 6 6 MINUTES on HIGH, or until fish flakes easily and appears opaque. Garnish with toasted almonds.

SCALLOP CURRY

4 servings
1½-quart casserole

1 pound fresh or frozen scallops, defrosted
1 tablespoon butter or margarine
¼ cup sliced green onions
1½ teaspoons corn starch
1½ teaspoons curry powder
¼ teaspoon salt
2 cups hot cooked rice

Rinse scallops in cold water and drain.

Place butter in 1½-quart casserole. MICROWAVE on HIGH until melted. Add onions and scallops. MICROWAVE 4 MINUTES on '8', stirring after 2 minutes.

Place 2 tablespoons butter-scallop liquid in small cup. Stir in corn starch, curry powder and salt until dissolved. Add to scallop mixture. Stir until well blended. MICROWAVE 2 MINUTES on HIGH.

Add cooked rice. Mix lightly with fork. MICROWAVE 30 SECONDS to 1 MINUTE, or until heated through. Serve with tomato slices and chutney.

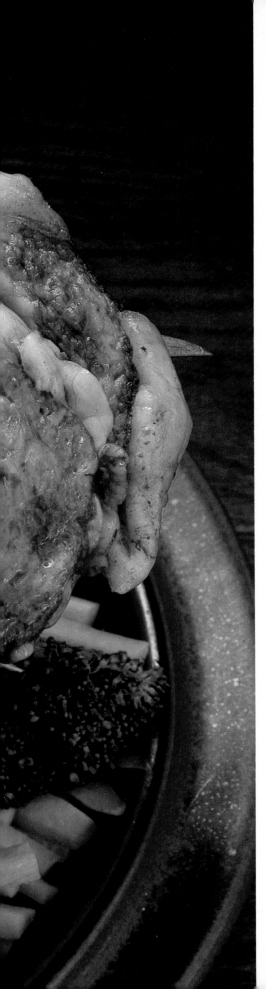

Beef

Tender, juicy roast beef is prepared with a minimum of time and attention. Flavor-blended, roasts and stews, quick meat loaves and ground beef dishes are all possible with heat control microwave ovens. Even frozen pot roast goes from freezer to table in a surprisingly short time.

If some of your guests or family prefer rare beef and others well done, the microwave oven solves that problem easily. After the roast is carved, a few seconds in the microwave oven will bring rare meat to medium or well done.

ROAST BEEF

12 x 8-inch utility dish,
with microwave roasting rack

Beef rib roast

Place roast fat side down on microwave roasting rack in (12 x 8-inch) utility dish. MICROWAVE 5 MINUTES on HIGH.

Reduce setting. MICROWAVE on '6' or '5' for half the roasting time, (see chart, page 100). Turn roast fat side up. MICROWAVE on '6' or '5' until internal temperature of thickest part of meat registers 120° to 150°, depending on desired doneness. Let stand 10 minutes, tented with aluminum foil, shiny side in. Roast will continue to cook while standing.

NOTE: If thickness of rolled roast is greater than 5-inches, turn roast over 4 times, top to bottom and end to end.

When cooking a standing rib roast, turn meat over 3 times, side to side and fat side up, (see chart, page 100).

Do not use a meat thermometer in the microwave oven unless you have a special microwave meat thermometer.

Inverted saucers may be substituted for a roasting rack.

BEEF BASICS

Recipes are provided for three types of beef: tender cuts, less tender cuts and ground beef.

Tender cuts, such as roast or steak, cook very rapidly. Because of its size and length of cooking time, a roast has time to brown in the microwave oven, but smaller cuts, such as steak, do not. If browning is desired, use the browning dish, or conventional fry pan to sear meat before finishing in the microwave oven.

Test roast beef for doneness with a meat thermometer. Unless you use a special microwave thermometer, do not use meat thermometer in the oven while cooking. During the last third of estimated cooking time, remove meat from the oven and test by inserting a meat thermometer in the thickest part, without touching bone. Remember that meat is easier to carve after standing, and will continue to cook. Remove meat from the oven when internal temperature registers 15 degrees lower than desired doneness.

The suggested times in our chart may be a little short for some tastes. Since power levels and personal preferences differ, we have given shorter times to prevent overcooking. It's easy to cook meat a little longer, but nothing can bring back an over done roast.

SUGGESTED COOKING TIMES FOR TENDER CUTS OF BEEF

CUT	SET ON	MINUTES PER LB.			MICROWAVE INSTRUCTIONS Use 8 x 12-inch utility dish and microwave roasting rack.	STANDING TIME
		RARE Remove at 120-125°	MED. Remove at 125°	WELL Remove at 130°		
Whole Beef Tenderloin	6	4-6	6-8	8-10	MICROWAVE fat side down for ½ of total cooking time. (Begin with 5 min. on HIGH then reduce to '6'). TURN fat side up and MICROWAVE on '6' until done. Remove from oven.	INSERT meat thermometer. TENT with foil (shiny side in). LET STAND 10 min.
Small Rolled Rib Roast (less than 5-inches in diameter)	6	8-10	10-12	12-14	MICROWAVE fat side down for ½ of total cooking time. (Begin with 5 min. on HIGH then reduce to '6'). TURN fat side up and MICROWAVE on '6' until done. Remove from oven.	INSERT meat thermometer. TENT with foil (shiny side in). LET STAND 10 min.
Large Rolled Rib Roast (more than 5-inches in diameter)	6	6-8	8-10	10-12	MICROWAVE fat side down for ¼ of total time. (Begin with 5 min. on HIGH then reduce to '6'). TURN fat side up and MICROWAVE on '6' for ¼ of total time. TURN one end up and MICROWAVE on '6' for ¼ of total time. TURN other end up and MICROWAVE on '6' until done. Remove from oven.	INSERT meat thermometer. TENT with foil (shiny side in). LET STAND 15-20 min.
Standing Rib Roast	6	7-9	9-11	11-13	MICROWAVE cut side up for ⅓ of total cooking time. (Begin with 5 min. on HIGH then reduce to '6'). TURN roast top to bottom and MICROWAVE on '6' for ⅓ of total time. TURN fat side up (as shown) and MICROWAVE on '6' until done. Remove from oven.	INSERT meat thermometer. TENT with foil (shiny side in). LET STAND 10 min.

With lower heat control settings, less tender cuts, such as round steak, chuck roast or stew meat simmer to fork tenderness. With small tender cuts, meat is medium rare when beads of juice begin to appear on surface; medium when surface is moist with juice; well done when juice begins to retreat. Less tender cuts should be cooked until fork tender.

Cooking Beef At Other Settings

You may roast tender cuts of beef on the high setting, if you need to cook them quickly. Watch carefully. You may want to rotate the dish as well as turn the meat, to assure even cooking.

With variable heat control ovens, meats may also be roasted at lower settings such as '4'. This is a good choice when you have time to cook the roast, but are too busy to attend to it at short intervals. Less tender cuts should always be cooked on '6' or lower, since they need time to become tender.

Since power levels and personal preferences differ, recipes are for a minimum cooking time. You may find some of the timings short. If necessary, cook a little longer to bring meat to desired doneness.

Cooking Hints for Less Tender Cuts

Grades of meat differ. Better meat is marbled with fat and will be more tender cooked by microwave. If
meat is very lean or tough it will need some special techniques to help it to become more tender.

If the meat has no layer of fat, bacon strips or a dry soup mix on top will help. These cuts can also be marinated in acid based marinades such as wine, tomato juice, fruit juices, soy sauce or one of the commercial marinades.

Piercing the meat with a fork will also help tenderize it.

Cooking bags can be used. Replace the metal twist ties with loosely tied string.

Freezer to Table Beef

With this new method of variable heat cooking, you cannot only microwave a less tender cut of beef, but you can take it from freezer to oven to table without separate defrosting. Cooking time is at least an hour less than by conventional methods, and meat needs only a minimum of attention.

Select a casserole just large enough to hold meat comfortably. A tight cover is essential. If the casserole lid is loose, cover the casserole with plastic wrap and place the lid over it firmly.

Standing time after cooking is also important. It helps make the meat tender and flavorful.

Page 103 will give you some specific suggestions for freezer to table meats.

SUGGESTED COOKING TIMES FOR LESS TENDER CUTS OF BEEF

CUT	CONTAINER	SPECIAL INSTRUCTIONS	SETTING	MINUTES PER POUND	STANDING TIME
Rump roast or Sirloin tip	12 x 8 utility dish	Microwave on rack, fat side down, turn halfway through	6	12-16	15 min. under foil tent (foil shiny side in)
Round bone chuck pot roast	2-quart covered casserole	Microwave covered, turn halfway through	6	15-20	5 min. covered
Eye of round	12 x 8 utility dish	Wrap with bacon, turn halfway through	4	Rare 9-10 Med. 10-12	

Meat thermometer is not a satisfactory test for doneness when cooking less tender cuts of beef. The internal temperature of a less tender cut will reach "well done" in the same time as a tender one, but the meat will still need additional gentle roasting or simmering in liquid before it will be tenderized.

EVERY DAY POT ROAST

6 to 8 servings
Shallow 2-quart casserole

3 to 4 pound beef chuck pot roast, trimmed of fat
1 envelope (¾-ounce) gravy mix
1 onion, thinly sliced
2 teaspoons instant beef bouillon, dissolved in 1 cup hot water
4 boiling potatoes, peeled and cut in ½-inch slices
4 carrots, quartered

Place pot roast in 2-quart casserole. Sprinkle gravy mix over roast. Spread onion slices on top. Add bouillon, potatoes and carrots. Cover.

MICROWAVE 50 to 60 MINUTES on '6', or until meat is fork tender, turning meat over after 30 minutes. Let stand 5 minutes, covered.

FRONTIER POT ROAST

6 to 8 servings
1-quart measure
12 x 8-inch utility dish with microwave roasting rack

3 tablespoons butter or margarine
½ cup soy sauce
½ cup Worcestershire sauce
½ cup water
1 large onion, chopped
4 to 5 pound beef rump roast or 2-inch chuck pot roast

Place butter in 1-quart measure. MICROWAVE on HIGH until melted. Add soy sauce, Worcestershire sauce, water and onion. Place roast in plastic storage bag. Pour in marinade. Seal bag tightly with twist tie. Let stand overnight at room temperature.

To cook, place roast on microwave roasting rack in (12 x 8-inch) utility dish (If roast has layer of fat, place fat side down.) MICROWAVE 60 to 65 MINUTES on '6', or until fork tender, turning roast over after 30 minutes.

Let stand 15 minutes, covered with tent of aluminum foil.

NOTE: Inverted saucers may be substituted for roasting rack.

SAUERBRATEN

6 to 8 servings
2-2½ quart casserole
with cover

3 pound sirloin tip roast
1½ cups water
½ cup red cooking wine
½ cup vinegar
½ lemon, sliced
2 large onions
2 tablespoons sugar
2 tablespoons mixed pickling spices
½ teaspoon salt
  Flour
1 tablespoon vegetable oil
¼ cup butter or margarine
¼ cup flour
2 teaspoons light brown sugar
10 gingersnaps, crushed

Mix together wine, vinegar, water, onion, lemon, pickling spice, salt and sugar. Place meat in a deep bowl and pour the liquid mixture over the meat. Cover and refrigerate for 48 hours, turning the meat twice a day. Remove meat from the refrigerator 1 hour before cooking. Drain the meat and reserve the liquid.

Pat the meat dry with paper towels and rub it lightly with flour. PREHEAT the large browning dish for 4½ to 5 MINUTES. Add oil and meat. MICROWAVE 1 MINUTE on each side. (You can brown the meat conventionally if desired.)

Place meat in a 2-2½ quart covered casserole. PROGRAM TO MICROWAVE for 30 MINUTES on '5'. Turn meat over, add 1 cup strained marinade. MICROWAVE for 20 MINUTES on '5' or until tender.

In a small bowl, microwave butter until melted. Stir in flour and brown sugar to make a smooth paste. Add 1 cup strained marinade, stirring constantly. MICROWAVE 2 to 2½ MINUTES on HIGH, stirring twice. Remove meat to a warm platter. Stir the sauce into the liquid in the casserole. MICRO-WAVE on HIGH for 3 MINUTES, stir once. Add crushed gingersnaps, stir until smooth. Serve with thinly sliced meat.

FREEZER TO TABLE RUMP ROAST ❄️

6 servings
Shallow 2½-quart casserole
with tight-fitting cover

3 *pound beef boneless rump roast, frozen*
1 *envelope (⅞-ounce) onion gravy mix*
6 *medium carrots, halved crosswise and lengthwise*
6 *small onions*
6 *stems celery, sliced coarsely*

Place frozen roast in 2½-quart casserole. Cover tightly. MICROWAVE 30 MINUTES on '5'.

Turn roast over. Cover tightly. MICROWAVE 30 MINUTES on '5'.

Drain liquid. Turn meat over. Sprinkle with gravy mix. Spread vegetables over meat. Cover tightly. MICROWAVE 25 to 30 MINUTES on '5', or until meat is fork tender. Let stand 10 minutes, tightly covered.

NOTE: If potatoes are desired, cook them while beef stands. Cooking potatoes with meat increases cooking time.

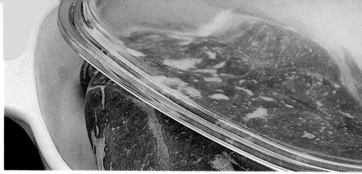

Place frozen meat in 2½-quart casserole. Cover tightly.

Sprinkle with soup mix and spread evenly.

FREEZER TO TABLE SWISS STEAK ❄️

4 to 6 servings
Shallow 1½-quart casserole
with tight-fitting cover

2 *pound beef round steak, frozen*
1 *can (8-ounces) tomato sauce*
1 *can (4-ounces) mushroom stems and pieces, drained*
Salt and pepper

Place frozen round steak in 1½-quart casserole. Cover tightly. MICROWAVE 15 MINUTES on '5'.

Drain liquid. Turn meat over. Add tomato sauce and mushrooms. Spread over meat. Cover tightly. MICROWAVE 20 to 25 MINUTES on '5', or until fork tender. Season with salt and pepper. Let stand 5 minutes, tightly covered.

Sprinkle onion rings over meat. Cover tightly.

FREEZER TO TABLE POT ROAST ❄️

4 to 6 servings
Shallow 2½-quart casserole
with tight-fitting cover

3 *pound beef round-bone chuck roast, frozen*
1 *envelope (1 to 1¼-ounces) onion soup mix*
1 *onion sliced and separated into rings*

Place frozen meat in 2½-quart casserole. Cover tightly. MICROWAVE 40 MINUTES on '5'.

Drain liquid. Turn meat over. Sprinkle with soup mix and spread evenly to edges. Cover tightly. MICROWAVE 30 to 40 MINUTES on '5', or until meat is fork tender.

Sprinkle onion rings over meat. Let stand 10 minutes, tightly covered.

NOTE: Heat from the meat will cook onion rings during standing time.

A Rib-eye Steak is perfect for the microwave browning dish

BROWNING DISH BASICS

Browning dishes and grills come in many sizes. They work best with steaks up to ¾-inch thick and from 8 to 16-ounces.

Meat works better in a browning dish if it is brought to room temperature first. To avoid a steamed taste, do not cover during the cooking process. If you are not completely satisfied with your results, vary the preheat times to obtain desired results.

ONION PEPPER STEAK FINGERS

4 servings
10½-inch browning dish

1 *pound sirloin tip steak*
1 *tablespoon salad oil*
1 *package (1 to 1¼-ounce) onion soup mix*
1 *teaspoon seasoned pepper*

Cut steak into 3-inch pieces, (½-inch width). Preheat browning dish 7 minutes. Mix onion soup and pepper together in a mixing bowl. Roll steak fingers into mixture, pressing it lightly into the meat. Add the oil to the preheated browning dish. Add coated steak fingers. MICROWAVE 1 MINUTE on HIGH. Turn steak fingers over. MICROWAVE 1 MINUTE on HIGH. Allow to stand 2 minutes.

RIB EYE STEAKS

2 servings
10½-inch browning dish

2 *8-ounce rib eye steaks*

Preheat browning dish for 7 minutes. Place steaks in browning dish. MICROWAVE 1 MINUTE on HIGH. Turn over. MICROWAVE 1 MINUTE on HIGH, or until done to taste. Steaks are better if brought to room temperature before microwaving.

MARINATED CUBE STEAK

4 servings
6x9-inch utility dish
10½-inch browning dish

4 *cube steaks, (approximately 1-pound total)*
½ *cup soy sauce*
½ *cup Worcestershire sauce*

Place steaks in 6x9-inch utility dish. Combine soy sauce and Worcestershire sauce and pour over steaks. Allow to sit in marinade for 10 minutes. Preheat browning dish 7 minutes. Drain marinade from steaks. Place in hot browning dish. MICROWAVE 1 MINUTE on HIGH. Turn over. MICROWAVE 1 MINUTE on HIGH, or until done to taste.

PEPPER STEAK

4 servings
Browning dish

1 *tablespoon salad oil*
1 *to 1½ pounds beef top round steak sliced and cut into strips ½-inch wide by 1½-inches long*
1 *clove garlic, pressed or finely chopped*
½ *teaspoon sliced candied ginger, or ¼ teaspoon ginger*
½ *cup water*
1 *teaspoon instant beef bouillon*
2 *cups 1-inch chunks green pepper*
1 *medium onion, thinly sliced*
2 *large stems celery, sliced diagonally*
1 *jar (2-ounces) chopped pimiento*
1 *teaspoon salt*
¼ *teaspoon pepper*
2 *teaspoons cornstarch dissolved in 2 tablespoons soy sauce*

Place browning dish in oven. MICROWAVE 5 MINUTES on HIGH. Add oil and beef strips. MICROWAVE 2 to 3 MINUTES on HIGH, or until meat is brown, stirring after 1 minute.

Add garlic and ginger. Cover. MICROWAVE 7 MINUTES on '6'.

Stir in remaining ingredients. Cover. MICROWAVE 7 to 10 MINUTES on '6', or until vegetables are tender-crisp.

SIRLOIN STEAK

3 servings
Browning dish

1 *pound sirloin steak, cut in three pieces*

Place empty browning dish in oven. MICROWAVE 5 MINUTES on HIGH. Without removing browning dish from oven, drop steak pieces into dish. MICROWAVE 5 to 7 MINUTES on HIGH, or until desired doneness, turning meat over after 3 to 4 minutes.

NOTE: This recipe is a pattern for doing small steaks in the browning dish. If not using browning dish, pre-sear conventionally and cook on microwave roasting rack.

MOCK FILETS

4 servings
Browning dish
Paper towels

4 *cube steaks*
4 *strips of bacon*
8 *ounces sliced fresh mushrooms*
1 *medium onion, sliced*

Place bacon on several layers of paper towel. MICROWAVE 2 MINUTES on HIGH. Cool slightly. Wrap bacon around circumference of cube steaks. Secure with a toothpick.

Preheat browning dish 6 minutes. Add bacon-wrapped cube steaks. MICROWAVE 1 MINUTE, 30 SECONDS on HIGH. Turn over. MICROWAVE 1 MINUTE, 30 SECONDS on HIGH. Remove steaks from browning dish, add mushrooms and onions to drippings. MICROWAVE 2 MINUTES on HIGH. Top Mock Filets with onions and mushrooms before serving.

Pepper Steak

COUNTRY STYLE SHORT RIBS

4 servings
3-quart casserole

¼ cup all-purpose flour
1 teaspoon salt
¼ teaspoon pepper
3½ pounds beef short ribs
1 large onion, sliced
1 medium green pepper, chopped
1 can (8-ounces) tomato sauce
1 teaspoon instant beef bouillon dissolved in 1 cup
  hot water
2 tablespoons dried parsley
½ teaspoon dry mustard
3 tablespoons vinegar
2 teaspoons Worcestershire sauce

Combine flour, salt and pepper. Coat short ribs with mixture. Place ribs in 3-quart casserole. Add onion, green pepper, tomato sauce, bouillon, parsley, mustard, vinegar and Worcestershire sauce. Mix gently. Cover. MICROWAVE 10 MINUTES on HIGH.

Reduce setting. MICROWAVE 40 to 45 MINUTES on '6', or until meat and vegetables are tender. Let stand 10 minutes, covered. Thicken gravy before serving, if desired.

BEEF WITH ONIONS

6 servings
Browning dish

2 tablespoons butter or margarine
2 tablespoons olive oil
2 pounds bottom round beef steak, cut in ¾-inch
  cubes
3 small onions, quartered
4 firm, ripe tomatoes, quartered, or 1 can
  (16-ounces) tomatoes
2 cloves garlic, pressed or finely chopped
3 tablespoons wine vinegar
2 bay leaves
  Salt and pepper to taste

Place browning dish in oven. MICROWAVE 5 MINUTES on HIGH. Add butter, olive oil and beef cubes. MICROWAVE 3 to 4 MINUTES on HIGH, or until brown, stirring twice.

Add onions, tomatoes, garlic, vinegar and bay leaves. Cover. MICROWAVE 50 MINUTES on '6', or until fork tender, stirring 3 times. Season with salt and pepper to taste. Remove bay leaves before serving.

SPICY TEXAS SHORT RIBS

4 servings
8 x 8-inch baking dish

3 pounds beef short ribs
1 cup catsup
¼ cup cider vinegar
1 tablespoon Worcestershire sauce
2 tablespoons finely chopped onion
2 tablespoons firmly packed brown sugar
1 tablespoon paprika
1 teaspoon sugar
1 teaspoon hickory salt
  Pepper to taste
1 teaspoon hot sauce

Arrange ribs in (8 x 8-inch) baking dish. Combine remaining ingredients in a 1-quart bowl. MICROWAVE on HIGH for 2 MINUTES. Pour over ribs. Cover with plastic wrap. MICROWAVE 40 MINUTES on '6'.

BEEF BIRDS

6 to 8 servings
1-quart measure
12x8-inch baking dish

2 pounds beef round steak, cut ½-inch thick
  and pounded
2 tablespoons butter or margarine
½ cup chopped celery with leaves
3 tablespoons chopped onion
1 cup soft bread crumbs
¼ teaspoon rosemary
¼ teaspoon thyme
⅛ teaspoon pepper
1 can (10¾-ounces) condensed cream of mushroom
  soup, undiluted

Cut round steak in 3x4-inch rectangles. Set aside.

Combine butter, celery and onion in 1-quart measure. MICROWAVE 2 to 3 MINUTES on HIGH, or until onion is transparent. Stir in bread crumbs, rosemary, thyme and pepper.

Spoon stuffing on end of beef strips. Roll up and secure with wooden pick. Arrange rolls in baking dish.

Spoon soup over rolls. Cover. MICROWAVE 20 MINUTES on '6', or until meat is fork tender. Let stand 5 minutes, covered.

FLANK STEAK ROLL-UP

4 to 6 servings
1-quart measure
8x8-inch baking dish

2 pounds beef flank steak
¼ cup butter or margarine
1 medium onion, finely chopped
½ cup finely chopped celery
2 cups dried bread cubes, lightly crushed
1 teaspoon salt
½ teaspoon poultry seasoning
1 cup beef bouillon or 1 teaspoon instant bouillon
  dissolved in 1 cup hot water
2 teaspoons Worcestershire sauce

Cut flank steak in half crosswise. Score on both sides by slashing lightly in criss-cross pattern. Set aside.

Combine butter, onion and celery in 1-quart measure. MICROWAVE 4 to 5 MINUTES on HIGH, or until onions are transparent. Add crushed bread cubes, salt and poultry seasoning, toss lightly.

Spread half of stuffing across center of each flank steak. Fold short sides over stuffing. Secure with string or wooden picks.

Place rolls in (8x8-inch) baking dish, seam side down. Mix together bouillon and Worcestershire sauce. Pour over flank steak. Cover with plastic wrap. MICRO-WAVE 30 to 35 MINUTES on '6', or until fork tender, turning rolls over after 15 minutes.

Let stand 10 minutes, covered.

PIZZA STEAKS

4 servings
10½-inch browning dish

1 pound round steak
1 tablespoon olive oil
1 medium onion, sliced in rings
1 jar (10-ounces) pizza sauce
4 slices mozzarella cheese

Cut round steak into 4 pieces and pound to tenderize. Preheat 10½-inch browning dish 7 minutes. Add olive oil and steaks. MICROWAVE 1 MINUTE on HIGH. Turn over. MICROWAVE 1 MINUTE on HIGH. Top steak with onion rings and cover with pizza sauce. Cover. MICROWAVE 6 MINUTES on '8'. Top each steak with a slice of mozzarella cheese. Cover. Let stand 5 minutes.

SWISS STEAK

6 servings
Browning dish
12x8-inch baking dish

2 pounds beef round steak, cut ½-inch thick
  Flour
2 tablespoons salad oil
1 onion, sliced
1 can (16-ounces) stewed tomatoes
1 tablespoon parsley flakes
  Salt and pepper to taste

Sprinkle one side of meat with flour. Pound in. Turn meat, sprinkle with flour and pound in. Cut meat into serving pieces.

Place browning dish in oven. MICROWAVE 5 MIN-UTES on HIGH. Add oil and enough meat pieces to fit bottom without overlapping.

MICROWAVE 2 to 3 MINUTES on HIGH, or until browned, turning meat after 1 minute.

Remove meat to (12x8-inch) baking dish. Brown any remaining meat. (Preheat browning dish 2 to 3 min-utes, if necessary.)

Spread sliced onions on top of meat. Pour canned tomatoes over top. Sprinkle with parsley flakes. Cov-er with plastic wrap. MICROWAVE 50 MINUTES on '6', or until meat is fork tender. Season with salt and pepper before serving.

CASSEROLE BEEFSTEAK

4 to 6 servings
3-quart casserole

1½ pounds boneless beef round steak
⅓ cup flour
2 cups peeled and thinly sliced potatoes
3 tablespoons finely chopped onion
6 small cabbage leaves, cut in strips
1 cup sliced carrots
6 peppercorns
⅔ cup beef bouillon
3 tomatoes, sliced

Dredge beef in flour and pound in. Cut into 2 x ½-inch strips. Place in 3-quart casserole.

Layer potatoes, onion, cabbage and carrots over beef. Scatter peppercorns on top. Pour in bouillon. Cover. MICROWAVE 5 MINUTES on HIGH.

Reduce setting. MICROWAVE 20 MINUTES on '6', or until meat and potatoes are tender. Arrange tomatoes over top. Let stand 5 minutes, covered.

Basic Beef Casserole

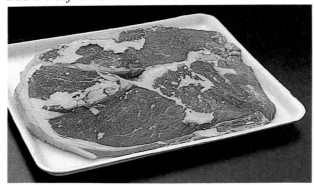

Freeze meat to make cutting easier.

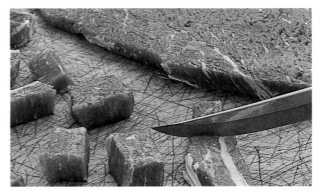

Cut frozen meat into ¾-inch cubes.

Toss beef cubes in bag with flour to coat evenly.

Combine all ingredients in 3-quart casserole.

BASIC BEEF CASSEROLE

4 to 6 servings
3-quart casserole

  3 *tablespoons flour*
1½ *pounds beef round steak, cut in ¾-inch cubes*
  ½ *cup finely chopped onion*
  1 *cup finely sliced carrots*
2½ *cups water*
  1 *teaspoon instant beef bouillon*
  1 *teaspoon salt*
  1 *teaspoon pepper*

Measure flour into paper or plastic bag. Add beef cubes and toss to coat evenly.

Combine all ingredients in 3-quart casserole. Cover. MICROWAVE 5 MINUTES on HIGH.

Reduce setting. MICROWAVE 30 MINUTES on '6', or until meat and vegetables are tender.

Variations:

ENGLISH BEEF

Add:
1 *small turnip, peeled and finely chopped*
2 *stems celery, finely chopped*
1 *cup fresh shelled peas*
2 *tomatoes, peeled and coarsely chopped*
  Garnish with snipped parsley

Serve with boiled or baked potatoes.

NOTE: 1 cup frozen peas may be substituted for fresh. Add during last 5 minutes of cooking.

HUNGARIAN BEEF

Add:
4 *medium carrots, thinly sliced*
4 *medium boiling potatoes, sliced*
1 *tablespoon paprika*
1 *clove garlic, pressed or finely chopped*
  Stir in 3 tablespoons dairy sour cream just before
   serving

Serve with macaroni, noodles or rice. Top each serving with additional sour cream, if desired.

Variations Continued:

AUSTRALIAN BEEF

Add:
¼ *cup firmly packed brown sugar*
1½ *tablespoons Worcestershire sauce*
1½ *tablespoons catsup*
1½ *tablespoons vinegar*
½ *teaspoon nutmeg*

Serve with a green vegetable and mashed or baked potatoes.

INDIAN BEEF

1 *to* 1½ *tablespoons curry powder (add with flour)*
2 *tomatoes, peeled and chopped*
1 *apple, peeled, cored and chopped*
  Stir in 1 tablespoon lemon juice and 2 tablespoons fruit chutney just before serving

Serve with rice, sliced bananas in lemon juice and fruit chutney.

STROGANOFF SPECTACULAR

4 servings
Browning dish

3 *tablespoons butter or margarine*
1 *pound sirloin beef steak sliced and cut into strips ½-inch wide by 1½-inches long*
1 *can (3 to 4-ounces) sliced mushrooms or stems and pieces, drained*
½ *cup chopped onion*
½ *teaspoon dry mustard*
  Pepper to taste
⅔ *cup milk*
1 *package (8-ounces) cream cheese, softened to room temperature*
  Hot noodles with snipped parsley

Place browning dish in oven. MICROWAVE 5 MINUTES on HIGH.

Add butter and beef strips. MICROWAVE 2 to 3 MINUTES on HIGH, or until meat is brown, stirring after 1 minute.

Add mushrooms, onion, mustard and pepper. MICROWAVE 3 MINUTES on HIGH, or until onion is transparent.

Stir in milk and cream cheese. MICROWAVE 6 MINUTES on HIGH, or until mixture comes to a boil. Stir. Cover.

Reduce setting. MICROWAVE 5 MINUTES on '6', or until cheese is creamy and hot. Stir to distribute heat. Serve over noodles garnished with parsley.

FLEMISH STEW

4 to 6 servings
4-quart casserole

2 *medium onions, chopped*
2 *cloves garlic, pressed or finely chopped*
1 *tablespoon butter or margarine*
1½ *pounds stew meat, cut in 1-inch cubes*
½ *cup brown sugar*
1 *can (14½-ounces) stewed tomatoes*
1 *can (12-ounces) beer*
½ *cup flour*
1 *tablespoon seasoned salt*
4 *medium turnips, diced*
5 *medium carrots, sliced*

In a 4 to 5-quart casserole, MICROWAVE onions and garlic in butter on HIGH for 3 MINUTES or until onions are transparent.

Coat beef chunks in flour.

Combine remaining ingredients in the 4 to 5-quart casserole and mix well.

PROGRAM TO MICROWAVE on HIGH for 15 MINUTES, then on '6' for 20 MINUTES and on '2' for 20 MINUTES.

BEEF BOURGUIGNONNE

6 servings
2-quart casserole

4 *slices bacon, quartered*
2 *pounds lean beef sirloin or top round steak, cut in ¾-inch cubes*
¼ *cup all-purpose flour*
1 *package (8-ounces) fresh mushrooms, sliced or 2 cans (4-ounces each) sliced mushrooms, drained*
1 *medium onion, cut in eighths*
1 *clove garlic, pressed or finely chopped*
1 *bay leaf*
1 *tablespoon snipped parsley*
½ *teaspoon thyme*
1¼ *cups burgundy wine*
2 *teaspoons instant beef bouillon*
1 *teaspoon salt*
¼ *teaspoon pepper*

Place bacon in 2-quart casserole. MICROWAVE 2 MINUTES on HIGH. Do not drain. Coat beef cubes with flour. Add to bacon and drippings. Toss to coat with fat. Sprinkle any remaining flour over meat. Add mushrooms, onion, garlic, bay leaf, parsley and thyme. Stir in wine and bouillon. Cover. MICROWAVE 5 MINUTES on HIGH.

Reduce setting. MICROWAVE 30 MINUTES on '6', or until beef is fork tender, stirring once. Season with salt and pepper. Let stand 10 minutes, covered. Remove bay leaf. Serve over noodles.

Ground Beef

GROUND BEEF BASICS

Most of these recipes call for lean ground beef. If you prefer to use regular ground beef, drain fat before adding sauce ingredients. Ground beef cooks quickly. When trying out ground beef for a casserole, microwave only until meat is set. It will finish cooking with the sauce.

MEATLOAF

4 to 5 servings
9x5-inch loaf dish

 1 *egg, slightly beaten*
 2 *tablespoons Worcestershire sauce*
1½ *pounds lean ground beef*
 1 *cup crushed cracker crumbs*
 ½ *cup chopped onion*
 1 *teaspoon salt*
 ¼ *teaspoon pepper*

Mix all ingredients thoroughly in (9x5-inch) loaf dish. Spread mixture evenly in dish. MICROWAVE 16 to 20 MINUTES on '6', or until set in center. Let stand 5 minutes. Garnish with slices of cherry tomato and parsley sprigs, if desired.

Variations:
SAUCED LOAF

Before baking, spread ½ cup barbecue sauce, chili sauce or catsup over top of loaf.

MUSTARD LOAF

Reduce Worcestershire sauce to 1 tablespoon. Add 1 tablespoon prepared mustard, ½ teaspoon horseradish and ¼ teaspoon garlic salt.

SEASONED LOAF

Add ¼ cup chopped celery, 2 tablespoons catsup and 2 teaspoons dried parsley flakes. Serve with dairy sour cream and crumbled bacon.

CURRIED MEAT LOAF

Omit Worcestershire sauce. Add ¼ cup finely chopped green pepper and 2 tablespoons chili sauce. Top with 1 can (8¾-ounces) crushed pineapple, drained, mixed with ¼ teaspoon curry powder.

LAYERED MEATLOAF

6 to 8 servings
Microwave bundt pan

 2 *pounds ground beef*
 2 *eggs, slightly beaten*
1½ *cups crushed cracker crumbs*
 ½ *cup chopped onions*
 2 *tablespoons Worcestershire sauce*
1½ *teaspoons salt*
 ½ *teaspoon pepper*

Filling:
 8 *ounces fresh mushrooms, sliced*
 1 *medium onion, chopped*
 2 *tablespoons butter or margarine*
 1 *teaspoon thyme*
 1 *teaspoon cumin*
 1 *cup sour cream*
 1 *cup bread crumbs*

Mix meatloaf ingredients thoroughly. Set aside while preparing filling.

Saûté mushrooms and onions in butter. MICROWAVE 3 MINUTES on HIGH. Add thyme, cumin, sour cream and bread crumbs.

Spread ⅓ of meat mixture in bottom of bundt pan, top with ½ of filling, ⅓ of meat mixture, rest of filling ending with the last of meat mixture. MICROWAVE 5 MINUTES on HIGH, reduce setting to '6' for 10 to 15 MINUTES, or until internal temperature reaches 140°. Rotate once or twice during cooking time.

Clockwise from top: Layered Meatloaf, Rolled Stuffed Meatloaf, Twin Meatloaves

ROLLED STUFFED MEATLOAF

6 servings
9 x 5 loaf dish

1½ *pounds lean ground beef*
 1 *egg, slightly beaten*
 1 *teaspoon salt*
¼ *teaspoon pepper*
 3 *slices boiled ham*
 2 *slices mozzarella cheese*
½ *cup chopped green olives*

Mix ground beef, egg, salt, and pepper thoroughly. On waxed paper, roll meat mixture out onto ½-inch thick rectangle (about 8 x 11-inch).

Lay ham slices crosswise, then cheese. Sprinkle with chopped olives. Roll meat into log shape. Secure the ends and seam by pinching them together. Place seam side down in (9 x 5-inch) loaf pan.

Insert Automatic Thermometer into center of the meatloaf. Connect thermometer. PROGRAM TO MICROWAVE on HIGH for 5 MINUTES or until the internal temperature reaches 105°, then on '5' for 16 MINUTES or until internal temperature reaches 135°, then on '4' 4 MINUTES or until 155°.

SARA'S MEATBALLS ❄

2 to 2½ dozen meatballs
12 x 8-inch baking dish

 1 *pound lean ground beef*
½ *pound lean ground pork*
½ *cup finely chopped onion*
½ *cup uncooked rice*
½ *cup bread or cracker crumbs*
 1 *egg*
½ *teaspoon salt*
⅛ *teaspoon pepper*
 1 *can (10¾-ounces) condensed tomato soup, diluted*

Combine ground meats, onion, rice, bread crumbs, egg, salt and pepper in medium bowl. Mix well. Form into 2-inch balls. Place in (12 x 8-inch) baking dish. Pour diluted soup over meatballs. Cover. MICROWAVE 14 to 16 MINUTES on '8', or until rice is tender, rearranging meatballs carefully after 8 minutes.

NOTE: Can be made ahead and refrigerated. To reheat from refrigerated state, MICROWAVE 3 to 5 MINUTES on '8'.

TWIN MEATLOAVES

4 servings
9 x 6-inch utility dish

 2 *eggs, slightly beaten*
 2 *tablespoons Worcestershire sauce*
1½ *pounds lean ground beef*
 1 *cup crushed cracker crumbs*
½ *cup chopped onion*
 1 *teaspoon salt*
¼ *teaspoon pepper*
½ *cup steak sauce or ½ cup catsup*
 1 *tablespoon Worcestershire sauce*

Combine eggs, Worcestershire sauce, ground beef, cracker crumbs, onion, salt and pepper in a 2-quart bowl. Divide mixture in half and shape into two loaves. Arrange loaves in the utility dish and coat the top and sides with the catsup and Worcestershire sauce or steak sauce. MICROWAVE on HIGH 18 to 20 MINUTES.

Variation:

Basic Meatballs

Form meat mixture into meatballs. To preheat browning dish MICROWAVE 6 MINUTES on HIGH. Add meatballs, MICROWAVE on HIGH 6 to 8 MINUTES, turning meatballs over every 2 minutes.

TOMATO SAUCED MEATLOAF

6 to 8 servings
9 x 5-inch loaf dish

 1 *pound lean ground beef*
¼ *pound lean ground pork*
¼ *pound lean ground veal*
 1 *can (8-ounces) tomato sauce*
½ *cup finely chopped onion*
 1 *egg, beaten*
½ *cup bread crumbs or quick rolled oats*
 1 *teaspoon salt*
⅛ *teaspoon pepper*

Combine ground meats, ½ cup tomato sauce, onion, egg, bread crumbs, salt and pepper in large bowl. Mix thoroughly. Spread mixture in loaf pan.

Pour remaining tomato sauce over loaf. MICRO-WAVE 20 to 25 MINUTES on '6', or until set in center. Let stand 5 minutes.

SWEDISH MEATBALLS

4 servings
Browning dish

1 cup milk
½ cup crushed dry bread crumbs
½ pound lean ground beef
½ pound lean ground pork
1 egg, slightly beaten
1 small onion, chopped
1 tablespoon Worcestershire sauce
½ teaspoon salt
¼ teaspoon pepper
⅛ teaspoon cloves
2 tablespoons cooking oil
¼ cup all-purpose flour
½ cup cream
½ teaspoon instant beef bouillon dissolved in ½ cup hot water

Pour milk over bread crumbs in medium mixing bowl. Let stand 10 minutes. Add ground meats, egg, onion, Worcestershire sauce, salt, pepper and cloves. Blend well with fork. Form into 1-inch balls. To preheat browning dish, MICROWAVE 5 MINUTES on HIGH. Add oil and meatballs. MICROWAVE 4 MINUTES on HIGH, turning meatballs over once. Remove meatballs. Set aside.

Stir flour into drippings until smooth and well blended. Gradually stir in cream and bouillon. Return meatballs to browning dish. Cover. MICROWAVE 6 to 8 MINUTES on '6', or until sauce is thickened and meatballs are cooked through. Let stand 5 minutes, covered.

SALISBURY STEAK

4 to 5 servings
Browning dish

1½ pounds lean ground beef
1 package (¾-ounce) brown gravy mix
1 cup water
1 small onion, thinly sliced
1 teaspoon salt
¼ teaspoon pepper

Form ground beef into 4 to 5½-inch thick patties.

To preheat browning dish, MICROWAVE 4 MINUTES on HIGH. Add patties. MICROWAVE 4 MINUTES on HIGH, turning patties over after 2 minutes.

Add gravy mix, water and onion. Cover. MICROWAVE 6 to 8 MINUTES on HIGH, or until meat reaches desired doneness. Season with salt and pepper.

Variations:
SOUR CREAM SALISBURY STEAK

½ cup dairy sour cream
1 jar (2-ounces) mushroom stems and pieces, drained

Add sour cream and mushrooms during last 2 minutes of cooking. Heat until bubbly.

TASTY HERBED SALISBURY STEAK

Add 1 to 2 teaspoons of either parsley, basil or thyme with gravy mix.

SAUCY SALISBURY STEAK

¼ cup catsup
2 teaspoons Worcestershire sauce

Add catsup and Worcestershire sauce with gravy mix.

Basic Meatballs, Sara's Meatballs and Swedish Meatballs

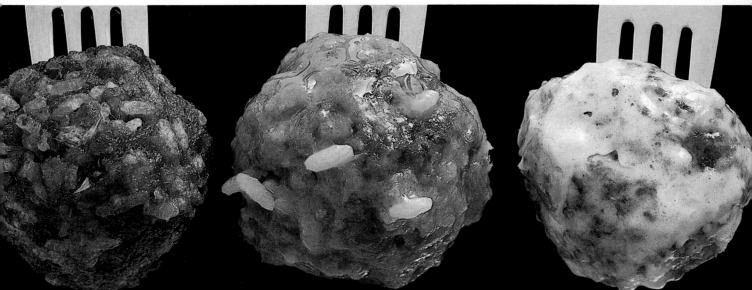

STUFFED CABBAGE ROLLS

8 servings
12 x 8-inch baking dish

8 *large cabbage leaves*
1 *pound lean ground beef*
1 *cup cooked rice*
1 *egg*
1 *teaspoon instant minced onion*
½ *teaspoon sage*
1 *can (8-ounces) tomato sauce*
2 *tablespoons brown sugar*
2 *tablespoons lemon juice or vinegar*
2 *tablespoons water*

To remove leaves from cabbage, place whole cabbage in microwave oven. MICROWAVE 2 to 3 MINUTES on HIGH, or until outer leaves peel off easily. Save remaining cabbage for soups or salads. With a sharp knife, cut hard cores from softened leaves.

Combine ground beef, rice, egg, onion, and sage in medium mixing bowl. Mix throughly. Form into 8 small loaves. Overlap cut edges of cabbage leaf. Place loaf in center. Fold sides of loaf over stuffing and roll up ends to form neat package. Arrange cabbage rolls, seam side down, in (12 x 8-inch) baking dish.

Mix tomato sauce, brown sugar, lemon juice and water in 2-cup measure. Pour sauce over cabbage rolls. Cover with plastic wrap. MICROWAVE 3 MINUTES on HIGH.

Reduce setting. MICROWAVE 10 MINUTES on '6', until cabbage is tender and stuffing is cooked through.

NOTE: If large cabbage leaves are not available, stuffing may be divided between smaller leaves.

SPAGHETTI SAUCE

6 to 8 servings
4 to 5-quart bowl

1 *pound lean ground beef*
1 *medium onion, chopped*
3 *cloves garlic, pressed or finely chopped*
4 *stems celery with leaves, chopped*
2 *cans (16-ounce) tomatoes*
1 *cup water*
1 *can (6-ounce) tomato paste*
½ *cup red wine or cooking wine*
¼ *cup chopped fresh parsley*
1 *teaspoon oregano*
1 *teaspoon salt (omit the salt if using cooking wine)*
2 *bay leaves*
¾ *teaspoon basil*
¼ *teaspoon fennel seed*

In a 4 or 5-quart bowl combine meat, onion, garlic and celery. MICROWAVE on HIGH for 5 to 8 MINUTES or until meat is set. Drain.

Add remaining ingredients and mix well. PROGRAM TO MICROWAVE uncovered on HIGH for 8 MINUTES, stir, then MICROWAVE on '5' for 45 MINUTES.

SPEEDY SHEPHERD'S PIE

4 to 5 servings
9-inch pie plate

1 *pound lean ground beef*
2 *slices soft white bread, torn into coarse crumbs*
⅔ *cup milk*
1 *egg, slightly beaten*
¼ *cup finely chopped onion*
1 *tablespoon Worcestershire sauce*
1 *teaspoon salt*
3 *cups hot mashed potatoes*
1 *cup finely diced American process cheese*

Combine beef, bread, milk, egg, onion, Worcestershire sauce and salt in medium bowl. Spread evenly in 9-inch pie plate. MICROWAVE 7 MINUTES on '8'.

Mask meat with mashed potatoes. Sprinkle with cheese. MICROWAVE 5 MINUTES on '8', or until cheese is melted. Let stand 3 minutes.

HAMBURGER CREOLE

4 servings
2-quart casserole

3 *slices bacon, chopped*
½ *cup chopped onion*
1 *pound lean ground beef*
½ *cup chopped celery*
¼ *cup chopped green pepper*
2 *tablespoons flour*
1 *can (8-ounces) stewed tomatoes*
1 *teaspoon salt*

Combine bacon and onion in a 2-quart casserole. MICROWAVE 2 to 3 MINUTES on HIGH, or until onion is transparent. Crumble ground beef into casserole. Mix well. MICROWAVE 3 MINUTES on HIGH, or until meat is set, stirring once.

Add remaining ingredients. Mix well. Cover. MICROWAVE 5 to 8 MINUTES on HIGH, stirring once. Serve over rice.

TACO PIE

6 servings
9-inch pie plate

3 *cups taco chips, crushed*
1 *can (16-ounces) refried beans*
1 *pound ground chuck*
1 *packet taco seasoning mix*
1 *cup shredded lettuce*
1 *large tomato, chopped*
½ *cup grated Cheddar cheese*
  Taco sauce (optional)

Crush taco chips in paper or plastic bag, using a rolling pin to lightly go over chips 2 or 3 times. Place in pie plate.

Press refried beans against taco chips, using a wooden spoon, to form a shell. Set aside.

Brown ground beef in a mixing bowl. MICROWAVE 5 to 6 MINUTES on HIGH, stirring occasionally. Add taco seasoning mix and recommended amount of water according to package directions. MICROWAVE 3 MINUTES on HIGH until mixture is at a boil. Reduce setting to '6' for 2 to 3 MINUTES or until mixture thickens.

Fill taco and bean "crust" with beef filling. MICROWAVE 2 to 3 MINUTES on '8' or until hot.

Top with lettuce, tomato, cheese and taco sauce if desired. Cut in wedges and serve.

Stuffed Pepper Pots

STUFFED PEPPER POTS

4 servings
Browning dish or
1½-quart casserole
4 squares plastic wrap or
8x8-inch baking dish

4 *large green peppers*
1 *pound lean ground beef, crumbled*
1 *small onion, chopped*
2 *cups cooked rice*
1 *can (8-ounces) tomato sauce*
2 *tablespoons chopped celery*
  Seasoned salt to taste

Cut thin slice from stem end of each pepper. Remove seeds and membrane. Rinse and drain.

(Preheat browning dish 4 MINUTES on HIGH, if used.) Combine beef and onion in browning dish or 1½-quart casserole. MICROWAVE 2 to 3 MINUTES on HIGH, or until onion is transparent, stirring after 1 minute.

Add rice, tomato sauce, celery and salt. Mix well. Stuff peppers with mixture. Garnish with ½ cherry tomato, if desired. Place each pepper on square of plastic wrap. Bring up corners and twist to seal tightly, or place peppers in (8x8-inch) baking dish and cover with plastic wrap. MICROWAVE 12 MINUTES on '8'.

NOTE: 1 cup diced, cooked beef may be substituted for ground beef. Omit browning dish and add beef with rice. Peppers and stuffing may be assembled for later cooking.

Veal Limone

Veal

VEAL VALENCIA

4 servings
Browning dish

¼ *cup flour*
1½ *pounds veal, cut in ¾-inch chunks*
2 *tablespoons butter or margarine*
1 *can (16-ounces) tomatoes*
½ *cup finely chopped onion*
1 *jar (2½-ounces) button mushrooms*
1½ *cups beef stock or bouillon*
1 *bay leaf, crumbled*

Place flour in paper bag. Add veal and shake to coat. Place browning dish in oven. MICROWAVE 5 MINUTES on HIGH.

Add butter and veal. MICROWAVE 2 to 4 MINUTES on HIGH, or until veal is brown, stirring twice.

Add remaining ingredients. Cover. MICROWAVE 5 MINUTES on HIGH. Stir and cover.

Reduce setting. MICROWAVE 12 MINUTES on '6', or until veal is fork tender. Serve over hot fluffy rice or buttered noodles.

VEAL LIMONE

4 servings
10-inch browning dish

2 *tablespoons butter or margarine*
¼ *cup flour*
1 *teaspoon salt*
½ *teaspoon pepper*
1 *pound boneless veal, thinly sliced*
1 *tablespoon flour*
1 *tablespoon lemon juice*
½ *cup mushrooms*
½ *cup water*
½ *teaspoon beef bouillon*

Combine flour, salt and pepper. Set aside.

Pound veal to ¼-inch thick. Roll in flour mixture.

To preheat browning dish, MICROWAVE 5 MINUTES on HIGH. Add 2 tablespoons butter. Stir. Add veal. Cover. MICROWAVE 4 MINUTES on HIGH.

Push veal to one side. Add flour, lemon juice, mushrooms, water and bouillon. Stir well. MICROWAVE 2 to 3 MINUTES on HIGH.

VEAL STEAKS IN ONION SAUCE

4 servings
Browning dish

½ cup flour
2 teaspoons dry mustard
½ teaspoon garlic salt
⅛ teaspoon pepper
4 veal arm steaks, ½-inch thick
2 tablespoons salad oil
1 envelope (1 to 1¼-ounces) onion soup mix
½ cup water
½ cup chili sauce
2 tablespoons Worcestershire sauce
½ teaspoon salt

Mix flour, mustard, garlic salt and pepper together. Coat steaks on both sides in seasoned flour mixture.

To preheat browning dish, MICROWAVE 4 MINUTES on HIGH. Add oil and 2 steaks. MICROWAVE 4 to 6 MINUTES on HIGH, turning steaks over after 2 to 3 minutes. Set aside. Preheat browning dish again, if necessary. Brown remaining steaks. Return first two steaks to browning dish.

Combine soup mix, water, chili sauce, Worcestershire sauce and salt in small bowl. Pour over steaks. Cover. MICROWAVE 12 to 15 MINUTES on '6', or until steaks are fork tender.

VEAL MARENGO

4 servings
3-quart casserole

1 pound veal, or 4 veal cutlets, cut into 1-inch cubes
1 medium onion, chopped
3 stems celery, thinly sliced
⅛ teaspoon garlic
1 can (8-ounces) tomato sauce
¼ cup white wine
2 bay leaves
1 teaspoon oregano
1 teaspoon rosemary
1 teaspoon salt
½ teaspoon pepper
8 ounces fresh mushrooms, sliced
2 tablespoons lemon juice
2 sprigs parsley, chopped

Combine veal, onion, celery and garlic. MICROWAVE for 5 MINUTES on HIGH, or until onion is transparent.

Add tomato sauce, wine, bay leaf and spices. MICROWAVE 5 MINUTES on HIGH, or until mixture boils.

Toss mushrooms with lemon juice. Add. Cover. MICROWAVE 10 MINUTES on '5'. Sprinkle with parsley before serving.

VEAL CHOPS PARMIGIANA

4 servings
12x8-inch baking dish

1 egg, beaten
¼ cup flour
½ cup zwieback or fine cracker crumbs
1 teaspoon salt
¼ teaspoon pepper
½ teaspoon paprika
4 veal loin chops, ¾-inch thick
4 slices mozzarella cheese
3 cans (4-ounces each) tomato sauce (1½ cups)
¼ cup grated Parmesan cheese

Beat egg in pie plate. Combine flour, crumbs, salt, pepper and paprika in shallow dish. Dip chops in beaten egg, then in flour mixture, coating well. Place in (12x8-inch) baking dish. Cover loosely. MICROWAVE 10 MINUTES on '8'.

Place slice of cheese on each chop. Cover with tomato sauce. Sprinkle with Parmesan cheese. MICROWAVE 8 to 10 MINUTES on '6', or until cheese is melted and chops are fork tender.

CREAMY VELVET VEAL

6 servings
Browning dish

1 can (10¾-ounces) condensed cream of
   mushroom soup, undiluted
¼ cup water
2 tablespoons red wine
2 teaspoons lemon juice
   Dash pepper
2 tablespoons butter or margarine
1 medium onion, sliced
1 clove garlic, finely chopped
1½ pounds thinly sliced veal, cut in serving pieces
½ teaspoon paprika

Combine soup, water, wine, lemon juice and pepper in 1-quart measure. Set aside.

To preheat browning dish, MICROWAVE 4 MINUTES on HIGH. Add butter, onion and garlic. Stir. Add veal. MICROWAVE 4 MINUTES on HIGH, turning veal over after 2 minutes.

Pour sauce over veal. Cover. MICROWAVE 4 to 6 MINUTES on '6', or until sauce is hot and veal is fork tender. Sprinkle with paprika. Serve over buttered noodles, if desired.

Pork

CROWN ROAST OF PORK

8 to 10 servings
2-quart utility dish

8 *to* 10 *pound crown roast*
 (14 to 16 ribs)
 Apple sausage stuffing

Insert Automatic Thermometer into the thickest part of meat, being careful not to touch fat or bone. Place roast, wide end up, on a roasting rack in a 2-quart utility dish. Connect Automatic Thermometer to the oven. PROGRAM TO MICROWAVE on '6' until it reaches 110°, or approximately 30 minutes.

Prepare apple sausage stuffing.

Turn roast narrow end up, baste with meat juices. Stuff cavity lightly.

Place remaining stuffing around the bottom of the roast. Reposition the Automatic Thermometer.

PROGRAM TO MICROWAVE on '6' until it reaches 165°, then on '2' until it reaches 175°, or remove from microwave, tent with foil and let stand 15 minutes before serving.

APPLE SAUSAGE STUFFING

 1 *pound ground pork*
 1 *large onion, chopped*
 2 *apples, peeled, cored and chopped*
 2 *stems celery, thinly sliced*
 2 *tablespoons butter or margarine*
 1 *cup hot water*
 1 *cube chicken bouillon*
 1 *tablespoon parsley flakes*
1½ *teaspoons seasoned salt*
 2 *cups seasoned stuffing mix*

MICROWAVE pork on HIGH for 3 MINUTES, or until set. Drain fat and set aside.

MICROWAVE onion, apples, celery and butter on HIGH for 4 to 5 MINUTES or until onion is transparent.

Combine remaining ingredients and mix well.

Place meat in dish meaty side up. Insert automatic thermometer into heavy fleshy part.

Prepare stuffing, tossing lightly. Stuffing will be slightly dry. It will pick up moisture from the meat as it cooks.

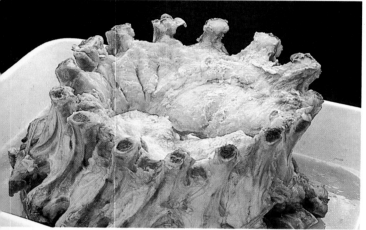

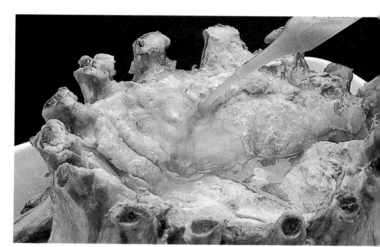

Remove automatic thermometer. Turn roast rib end up.

Baste with meat juices, being careful to cover entire roast. Reposition automatic thermometer into meaty section.

Loosely fill center of roast with stuffing.

Place additional stuffing around roast in dish. Place in oven, microwave until thermometer reaches 165°.

SUGGESTED COOKING TIMES FOR PORK

CUT	COOKING CONTAINER	SPECIAL INSTRUCTIONS	SETTING	MINUTES PER POUND	STANDING TIME
Loin Roast, boneless	8 × 12 × 2 utility dish	Microwave fat side down on rack, 5 min. on High. Reduce setting and proceed as per chart, turning halfway through.	6	10 - 13	10 min. under foil tent. Foil shiny side in.
Loin Roast, bone in	8 × 12 × 2 utility dish		6	9 - 12	
Pork Chops	8 x 12 x 2 utility dish	Coat with Shake and Bake mixture, or cover with soup or sauce.	6	6 - 8	5 Min. Covered

Meat thermometer reads 160° to 170° on removal and 180° after standing.

ROAST PORK

12x8-inch baking dish with microwave roasting rack

Pork loin roast
Salt and pepper

Rub seasonings into meat. Place roast fat side down on microwave roasting rack in (12x8-inch) utility dish. MICROWAVE 5 MINUTES on HIGH.

Reduce setting. MICROWAVE on '6' or '5' for half the roasting time.

Turn roast fat side up. MICROWAVE on '6' or '5' until internal temperature of thickest part of meat registers 160°. Let stand 15 minutes, tented with aluminum foil, shiny side in. Roast will continue to cook while standing.

NOTE: Do not use meat thermometer in microwave oven. Inverted saucers may be substituted for roasting rack.

Variations:

GARLIC STUDDED PORK

Make incisions in pork with sharp knife. Press 2 or 3 cloves garlic, peeled and quartered, into incisions.

HERBED PORK

Rub 1 clove garlic (halved), thyme and basil or sage, into meat.

SMOTHERED PORK TENDERLOINS

4 to 6 servings
12x8-inch baking dish
Medium mixing bowl

2 *pork tenderloins, about 1 to 1½-pounds each*
  Salt and pepper
3 *tablespoons butter or margarine*
1 *medium onion, chopped*
1 *can (8-ounces) crushed pineapple with juice*
2 *teaspoons soy sauce*
½ *teaspoon ginger*
2 *cups dried bread crumbs*

Place pork tenderloins in (12x8-inch) baking dish. Season with salt and pepper. Set aside.

Place butter in mixing bowl. MICROWAVE on HIGH until butter melts. Mix in onion, pineapple and juice, soy sauce, ginger and bread crumbs. Spread mixture over tenderloins. MICROWAVE 35 to 40 MINUTES on '6', or until meat is fork tender, or internal temperature registers 180°.

PORK CHOPS

4 servings
Browning dish

4 1-*inch cut pork chops*
1 *tablespoon oil*
1 *cup wine*
1 *teaspoon chicken bouillon*

Preheat browning dish for 7 MINUTES. Add oil and chops to browning dish. MICROWAVE 2 MINUTES on HIGH. Turn and MICROWAVE 4 MINUTES on HIGH. Add wine and bouillon to chops. Cover. MICROWAVE 20 MINUTES on '6'.

BARBECUED PORK CHOPS

4 servings
8 x 8-inch baking dish

4 *pork chops, cut ½-inch thick*
⅓ *cup chopped celery*
2 *tablespoons firmly packed brown sugar*
2 *teaspoons lemon juice*
½ *teaspoon mustard*
½ *teaspoon salt*
⅛ *teaspoon pepper*
1 *can (12-ounces) tomato sauce*
½ *cup water*

Arrange pork chops in (8 x 8-inch) baking dish. Sprinkle with celery, brown sugar, lemon juice, mustard, salt and pepper. Pour tomato sauce and water over chops. Cover with plastic wrap. MICROWAVE 5 MINUTES on HIGH. Reduce setting. MICROWAVE 15 to 18 MINUTES on '6', or until pork chops are fork tender.

STUFFED PORK CHOPS IN WINE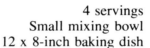

4 servings
Small mixing bowl
12 x 8-inch baking dish

2 *tablespoons butter or margarine*
1 *medium onion, finely chopped*
¼ *cup finely chopped celery*
1 *cup dried bread crumbs*
2 *tablespoons snipped parsley*
⅛ *teaspoon sage*
⅛ *teaspoon celery seed*
4 *pork chops, 1½-inches thick, with pocket*
2 *tablespoons flour*
1 *cup chicken stock, or 2 teaspoons instant chicken*
    bouillon dissolved in 1 cup boiling water
½ *cup dry white wine*

Combine butter, onion and celery in small mixing bowl. MICROWAVE 3 to 5 MINUTES on HIGH, or until onion is transparent.

Stir in bread crumbs, parsley, sage and celery seed. Fill pockets of pork chops with stuffing. Secure openings with wooden picks.

Arrange chops in (12 x 8-inch) baking dish, meatiest portions to outside. Sprinkle with flour. Pour chicken broth and wine over chops. Cover. MICROWAVE 35 to 40 MINUTES on '6', or until chops are fork tender.

BARBECUE BEEF OR PORK

4 servings
2-quart bowl

4 *cups chopped cooked beef or pork*
1½ *cups barbecue sauce*

Combine beef or pork and barbecue sauce in a 2-quart bowl. Cover. MICROWAVE 6 MINUTES on HIGH, or until mixture just starts to bubble. Serve on hamburger buns.

SHAKE AND BAKE PORK CHOPS PLAIN OR BARBECUE STYLE

3 to 4 servings
8 x 8-inch baking dish

4 *pork chops, cut ½-inch thick*
1 *package Shake and Bake Coating Mix (Plain or*
    Barbecue Style)

Coat pork chops with Shake and Bake mixture. Arrange the chops in baking dish and MICROWAVE 20 MINUTES on '6'.

OLD CHINA TOWN PORK BURGER

6 servings
10½-inch browning dish

1 *pound pork sausage*
1 *cup soft bread crumbs*
⅓ *cup finely chopped green onion*
⅓ *cup finely chopped green pepper*
1 *can (6½-ounces) water chestnuts, drained*
    and chopped
1 *large egg*
2 *tablespoons dry sherry*
2 *tablespoons soy sauce*
1 *small clove garlic, pressed or finely chopped*
¼ *teaspoon ginger*

Combine, mix well, form into 6 patties. Preheat browning dish 5 MINUTES on HIGH. MICROWAVE 6 MINUTES on HIGH.

Top with sauce and serve on toasted buttered buns.

SWEET 'N SOUR SAUCE

½ *cup crushed pineapple, drained*
⅓ *cup catsup*
2 *tablespoons vinegar*
2 *tablespoons orange marmalade*
1 *tablespoon prepared mustard*

Combine all ingredients. MICROWAVE 2 to 3 MINUTES on HIGH.

PORK CHOPS CREOLE

4 servings
12 x 8-inch baking dish

4 *lean pork chops*
1 *medium onion, chopped*
1 *small green pepper, chopped*
¼ *cup chopped celery*
2 *teaspoons parsley flakes*
1 *teaspoon salt*
½ *teaspoon pepper*
1 *can (8-ounces) tomato sauce*
  Dash hot pepper sauce

Arrange chops in (12 x 8-inch) baking dish with meatiest portions to outside of dish. Top with onion, green pepper and celery. Sprinkle with parsley, salt and pepper. Pour in tomato sauce. Add pepper sauce. Cover. MICROWAVE 5 MINUTES on HIGH.

Reduce setting. MICROWAVE 15 to 18 MINUTES on '6', or until chops are fork tender. Serve with rice.

PORK CHOPS IN SOUR CREAM

4 servings
Small mixing bowl
Browning dish

4 *pork chops*
  Seasoned bread crumbs
1 *tablespoon oil*
1 *cup dairy sour cream*
¼ *cup water*
2 *tablespoons vinegar*
1 *tablespoon sugar*
1 *small bay leaf*
¼ *teaspoon savory or basil*

Dredge chops in bread crumbs.

Preheat browning dish on HIGH for 5 MINUTES. Add oil and spread evenly in dish. Add chops and MICROWAVE on HIGH for 1 MINUTE on each side. Drain if needed.

In a separate bowl, combine remaining ingredients and pour over chops. Cover. PROGRAM TO MICROWAVE on HIGH for 5 MINUTES, then on '6' for 18 MINUTES or until chops are tender.

Spoon gravy over chops and serve with rice or egg noodles.

Pictured top to bottom: Shake and Bake Pork Chops-Plain, Barbecued Pork Chops, Pork Chops in Wine and Shake and Bake-Barbecue.

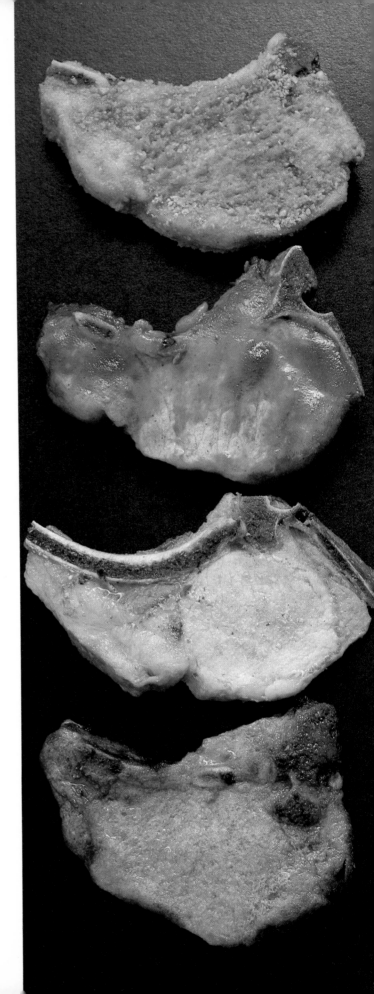

Barbecued Spareribs

ORIENTAL RIBS

4 servings
12x8-inch baking dish
1-quart measure

2 *pounds pork spareribs, cut into 2 to 2½-inch pieces*
1 *cup dried apricots, chopped*
1 *clove garlic, pressed or finely chopped*
2 *tablespoons sugar*
½ *cup water*
1 *teaspoon salt*
¼ *teaspoon pepper*
1 *teaspoon ginger*
¼ *teaspoon cloves*
1 *tablespoon vinegar*
½ *teaspoon lemon juice*

Place ribs in (12x8-inch) baking dish. Cover with wax paper. MICROWAVE 5 MINUTES on HIGH. Drain excess juices. Rearrange ribs. In 1-quart measure combine apricots, garlic, sugar, water, salt, pepper, ginger, cloves, vinegar and lemon juice. MICROWAVE 4 to 6 MINUTES on HIGH, or until mixture comes to a full boil. Stir. Pour over ribs. Cover with wax paper. MICROWAVE 30 to 35 MINUTES on '8', or until tender. Rearrange once during cooking period.

BARBECUED SPARERIBS

4 servings
2-quart utility dish or
8 x 8-inch baking dish

2 *pounds spareribs*
2½ *cups catsup*
½ *cup firmly packed brown sugar*
½ *cup cider vinegar*
1 *tablespoon horseradish*
1 *tablespoon Worcestershire sauce*
1 *teaspoon garlic salt*

Place spareribs bone side down in 2-quart dish. Mix remaining ingredients in 1-quart measure. Pour over ribs. Cover. MICROWAVE 5 MINUTES on HIGH.

Reduce setting. MICROWAVE 35 MINUTES on '6', or until meat is tender, turning ribs over after 15 minutes. Let stand 3 minutes.

Variation:
Use country style spareribs. Add 5 to 10 minutes to final cooking time.

NOTE: If you have a favorite sauce recipe, substitute for the above.

PORK AND APPLE PIE

4 to 6 servings
9 x 5-inch loaf dish

1 *large onion, chopped*
1 *teaspoon sage*
½ *teaspoon salt*
⅛ *teaspoon pepper*
2 *pounds lean pork, cut in ¼ to ½-inch cubes*
3 *apples, peeled, cored and thinly sliced*
2 *cups mashed potatoes*

Mix onion, sage, salt and pepper together in small bowl. In (9 x 5-inch) loaf dish, alternate layers of pork and layers of apple, sprinkling each layer with onion mixture. Use half the pork, half the apples and half the onions for each layer. Cover with plastic wrap. MICROWAVE 10 MINUTES on HIGH.

Spread mashed potatoes over top of loaf. Do not cover. MICROWAVE 10 MINUTES on '6', or until potatoes are heated through and meat is tender.

BASIC PORK CASSEROLE

4 to 6 servings
3-quart casserole

1 *tablespoon butter or margarine*
1 *onion, sliced*
1½ *pounds lean boneless pork, cut in ¾-inch cubes*
¼ *cup flour*
2½ *cups water*
1 *teaspoon instant chicken bouillon*
1 *teaspoon salt*
¼ *teaspoon pepper*

Combine butter and onion in 3-quart casserole. MICROWAVE 3 MINUTES on HIGH, or until onion is transparent. Add pork. Sprinkle flour over pork. Toss to coat well. Add water, bouillon, salt and pepper. Cover. MICROWAVE 5 MINUTES on HIGH.

Reduce setting. MICROWAVE 30 MINUTES on '6', or until meat is fork tender.

Variations:

AMERICAN PORK

Add:
1 *can (16-ounces) baked beans or red kidney beans, drained and rinsed*
4 *slices bacon, cut in 1-inch pieces*

Serve with boiled potatoes

BELGIAN PORK

Substitute 1¼ cups wine for half the water
Add:
½ *pound pitted prunes*

Just before serving, stir in 1 tablespoon currant jelly. Sprinkle with snipped parsley.

CHINESE PORK

Substitute salad oil for butter
Add:
2 *tablespoons firmly packed brown sugar*
2 *tablespoons catsup*
2 *tablespoons vinegar*
2 *tablespoons soy sauce*
1 *carrot cut in julienne strips*
1 *green pepper, cut in julienne strips*

During last 15 minutes, add:
1 *cup unsweetened pineapple cubes*
Serve with boiled rice.

FRENCH PORK

Add:
1 *can (4-ounces) sliced mushrooms, drained*
1 *clove garlic, pressed or finely chopped*

Just before serving add:
2 *tablespoons brandy*
2 *tablespoons cream*

MICROWAVE 2 MINUTES on HIGH, or until hot, but not boiling. Garnish with snipped parsley. Serve with new potatoes or egg noodles. Follow with tossed green salad.

ENGLISH PORK

Substitute cider for half the water. During last 15 minutes add:

1 *teaspoon sage*
2 *apples, peeled, cored and sliced*

Serve with a green vegetable and mashed potatoes.

GERMAN PORK

During last 15 minutes add:
½ *pound frankfurters, cut in 1-inch pieces*
1 *cup drained sauerkraut*
½ *teaspoon caraway seeds*
1 *teaspoon German mustard*

Serve with boiled or sauteed potatoes

HUNGARIAN PORK

Add:
4 *carrots, sliced*
4 *medium boiling potatoes, peeled and sliced*
2 *tomatoes, peeled and quartered*
1 *tablespoon paprika*

Just before serving, stir in:
3 *tablespoons dairy sour cream*

SCANDINAVIAN PORK

During last 15 minutes add:
2 *apples, peeled, cored and chopped*
½ *pound cooked ham, diced*

Just before serving add:
⅓ *cup cream*

MICROWAVE 2 MINUTES on HIGH, or until hot, but not boiling. Serve with braised red cabbage and sautéed potatoes.

Spicy Ham Slice

SPICY HAM SLICE

4 to 6 servings
12x8-inch utility dish with
microwave roasting rack

1 *fully-cooked, center-cut, smoked ham slice,*
   1½-inches thick
1 *cup catsup*
2 *tablespoons prepared mustard*
3 *tablespoons finely chopped green onion and tops*
   Parmesan cheese

Slash edges of ham to prevent curling. Combine catsup, mustard and onions in 1-cup measure. Set aside. Place ham on microwave roasting rack in (12x 8-inch) utility dish. MICROWAVE 10 MINUTES on '6'.

Turn ham over. Spread with sauce. Sprinkle with Parmesan cheese. MICROWAVE 5 to 6 MINUTES on '6', or until ham is hot or internal temperature registers 150°. Let stand 3 minutes before serving. NOTE: Do not use meat thermometer in microwave oven.

Variations:

Substitute the following for catsup sauce:

 1 *cup apricot or peach preserves, or*
½ *cup whole cranberry sauce mixed with*
   ½ *cup applesauce*

FULLY-COOKED-HAM CHART

WEIGHT	TIME	
	SETTING '6'	SETTING '5'
2-4 Pounds	10-12 Min. per Pound	12-14 Min. per Pound
5-8 Pounds	8-10 Min. per Pound	10-12 Min. per Pound

BAKED HAM

12x8-inch utility dish with
microwave roasting rack

Fully cooked ham
One of the following glazes, if desired

Score ham, if desired.

Place ham fat side down on microwave roasting rack in (12x8-inch) utility dish. Do not cover. MICRO-WAVE on '6' or '5' for half the roasting time (see chart.)

Turn ham fat side up. Brush with glaze and stud with cloves, if desired. MICROWAVE on '6' or '5' for remaining time, or until internal temperature registers 140° to 150°. Let stand 15 minutes tented with aluminum foil, shiny side in. (Temperature will rise 10 degrees during standing.)

HAM GLAZES

¼ *cup honey*
½ *cup firmly packed brown sugar*

Measure honey in 1-quart measure. MICROWAVE 1 to 2 MINUTES on HIGH, or until hot. Stir in brown sugar. Glaze ham after turning.

½ *cup firmly packed brown sugar*
2 *teaspoons prepared mustard*
1 *can (8-ounces) pineapple rings*

Blend sugar and mustard together. Add enough pineapple juice to make smooth paste.

After turning ham, arrange pineapple rings on top. Spoon on glaze. Garnish with maraschino cherries, if desired.

BROWN SUGAR HAM

6 to 8 servings
Shallow baking dish

5 *pound canned ham*
1 *tablespoon whole cloves*
½ *cup firmly packed brown sugar*
2 *tablespoons bread crumbs*
1 *teaspoon prepared mustard*

Place ham in baking dish. Stud with cloves. Combine sugar, bread crumbs and mustard in a small bowl. Spread mixture on top of ham and press firmly. Cover with waxed paper. MICROWAVE 10 MINUTES on HIGH.

Rotate dish ½ turn. MICROWAVE 25 MINUTES on '6'. Let stand 10 minutes, covered with aluminum foil.

Variation:

1 *package (10-ounces) frozen raspberries,*
   defrosted
½ *cup sugar*
1 *teaspoon cinnamon*
¼ *teaspoon cloves*

Mix raspberries and sugar together in 1-quart measure. MICROWAVE 4 to 5 MINUTES on HIGH, or until mixture is syrupy. Stir in cinnamon and cloves. MICROWAVE 1 MINUTE on HIGH, or until hot. Glaze ham after turning.

Baked Ham with Orange Potato Shells, page 187

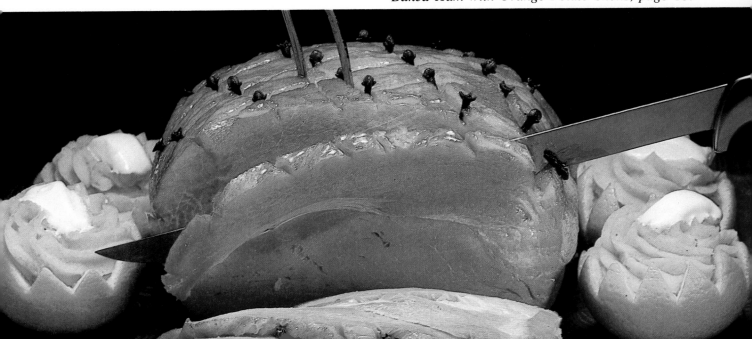

Lamb

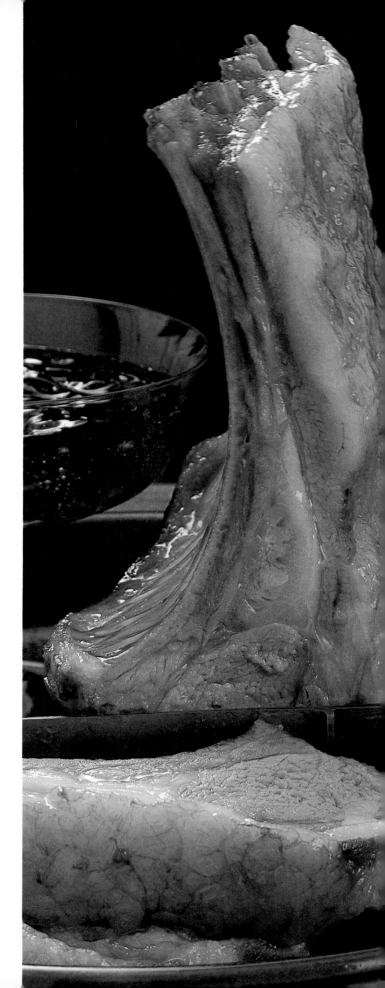

RACK OF LAMB (6 RIBS)

1 *rack of lamb (6 ribs)*
1 *clove garlic*

2 servings
12x8-inch utility dish
Microwave roasting rack

Cut garlic and rub it over the meat. Cut 5-6 slits in the fat side of the meat and insert thin slices of garlic.

Place on roasting rack with the bone resting on the rack. Connect the Automatic Thermometer to the oven.

Insert thermometer in the end muscle as close to the center of the meat as possible.

PROGRAM TO MICROWAVE on: Setting '6'—150°, Setting '2'—170°.

MINT JELLY GLAZE FOR LAMB

1½-cup
2-cup measure

12-*ounce jar mint jelly*

Spoon mint jelly into a 2-cup measure. MICRO-WAVE 3 MINUTES, 30 SECONDS to 4 MIN-UTES on HIGH.

Rack of Lamb with Mint Jelly

SUGGESTED COOKING TIMES FOR LAMB

CUT	COOKING CONTAINER	SPECIAL INSTRUCTIONS	MINUTES PER POUND	SETTING	TURN	STANDING TIME
Leg of Lamb	12×8 utility dish	Microwave fat side down on rack 5 min. on High Reduce setting and finish	9 - 11	6	Fat side up halfway through	10 min. under foil tent (foil shiny side in)
Lamb Chops	12 × 8 utility dish	Microwave on rack for 5 min. on High. Reduce setting to finish	7 - 9	6	Once	

These are approximate times for medium lamb. Adjust them if you prefer medium-rare or well-done lamb.

ROAST LEG OF LAMB

12x8-inch utility dish,
with microwave roasting rack

Leg of Lamb
1 *clove garlic, halved*

Rub lamb with garlic. Place fat side down on microwave roasting rack in (12x8-inch) utility dish. MICROWAVE 5 MINUTES on HIGH.

Reduce setting. MICROWAVE on '6' or '5' for half the roasting time.

Turn roast fat side up. MICROWAVE on '6' or '5' until internal temperature of thickest part of meat registers 150° to 160°, depending on desired doneness. Let stand 10 minutes tented with aluminum foil, shiny side in. Roast will continue to cook while standing.

NOTE: Use microwave meat thermometer in microwave oven. Inverted saucers may be substituted for roasting rack.

Variations:
GARLIC STUDDED LEG OF LAMB

Make incisions in lamb with sharp knife. Press 4 to 5 garlic cloves, peeled and quartered, into incisions.
HERBED LAMB

Rub 1 clove garlic, halved, and rosemary or thyme, into meat.

LEMON MARINATED LAMB CHOPS

4-servings
12 x 8-inch utility dish,
with microwave roasting rack
2-cup measure

4 *lamb chops, ¾-inch thick*
½ *cup salad oil*
½ *cup sherry*
⅓ *cup cider vinegar*
1 *medium onion, chopped*
2 *tablespoons lemon pepper seasoning*
1 *teaspoon lemon juice*
1 *clove garlic, pressed or finely chopped*
½ *teaspoon rosemary*
2 *teaspoons Worcestershire sauce*

Place lamb chops in (12 x 8-inch) utility dish.

Mix oil, sherry, vinegar, onion, lemon pepper seasoning, lemon juice, garlic, rosemary and Worcestershire sauce in 2-cup measure. MICROWAVE 1 MINUTE, 30 SECONDS on HIGH, or until hot. Pour over chops. Cover. Let stand 3 hours, or overnight, refrigerated.

Arrange marinated lamb chops on microwave roasting rack in (12 x 8-inch) utility dish. MICROWAVE 5 MINUTES on HIGH.

Turn chops over. MICROWAVE 10 to 15 MINUTES on '6', or until chops are of desired doneness.

LAMB RIBLETS
IN TOMATO HONEY SAUCE

4 servings
2-quart casserole

2 *pounds lamb riblets*
1 *medium onion, sliced*
1 *can (10½-ounces) condensed golden mushroom*
   soup, undiluted
1 *can (8-ounces) tomato sauce*
2 *tablespoons honey*
½ *teaspoon salt*
⅛ *teaspoon pepper*
¼ *teaspoon thyme*

Place riblets in 2-quart casserole. Cover with onion slices. MICROWAVE 10 MINUTES on '6'. Drain fat.

Stir in soup, tomato sauce, honey, salt, pepper and thyme. Cover. MICROWAVE 40 to 50 MINUTES on '6', or until riblets are tender, stirring twice.

Serve over rice, noodles or biscuits.

SHISH KABOB

4 servings
1-quart measure
2-quart utility dish with
microwave roasting rack

¼ *cup olive or salad oil*
2 *tablespoons light corn syrup*
2 *teaspoons lemon juice*
½ *teaspoon savory*
½ *teaspoon thyme*
1 *pound lamb cut in 1-inch cubes*
1 *green pepper cut in 1-inch squares*
4 *small onions*
4 *large fresh mushrooms*
4 *cherry tomatoes*

Combine olive oil, corn syrup, lemon juice, savory and thyme in 1-quart measure. MICROWAVE 3 MINUTES on HIGH. Stir. Cool slightly. Stir in lamb cubes. Marinate at least four hours or overnight.

Alternate lamb cubes and vegetables on each of 4 skewers. Lay carefully on roasting rack. MICROWAVE 8 to 10 MINUTES on '6', or until lamb is desired degree of doneness. Serve on a bed of rice or barley.

NOTE: Two inverted saucers may be substituted for roasting rack.

LAMB CURRY

6 to 8 servings
2-quart casserole

1 *tablespoon butter or margarine*
2 *teaspoons curry powder*
¼ *cup chopped onion*
1 *clove garlic, pressed or finely chopped*
1½ *pounds lamb, cut in ¾-inch cubes*
2 *cups chopped celery*
2 *tablespoons flour*
1 *can (14-ounces) unsweetened pineapple*
   tidbits
1 *teaspoon salt*
1 *teaspoon garlic salt*

Combine butter, curry powder, onion and garlic in 2-quart casserole. MICROWAVE 3 MINUTES on HIGH, or until onion is transparent. Add lamb cubes and celery. Sprinkle with flour. Toss to mix well.

Drain pineapple syrup into 1-quart measure. Add water to make 2 cups. Stir pineapple tidbits and liquid into lamb mixture. Cover. MICROWAVE 40 MINUTES on '6'. Add salts. Serve over rice.

Shish Kabobs

130

LAMB BURGER SPECIAL

4 servings
Browning dish

4 *slices bacon, cooked crisp and crumbled*
1 *pound ground lamb*
1 *teaspoon salt*
¼ *teaspoon pepper*
½ *teaspoon marjoram*
2 *teaspoons Worcestershire sauce*
4 *slices tomato*
⅓ *cup shredded cheddar cheese*

Mix bacon, lamb, salt, pepper, marjoram and Worcestershire sauce together in a medium bowl. Form into four ¾-inch thick patties. Set aside.

To preheat browning dish, MICROWAVE 4 MINUTES on HIGH. Add meat patties, MICROWAVE 5 to 6 MINUTES on HIGH, or until desired doneness, turning patties over once.

Top each with a tomato slice and shredded cheddar cheese. MICROWAVE 1 MINUTE on HIGH, or until cheese melts. Serve on roll or toast with tossed salad.

LAMB STEW

4 to 6 servings
Shallow 2-quart casserole

2 *pounds small boiling potatoes, peeled*
2 *large onions, sliced*
   Salt and pepper
2 *pounds lamb shoulder, cut in ¾-inch cubes,*
   excess fat removed
1 *to 2 cups water, as needed*
   Snipped parsley

Set aside half the potatoes. Slice remaining potatoes thinly. Spread sliced potatoes in bottom of 2-quart casserole. Layer half the onions over potatoes. Season lightly with salt and pepper.

Spread meat over onions. Season lightly. Layer with second half of onions. Arrange whole potatoes on top of onions. Add just enough water to cover. Cover tightly. MICROWAVE 30 to 40 MINUTES on '6', or until meat is fork tender. Let stand 10 minutes, covered. Sprinkle with parsley before serving in soup bowls.

NOTE: Use a casserole wide enough to take all the whole potatoes in one layer. Lamb shoulder is high in fat content. The whole potatoes absorb fat, enhancing their flavor, while improving the character of the sauce.

LAMB PILAF

4 servings
1-quart measure
1½-quart casserole

2 *cups chicken broth, or 3 teaspoons instant*
   chicken bouillon dissolved in 2 cups boiling
   water
3 *tablespoons butter or margarine*
2 *teaspoons lemon juice*
1 *teaspoon salt*
1 *bay leaf*
1 *cup uncooked white rice*
1 *medium onion, finely chopped*
1 *small green pepper, chopped*
2 *tablespoons butter or margarine*
1 *to 1½-cups cubed cooked lamb*
¼ *to ½-teaspoon thyme*

Combine chicken broth, 3 tablespoons butter, lemon juice, salt and bay leaf in medium sauce pan. Bring to boil on conventional range. Add rice. Cover tightly. Lower heat. Cook 18 to 20 minutes, or until rice is tender and all liquid absorbed. (Or cook rice in broth according to directions on page 199.) Remove bay leaf.

Combine onion, green pepper and 2 tablespoons butter in 1-quart measure. MICROWAVE 3 to 4 MINUTES on HIGH, or until onion is transparent and green pepper is tender-crisp.

Add lamb and thyme. Mix well. MICROWAVE 3 MINUTES on HIGH. Layer one third of cooked rice and half of the lamb mixture in 1½-quart casserole. Repeat layers. Top with remaining one third rice. Cover. MICROWAVE 5 MINUTES on '5', or until very hot.

LAMB CHOPS MARMALADE

4 servings
2-quart casserole

4 *loin lamb chops, cut ¾ to 1-inch thick*
   Garlic salt
½ *cup orange marmalade*

Sprinkle lamb chops with garlic salt on both sides. Arrange in 2-quart casserole, meatiest parts to outside of dish. Spoon marmalade over chops. Cover. MICROWAVE 5 MINUTES on HIGH.

Reduce setting. MICROWAVE 10 to 15 MINUTES on '6', or until chops are desired doneness.

Sausage, front: Ring Bologna, Bratwurst, back: Smokey sausage links and Polish sausage

Bacon, Sausage & Specialty Meats

BACON BASICS

A few slices of bacon can be cooked on a bed of paper towels for easy clean-up. If you wish to save drippings, cook bacon in a baking dish. Very salty cures do not cook well on paper towels.

For larger quantities of bacon, use a microwave roasting rack in a 12 x 8-inch utility dish. Larger amounts can be cooked on paper towels, but they render more fat than the towels can absorb, so you'll need to wipe up the oven floor. When cooking bacon, cover with a paper towel to prevent spatters.

The chart is for medium-sliced bacon. Thinly-sliced bacon should be microwaved for less time. Thick-sliced bacon will take a little longer. When microwaving special "home style" cures, reduce setting to '6' or '5' and experiment with times to suit your type of bacon.

SUGGESTED COOKING TIMES FOR BACON

NUMBER OF STRIPS	TIME	SETTING
2	2 min.	High
3	3½ min.	High
4	4-4½ min.	High
5	5-5½ min.	High
6	6-6½ min.	High

SAUSAGE COOKING INSTRUCTIONS

ITEM	AMOUNT		HEAT ON HIGH		HEAT ON HIGH
Sausage	2 links or patties	Preheat browning dish 5 MINUTES on HIGH.	1 minute	Turn for even heating.	1½-2 minutes
	4 links or patties		1 minute		2½-3 minutes
	6 links or patties		1 minute		3 minutes
Brown & Serve Sausage	2 links		30 seconds		45 seconds
	4 links		45 seconds		1 minute
	6 links		1 minute		1 minute
Little Sizzlers	2 links		1 minute		1 minute
	4 links		1 minute		1-2 minutes
	6 links		1 minute		2½ minutes

POLISH SAUSAGE A LA ORANGE

6 servings
10½-inch browning dish

1½ *pounds Polish sausage cut in ½-inch to
¾-inch slices*
3 *oranges, peeled and cut in 1-inch chunks*

Preheat browning dish for 6 MINUTES on HIGH. Add sausage and stir until the sizzling stops. Add oranges and stir. Leave uncovered.

MICROWAVE 3 MINUTES on HIGH, and then 8 MINUTES on '4'.

ORANGE-BERRY GLAZED LUNCHEON MEAT

4 servings
Plate

1 *can (12-ounces) luncheon meat*
¾ *cup cranberry-orange relish*

Make slashes in luncheon meat ¾-inch apart, cutting to within ¾-inch of bottom. Fill slits with cranberry-orange relish. Place ham on plate. Cover loosely with waxed paper. MICROWAVE 4 to 5 MINUTES on '6', or until heated through.

CHEESE SAUSAGE BEAN CASSEROLE

6 servings
2-quart casserole

4 *cups cooked macaroni*
1½ *pounds smoked sausage or ring bologna*
1 *cup chopped celery*
1 *cup chopped onion*
1 *can (16-ounces) stewed tomatoes*
1 *teaspoon chili powder*
1 *teaspoon cumin*
1 *can (16-ounces) garbanzo beans*
1 *can (16-ounces) whole kernel corn*
1 *jar (8-ounces) processed cheese spread*
1 *cup crushed corn flake crumbs*

Slice sausage into ½-inch slices. Place in 2-quart casserole with celery and onions. Cover. MICROWAVE 4 MINUTES on HIGH, or until celery is tender. Add tomatoes, chili, cumin, beans, corn and precooked macaroni. Mix well. Melt cheese spread. MICROWAVE 3 MINUTES on '5'. Pour over mixture. Top with corn flake crumbs. MICROWAVE 6 MINUTES on '6', uncovered.

SAUSAGE BUDGET DINNER

4 servings
10-inch browning dish

6 franks, large, sliced lengthwise
1 onion, thinly sliced and separated
2 carrots, thinly sliced
2 to 3 cups shredded Chinese cabbage
2 teaspoons chicken bouillon
1 cup water
1 teaspoon marjoram

Preheat browning dish 6 MINUTES on HIGH. Layer franks, onions, carrots and cabbage in dish. Dissolve bouillon in water, pour over combined ingredients, sprinkle marjoram on top. Cover. MICROWAVE 8 to 10 MINUTES on HIGH, or until carrots are tender-crisp.

SAUSAGE CASSEROLE DINNER

4 servings
10½-inch browning dish

1 pound Polish sausage or smoked sausage
1 medium onion, coarsely chopped
1 clove garlic pressed or finely chopped
3 cups, 1-inch pieces, yellow winter squash
1 package (10-ounces) frozen whole kernel corn
1 can (16-ounces) stewed tomatoes
2 teaspoons seasoned salt

Preheat browning dish 6 minutes. Slice sausage diagonally at 2-inch intervals, being careful not to cut through completely. Place in preheated browning dish. MICROWAVE 1 MINUTE on HIGH. Turn sausage over. MICROWAVE 1 MINUTE on HIGH. Add remaining ingredients. Cover. MICROWAVE 4 MINUTES on HIGH. Stir. Cover. MICROWAVE 8 MINUTES on '6', or until squash is tender.

SMOKED BRATWURST

4 to 5 servings
8 x 8-inch baking dish

1 pound smoked bratwurst

Place bratwurst in (8 x 8-inch) baking dish. MICROWAVE 5 MINUTES, 30 SECONDS to 6 MINUTES on '6', or until sausages are hot. Serve with pickle relish or sauerkraut on bun, or with German potato salad.

Variation:
Pour ½ cup beer over bratwurst. Cover. MICROWAVE 5 MINUTES, 30 SECONDS to 6 MINUTES on '6'.

SAUSAGE SKILLET

4 servings
10-inch browning dish

1 package (8-ounces) brown & serve sausages, cut in half
1 jar (16-ounces) German potato salad
1 can (16-ounces) sauerkraut

Preheat browning dish 6 MINUTES on HIGH. Add sausage. MICROWAVE 3 MINUTES on HIGH, turning halfway through. Drain sauerkraut. Add potato salad and sauerkraut to browning dish, stir. Cover. MICROWAVE 4 to 6 MINUTES on HIGH, or until potatoes are hot.

SAUSAGE RING

8 servings
Ring mold

2 packages bulk pork sausage
1½ cups cracker crumbs
2 eggs, slightly beaten
½ cup milk
1 medium onion, chopped
1 medium size tart apple, peeled and finely chopped

Mix all ingredients together and fit into ring mold. MICROWAVE 16 MINUTES on HIGH. Turn out onto plate, MICROWAVE 6 MINUTES on HIGH. Let stand for 5 minutes.

Serving Suggestion: Fill center with scrambled egg.

CORNED BEEF

6 to 8 servings
2-quart casserole

3 *pound beef corned brisket with seasoning packet*
2 *cups water*

Place beef in casserole. Sprinkle with seasonings. Pour water over meat. Cover. MICROWAVE 8 to 10 MINUTES on HIGH, or until water boils rapidly. Reduce setting. MICROWAVE 40 MINUTES on '6', or until fork tender, turning meat over after 20 minutes. Let stand 15 minutes in juices, covered. Serve with Horseradish Sauce.

NOTE: If cabbage is desired, cook during standing time, following directions on page 192.

HORSERADISH SAUCE

1½ cup
1-cup measure

1 *package (3-ounces) cream cheese*
2 *teaspoons horseradish*
1 *tablespoon cream*

Place cream cheese in 1-cup measure. MICRO-WAVE 2 MINUTES on '6', or until softened. Stir in horseradish and cream. MICROWAVE 1 MIN-UTE on '6'. Serve warm.

Corned Beef with Cabbage and Horseradish Sauce

QUICK BOLOGNA CASSEROLE

4 servings
2-quart casserole

1 *pound ring bologna*
1 *can (16-ounces) Irish potatoes*
1 *can (10-ounces) cream of mushroom soup*
1 *small onion, chopped*

Skin ring bologna. Place in 2-quart casserole. Cut into 8 pieces, retaining ring shape. Slice potatoes into ¼-inch slices. Place half the potatoes over bologna. Sprinkle with chopped onion. Add the remainder of potatoes. Top with cream of mushroom soup. Cover. MICROWAVE 4 MINUTES on HIGH, then MICROWAVE 8 MINUTES on '6'.

FRIED LIVER AND ONION

4 to 6 servings
Browning dish

¼ *cup all-purpose flour*
1 *teaspoon salt*
⅛ *teaspoon pepper*
1 *pound beef liver, cut in serving pieces*
2 *tablespoons salad oil*
2 *medium onions, sliced*

Combine flour, salt and pepper. Coat liver pieces with flour.

To preheat browning dish, MICROWAVE 4 MIN-UTES on HIGH. Add oil. Place half the liver and half the onion in browning dish. MICROWAVE 2 MINUTES on HIGH, depending on desired doneness, turning liver over once. Repeat with remaining liver and onions. Return all liver to browning dish. Spoon onions on top of liver, MICROWAVE 10 MINUTES to 12 MINUTES on '6', or until liver is tender.

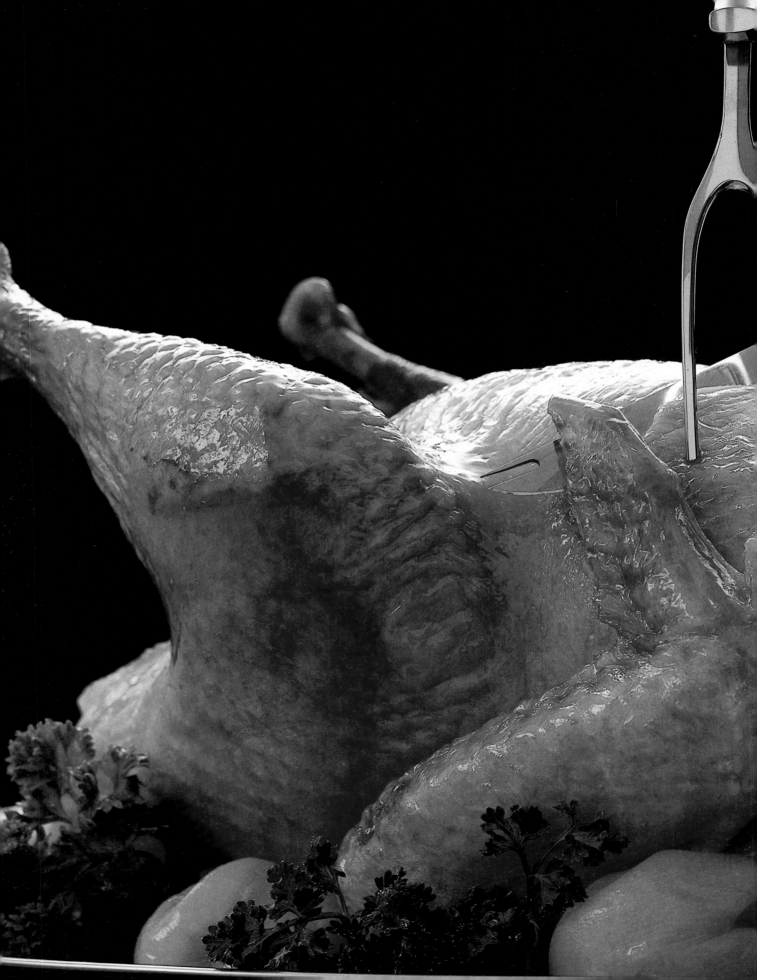

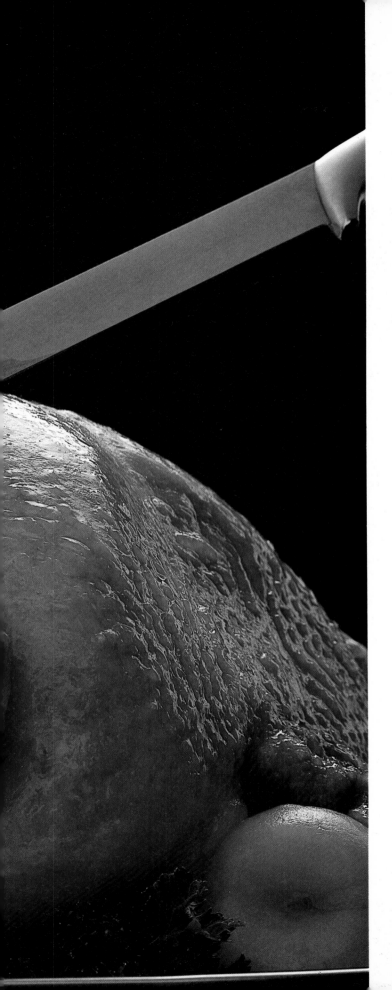

Poultry

Sautéed or braised chicken parts cook juicy and tender in about half the time it takes to cook them conventionally. With heat control microwave ovens poultry parts are cooked on high, while whole birds from Cornish hens to a 14 pound turkey are cooked on a low setting to minimize the need for shielding tender parts and for turning. When buying turkey over 14 pounds, ask your butcher to saw it into halves or quarters, and try the recipes for roasted turkey parts.

ROAST TURKEY
(12 to 14 pounds)

> 2-quart utility dish
> Roasting rack

To Defrost:

Remove any metal clasps from the outer wrapping. Place the turkey in a utility dish to keep the juices from running.

MICROWAVE 7 to 8 MINUTES per pound on '5' allowing the turkey to rest 5 minutes after every 15 minutes of defrosting. Rotate the turkey after each rest period.

When you can easily move the legs and open the cavity, run the turkey under cold water to clean and remove any remaining ice crystals.

NOTE: To insure complete defrosting run turkey under warm water and let stand 15 minutes.

To Cook:

Clean and stuff bird. Do not use metal skewers.

In a 2-quart utility dish turn the turkey on its side. MICROWAVE 15 MINUTES on HIGH. Turn it on its other side. MICROWAVE 15 MINUTES on HIGH.

Place the roasting rack in the utility dish and turn the turkey breast side down. MICROWAVE 35 MINUTES on '6'. Turn breast side up. MICROWAVE 35 MINUTES on '6'. Turn breast side down. MICROWAVE 30 to 40 MINUTES on HIGH, or until the internal temperature in the thigh reads 165° to 170° F.

Immediately wrap in foil and let stand 15 to 20 minutes to finish cooking.

POULTRY BASICS

To prepare whole birds for cooking, remove giblets, wash thoroughly and pat dry with paper towels. Do not stuff poultry until just before cooking.

You can try microwaving turkeys over 10 pounds, but large turkeys require less attention when roasted in a conventional oven. Roasting large birds conventionally frees the microwave oven for cooking side dishes, thus reducing over-all preparation time.

Poultry parts should be washed, cut into serving pieces if necessary, and dried with paper towels unless they are to be coated with crumbs. Arrange them in the dish with meatiest portions to the outside.

Fried chicken is best cooked conventionally. The amount of fat necessary to fry chicken becomes dangerously hot in the microwave oven.

The most reliable test for poultry doneness is a meat thermometer. Unless you have a special microwave thermometer, do not use a meat thermometer in the microwave oven while cooking. To test internal temperature of whole birds, insert thermometer in fleshy part of the inside thigh muscle without touching the bone. Remove bird from the oven when temperature registers 175°. Tent with foil and let stand to complete cooking.

Other tests for poultry doneness are:

Pierce inside thigh muscle deeply with fork. If juices run clear without a tinge of pink, poultry is done.

Press thickest part of drumstick meat between fingers, it should be very soft. With whole birds, move drumstick up and down. Joint should move freely or break when bird is done.

ROAST CHICKEN

4 to 6 servings
12x8-inch utility dish with
microwave roasting rack

5 *pound roasting chicken*
  Stuffing, if desired
¼ *cup honey*
 1 *teaspoon Worcestershire*
 1 *teaspoon soy sauce*

Remove giblets. Wash chicken well with cold water. Pat dry. Stuff cavity, packing loosely. Secure cavity with wooden picks or poultry skewers.

Place chicken breast-side down on microwave roasting rack in (12x8-inch) utility dish. MICROWAVE 10 MINUTES on HIGH.

Reduce setting. MICROWAVE 14 MINUTES on '6'.

Combine honey, Worcestershire sauce and soy sauce in 1-cup measure. Baste chicken with glaze.

Turn breast side up. Brush with glaze. MICROWAVE 22 MINUTES on '6', or until thickest part of inside thigh muscle registers 175°, rotating dish ½ turn if necessary. Let stand 15 minutes, tented with aluminum foil.

NOTE: Do not use meat thermometer in microwave oven. Cooking times are the same for unstuffed chicken.

TURKEY BREAST
(6 to 8 pounds)

2-quart utility dish,
and roasting rack

1 6 *to 8 pound turkey breast, defrosted*
  Wine jelly glaze

Place cleaned turkey breast on its side in utility dish with roasting rack inside. MICROWAVE 15 MINUTES on HIGH, turn to other side, MICROWAVE 15 MINUTES on HIGH. Turn breast side down, making sure breast is as flat as possible on rack, brush with glaze, MICROWAVE 20 MINUTES on '6'.

Turn breast side up, glaze, MICROWAVE 20 to 30 MINUTES on '6', or until internal temperature reaches 165° to 170° F. Brush on more glaze, and tent with foil. Let stand 15 minutes. Serve with warmed glaze in a dish.

NOTE: To insure complete defrosting run turkey under warm water and let stand for fifteen minutes.

SUGGESTED COOKING TIMES FOR POULTRY

ITEM	COOKING METHOD	MINUTES PER POUND		SETTING	TURN	STANDING TIME
Cornish Game Hen	8 x 8-inch baking dish. Start breast side down.	14 - 16		6	once	5 min.
Cornish Game Hens, 4 stuffed	12 x 8-inch baking dish or platter. Start breast side down.	6 - 8		High	once	7 min.
Duckling	2-quart utility dish on rack or inverted saucer	$^1/_5$ total cooking time on High, then…	9 - 11	6	once	10 min. under foil tent
Roasting Hen	12 x 8-inch baking dish on rack or inverted saucer	$^1/_5$ total cooking time on High, then…	9 - 11	6	once	15 min. under foil tent

NOTE: Meat thermometer reads 175° on removal and 195° after standing.

TURKEY ROAST

4 to 6 servings
Glass loaf pan

1 *pound, 11-ounce frozen turkey roast*

Place frozen turkey roast in loaf pan upside down. Cover with waxed paper. MICROWAVE 5 MINUTES on HIGH.

Turn turkey roast over. Reduce setting. MICROWAVE 28 MINUTES on '6', or until roast reaches an internal temperature of 175°, rotating dish halfway through cooking time. Let stand 15 minutes, covered with aluminum foil.

NOTE: If package includes gravy mix, add water to drippings as package directs. MICROWAVE on HIGH until boiling. Stir in mix. Let stand 2 to 3 minutes, or until thick. Do not use meat thermometer in microwave oven.

ORANGE-GLAZED TURKEY QUARTER

2 servings
8 x 8-inch baking dish

1 *cup orange juice*
1 *cup firmly packed brown sugar*
¼ *turkey (about 2-pounds)*

Combine orange juice and sugar in 2-cup measure. Mix well. Place dry turkey, skin side up, in (8 x 8-inch) baking dish. Brush with orange glaze. MICROWAVE 15 MINUTES on '6', rotating dish ½ turn (so that front is toward back of oven) after 10 minutes.

Turn turkey flesh side up. Brush with glaze. MICROWAVE 15 MINUTES on '6', rotating dish ½ turn after 10 minutes.

Turn turkey skin side up. Brush with glaze. MICROWAVE 5 MINUTES on '6'. Let stand 5 minutes.

DUCKLING A L'ORANGE

3 to 4 servings
2-quart utility dish with
microwave roasting rack

4 *to 5 pound fresh or frozen duckling, defrosted*
1 *orange, quartered*
1 *small onion, quartered*
2 *stems celery, cut in thirds*
   Orange sauce, below

Remove giblets and wash cavity. If duckling is defrosted, keep in original wrappings. Prick plastic bag with a fork near backbone.

Place duckling on rack in (2-quart) utility dish, breast side up. MICROWAVE 7 to 9 MINUTES on HIGH, or until duckling begins to exude fat. Let stand 5 minutes to allow fat to run out. Prepare orange sauce below.

Remove duckling from bag. Drain fat from utility dish. Secure neck skin of duckling to back with wooden picks. Lift wing tips up and over back. Fill cavity with orange and onion quarters and celery pieces.

Place duckling breast down on rack. MICROWAVE 12 to 17 MINUTES on '6'. Turn breast side up. Brush with orange sauce. MICROWAVE 20 to 25 MINUTES on '6'. Let stand 5 minutes, tented with aluminum foil, shiny side in. Serve with remaining orange sauce and garnish with orange segments if desired.

Orange Sauce

2-cup measure

1 *orange*
1 *cup orange juice*
2 *tablespoons cornstarch*
2 *tablespoons soy sauce*
¼ *cup orange liqueur or sherry*
3 *tablespoons honey*

Pare orange thinly, being careful not to take white membrane. Cut peel in julienne strips. Set aside.

Combine orange juice, cornstarch and soy sauce in 2-cup measure. Mix well. MICROWAVE 2 to 3 MINUTES on HIGH. Stir. Mix in orange peel, liqueur and honey. MICROWAVE 2 MINUTES on HIGH, or until sauce is thick and glossy.

GINGER PLUM SAUCE

1 *cup plum jelly*
1½ *teaspoons powdered ginger*

Put jelly in a 2-cup measure. MICROWAVE 3 MINUTES on '8'. Stir in ginger. MICROWAVE 2 MINUTES on '8'.

PHEASANT IN WINE CREAM SAUCE

6 to 8 servings
Shallow 3-quart casserole
Serving dish or platter

3 *pheasants, skinned and cut in serving pieces*
2 *teaspoons salt*
¼ *teaspoon pepper*
½ *teaspoon rosemary*
1 *cup finely chopped onion*
1 *cup chopped parsley*
½ *cup dry white wine*
1 *teaspoon instant chicken bouillon dissolved in 1 cup hot water*
¼ *cup cornstarch*
1 *cup light cream*
   Paprika

Place pheasants in 3-quart casserole. Season with salt, pepper and rosemary. Sprinkle with onion and parsley. Pour in wine and bouillon. Cover. MICRO-WAVE 60 to 70 MINUTES on HIGH, or until pheasants are fork tender, turning and rearranging pieces after 30 minutes.

Remove pheasants to serving dish. Set aside.

Blend cornstarch with cream until smooth. Stir into hot broth. MICROWAVE 5 to 6 MINUTES on '8', or until thickened, stirring once. Pour over pheasants. Sprinkle with paprika. MICROWAVE 2 to 3 MINUTES on '8', or until heated through.

CHICKEN MAJORCA

6 servings
12 x 8-inch baking dish

6 *chicken breasts*
1 *bottle (8-ounces) Italian salad dressing*
1 *jar (12-ounces) apricot preserves*

Place chicken in deep bowl. Pour Italian dressing over chicken and turn pieces to coat well. Cover. Marinate at least 2 hours at room temperature, or overnight in refrigerator.

Drain chicken and add apricot preserves to dressing. Mix well. Place chicken skin side up in (12 x 8-inch) baking dish. Pour glaze over and turn chicken to coat well. Cover with plastic wrap. MICROWAVE 36 MINUTES on '5', or until chicken is tender, turning breasts over after 18 minutes. Let stand 3 minutes.

NOTE: If chicken has been refrigerated, add a few minutes to cooking time.

CHICKEN BREASTS BLEU

6 servings
12x7 or 8x8-inch dish

8 *ounces fresh mushrooms, sliced*
1 *medium onion, chopped*
2 *tablespoons butter or margarine*
4 *ounces bleu cheese, crumbled*
½ *cup bread crumbs*
6 *chicken breast halves, boned and skinned*

In a 1-quart measure, combine mushrooms, onions and butter. MICROWAVE 3 to 4 MINUTES on HIGH, or until onions are transparent. Drain. Add bleu cheese and bread crumbs. Mix well. Set aside.

Pound chicken breasts until flat. Place 2 heaping tablespoons of bleu cheese mixture into dish, forming into a mound. Place a chicken breast half over the mound, tucking loose edges around the mixture. Repeat with other chicken breast halves. Cover with plastic wrap. MICROWAVE 15 to 20 MINUTES on '6', or until chicken breasts are fork tender. Cover each with 1 tablespoon bread crumb mixture. Let stand covered 3 minutes.

Bread Crumb Mixture:

¼ *cup bread crumbs*
2 *tablespoons chopped, fresh parlsey*
½ *teaspoon paprika*

TURKEY DIVAN

4 servings
8x8-inch baking dish

1 *package (10-ounces) frozen, chopped broccoli*
1 *can (11¾-ounces) cream of chicken soup, undiluted*
¼ *cup milk or light cream*
2 *tablespoons dry sherry*
6 *to 8 turkey slices*
⅓ *cup grated Parmesan cheese*

Place broccoli in baking dish. Cover tightly with plastic wrap. MICROWAVE 3 to 4 MINUTES on HIGH, or until hot. Drain.

Blend soup, milk and sherry in 1-quart measure. Spoon half over broccoli. Top with turkey slices. Add half the grated cheese to remaining soup. Spoon over turkey. Top with remaining cheese. Cover lightly. MICROWAVE 5 MINUTES on HIGH, or until sauce bubbles and cheese browns lightly.

OVEN FRIED CHICKEN

4 servings
2-quart utility dish

2 *pound cut up frying chicken*
1 *package seasoned coating for chicken*
1 *tablespoon grated Parmesan cheese*
½ *teaspoon garlic salt*
  Paprika

Wash chicken and pat dry.

Combine coating mix, Parmesan cheese and garlic salt in bag provided with coating mix. Coat the chicken with the mixture.

Arrange chicken in a 2-quart utility dish with the thickest part of the meat to the outside of the dish. Sprinkle with paprika. PROGRAM TO MICROWAVE on HIGH for 5 MINUTES, then on '7' for 15 to 20 MINUTES, or until meat is tender.

EASY-BAKE CHICKEN

4 servings
12x8-inch baking dish

1 *package (2⅜-ounces) seasoned coating mix*
  for chicken
2 *to 3 pound frying chicken, cut up*

Place coating mix in bag provided with mix. Add chicken pieces, two or three at a time, and shake until evenly coated. Arrange chicken in (12x8-inch) baking dish, with meaty pieces toward outside of dish. Cover with wax paper. MICROWAVE 20 to 30 MINUTES on HIGH, or until thickest pieces are fork tender.

Chicken left to right: uncoated, brushed with Kitchen Bouquet, Chicken Barbecue, Oven Fried Chicken, Easy Bake Chicken, Chicken Coated with Corn Flake Crumbs

CHICKEN BARBECUE

4 servings
12 x 8-inch baking dish

2 to 3-pound frying chicken, cut in serving pieces
¼ cup butter or margarine, melted
1½ cups Barbecue Sauce (page 202)

Arrange chicken in (12 x 8-inch) baking dish, with meatiest portions toward outside of dish. Brush with melted butter. Pour barbecue sauce over chicken. Cover with plastic wrap. MICROWAVE 25 to 30 MINUTES on HIGH. Let stand 5 minutes, covered.

CHICKEN COATED WITH CORN FLAKE CRUMBS

4 servings
12x8-inch baking dish

1 2½ to 3-pound frying chicken, cut in serving pieces
2 eggs, slightly beaten
⅓ cup melted butter or margarine
1 teaspoon salt
2 cups corn flake crumbs

Combine eggs, butter and salt in a small bowl. Combine chicken with egg mixture and then with corn flake crumbs. Arrange chicken in (12x8-inch) baking dish, with meatiest portions toward outside. Cover with wax paper. MICROWAVE 20 to 25 MINUTES on HIGH, or until thickest pieces are fork tender.

SHERRIED CHICKEN BREASTS

4 servings
10x8-inch utility dish

8 *ounces fresh mushrooms, sliced*
3 *tablespoons butter or margarine*
1 *tablespoon flour*
1 *cup whipping cream*
2 *tablespoons sherry*
4 *chicken breasts (1½-pounds)*

Combine mushrooms and butter in 1½-quart bowl. MICROWAVE 1 to 2 MINUTES on HIGH, or until butter melts and mushrooms soften. Stir in flour, cream and sherry, mixing until smooth. MICROWAVE 4 to 5 MINUTES on '6', or until mixture boils, stirring once. Set aside.

Arrange chicken breasts, skin side down, in (10x8-inch) utility dish, with meatiest portions to outside. Cover. MICROWAVE 10 MINUTES on HIGH, turning chicken over after 5 minutes.

Pour sauce over chicken. Cover. MICROWAVE 10 to 15 MINUTES on HIGH, or until chicken is fork tender.

CHICKEN MARENGO

4 to 6 servings
2-quart casserole

1 *cup all-purpose flour*
1 *teaspoon salt*
¼ *teaspoon pepper*
1 *teaspoon paprika*
2½ *to 3 pounds frying chicken, cut in serving pieces*
1 *clove garlic, pressed or finely chopped*
1 *teaspoon sugar*
½ *teaspoon basil*
8 *ounces fresh mushrooms, sliced*
1 *can (8-ounces) tomato sauce*
½ *cup sherry*
8 *to 10 stuffed olives*
1 *tablespoon olive brine*
¼ *cup almonds, toasted*
½ *pound mozzarella cheese, grated*

Combine flour, salt, pepper and paprika in a shallow dish. Coat chicken with flour mixture. Place in 2-quart casserole. Add garlic, sugar, basil and mushrooms. Mix in any remaining seasoned flour. Stir in tomato sauce, sherry, olives and brine. Sprinkle with almonds and cheese. Cover. MICROWAVE 25 MINUTES on HIGH, or until chicken is fork tender, stirring once. Let stand 5 to 10 minutes, covered.

CHICKEN PARISIENNE

4 servings
12 x 8-inch baking dish

4 *large chicken breasts (2½-pounds)*
1 *can (10¾-ounces) condensed cream of mushroom soup, undiluted*
1 *can (4-ounces) mushroom stems and pieces, drained*
1 *cup dairy sour cream*
½ *cup sherry*
  Paprika

Arrange chicken breasts skin side up in (12 x 8-inch) baking dish.

Stir together soup, mushrooms, sour cream and sherry in 1-quart bowl. Pour over chicken breasts. Sprinkle generously with paprika. Cover. MICROWAVE 35 to 40 MINUTES on '5', or until chicken is fork tender, rotating dish ½ turn after 15 minutes.

CHICKEN CACCIATORI

4 to 6 servings
3-quart casserole

3 *to 3½ pounds frying chicken, cut in serving pieces*
¼ *cup flour*
1 *can (16-ounces) Italian style tomatoes, drained*
1 *can (8-ounces) tomato paste*
2 *medium onions, sliced*
1 *clove garlic, pressed or finely chopped*
1½ *teaspoons oregano*
¼ *teaspoon thyme*
2 *teaspoons parsley flakes*
¼ *teaspoon pepper*
½ *cup red wine*
1½ *cups water*
1 *can (4-ounces) sliced mushrooms, drained*
1 *teaspoon salt*

Dredge chicken in flour.

Combine tomatoes, tomato paste, onions, garlic, oregano, thyme, parsley, pepper, wine and water. Stir until well-blended. Add chicken pieces, turning to coat well with sauce. Cover. MICROWAVE 25 to 30 MINUTES on HIGH, or until chicken is fork tender, stirring after 15 minutes. Stir in mushroom slices and salt. Let stand 5 minutes. Serve over spaghetti.

144

COQ AU VIN

4 to 6 servings
2-quart casserole

1 cup all-purpose flour
2 teaspoons salt
¼ teaspoon pepper
3 pound frying chicken, cut in serving pieces
3 slices bacon, cut in 1-inch pieces
1 large onion, cut in quarters
8 ounces fresh mushrooms, sliced
1 clove garlic, pressed or finely chopped
1 cup red wine
2 tablespoons brandy
1 bay leaf
1 tablespoon snipped parsley

Combine flour, salt and pepper in a shallow dish. Dredge chicken in flour mixture. Set aside.

Place bacon in 2-quart casserole. MICROWAVE 2 MINUTES on HIGH, or until almost crisp.

Add chicken and remaining seasoned flour to bacon and drippings. Mix in onion, mushrooms, garlic, wine, brandy, bay leaf and parsley. Cover tightly. MICROWAVE 15 MINUTES on HIGH.

Stir. Do not cover. MICROWAVE 10 MINUTES on HIGH, or until chicken is fork tender. Let stand 5 to 10 minutes, covered. Remove bay leaf before serving.

CHICKEN SALTIMBOCCA

4 servings
8x8-inch baking dish

4 chicken breasts (approx. 1½ lbs.), skinned and boned
3 tablespoons butter or margarine
Salt and pepper
4 thin slices boiled ham, 4x3-inches
4 thin slices mozzarella cheese, 4x3-inches
4 teaspoons grated Parmesan cheese

Place chicken breasts between 2 pieces of wax paper. Pound to flatten slightly.

Place 3 tablespoons butter in (8x8-inch) baking dish. MICROWAVE on HIGH, or until butter melts. Add chicken breasts, turning to coat with butter. Cover. MICROWAVE 8 to 10 MINUTES on HIGH, or until chicken is fork tender.

Drain and reserve broth from baking dish. Season chicken with salt and pepper. Top each breast with slice ham and slice of cheese. Sprinkle each with 1 teaspoon reserved broth and 1 teaspoon Parmesan cheese. MICROWAVE 3 MINUTES on HIGH, or until cheese melts.

CHICKEN BRAISED IN WINE

4 to 6 servings
3-quart casserole

2½ to 3 pounds frying chicken, cut in serving pieces
¼ cup flour
2 tablespoons butter or margarine
1 medium onion, sliced
4 green onions with tops, sliced
1 clove garlic, pressed or finely chopped
3 large carrots, thinly sliced
1 tablespoon chopped or snipped parsley
¼ teaspoon thyme
¼ teaspoon oregano
1 bay leaf
1 cup white or red wine
1 can (4-ounces) mushroom stems and pieces, drained
1 teaspoon salt

Coat chicken pieces thoroughly with flour. Set aside.

Combine butter, onion, green onion, garlic and carrots in 3-quart casserole. Place chicken on top. Sprinkle with parsley, thyme and oregano. Add bay leaf and wine. Cover. MICROWAVE 25 to 30 MINUTES on HIGH, stirring once.

Add mushrooms. Cover. MICROWAVE 3 to 5 MINUTES on HIGH, or until chicken and carrots are tender. Remove bay leaf and stir in salt before serving.

Coq Au Vin

STUFFED ROLLED CHICKEN BREASTS

4 servings
9x6-inch utility dish

4 large (1½ to 2 lbs.) boneless chicken breasts
1 cup mushrooms, chopped
1 cup chopped onion
2 tablespoons butter or margarine
1 teaspoon instant chicken bouillon
1 cup hot water
3 cups seasoned stuffing mix
1 cup dairy sour cream
1 can (10¾-ounces) cream of mushroom soup,
    undiluted
    Paprika

In a 2-quart measure or a mixing bowl, MICRO-WAVE mushrooms, onion and butter on HIGH for 2 to 3 MINUTES, or until onions are transparent. Add chicken bouillon, hot water and stuffing mix. Mix well. Set aside.

Lightly pound chicken breasts so they lie flat. Place a small roll of stuffing in the center of each chicken breast. Roll the chicken breasts around the stuffing. Place chicken breasts seam side down in the center of a 1½-quart utility dish. Place remaining stuffing along the sides of the dish.

In a small bowl, combine sour cream and mushroom soup. Mix well. Pour the soup mixture evenly over the chicken breasts and stuffing. Sprinkle with paprika. Cover tightly with plastic wrap. PROGRAM TO MICROWAVE on HIGH for 5 MINUTES, then on '5' for 5 MINUTES.

SINGLE CORNISH HEN

1 serving
8x8-inch baking dish

1 pound Cornish hen
1 cup stuffing
½ teaspoon Kitchen Bouquet mixed with ½ teaspoon
    water

Stuff Cornish hen. Secure cavity with wooden picks. Place hen breast-side down in (8x8-inch) baking dish. Brush with Kitchen Bouquet mixture. Cover with wax paper. MICROWAVE 5 MINUTES on '6', or until legs can be moved easily. Let stand 5 minutes, tented with aluminum foil.

Turn hen breast-side up. Brush with Kitchen Bouquet mixture. Cover with wax paper. MICROWAVE 9 to 11 MINUTES on '6', or until legs can be moved easily. Let stand 5 minutes, tented with aluminum foil.

HOT TURKEY SALAD

4 to 6 servings
1½-quart casserole

2 cups diced cooked turkey
2 cups finely chopped celery
½ small onion, thinly sliced
1 can (6-ounces) water chestnuts, drained and
    sliced
½ small green pepper, cut in short, thin strips
2 tablespoons chopped pimiento or stuffed olives
1 cup mayonnaise
2 tablespoons lemon juice
1 cup crushed corn chips
1 cup shredded sharp Cheddar cheese

Combine turkey, celery, onion, water chestnuts, green pepper, pimiento, mayonnaise and lemon juice in 1½-quart casserole. Cover. MICROWAVE 10 MINUTES on '8', stirring after 5 minutes. Sprinkle with corn chips and cheese. MICROWAVE 1 MINUTE on HIGH, or until cheese melts.

CHICKEN A LA KING

5 to 6 servings
1½-quart casserole

¼ cup butter or margarine
¼ cup flour
1 cup chicken broth
1 cup milk
1½ cups diced cooked chicken or turkey
1 cup frozen peas, defrosted
1 jar (2-ounces) chopped pimiento
½ teaspoon celery seed (optional)
⅛ teaspoon pepper
    Seasoned salt
1 tablespoon grated sharp cheese

Place butter in 1½-quart casserole. MICROWAVE on HIGH, until butter is melted. Stir in flour to make a smooth paste. Add chicken broth and milk, beating with wire whip. MICROWAVE 6 to 7 MINUTES on '8', or until thick, stirring after 4 minutes and again when thick.

Add chicken, peas, pimiento, celery seed and pepper. Cover. MICROWAVE 4 MINUTES on HIGH, or until hot. Just before serving, stir in seasoned salt to taste and grated cheese. Serve on biscuits, buttered toast or patty shells.

ROAST CORNISH HENS

4 servings
12x8-inch utility dish with
microwave roasting rack, if desired

4 1-pound Cornish hens
4 cups stuffing
½ cup cranberry-orange relish
1 tablespoon honey

Stuff Cornish hens. Secure cavity with wooden picks. Mix cranberry-orange relish and honey in small bowl.

Arrange hens breast-side down and at least 1-inch apart, in (12x8-inch) utility dish. Brush hens with glaze. Cover with wax paper. MICROWAVE 12 to 15 MINUTES on HIGH, rotating dish once if necessary.

Turn hens over so that breast sides are up and outside edges are reversed to inside of dish. Brush with glaze. Cover with wax paper. MICROWAVE 15 MINUTES on HIGH, or until internal temperature of thickest part of inside thigh muscle registers 175°. Let stand 7 minutes, tented with aluminum foil.

If desired, serve on bed of wild rice, garnished with green beans and spiced peaches.

CHICKEN LIVERS CHABLIS

4 servings
2-quart casserole

2 tablespoons butter or margarine
2 packages (8-ounces each) frozen chicken livers, defrosted
3 tablespoons flour
¼ cup finely chopped onion
2 tablespoons catsup
¾ cup chablis or white grape juice with 1 teaspoon lemon juice

Place butter in 2-quart casserole. MICROWAVE on HIGH until melted.

Dredge livers in flour. Arrange in casserole in single layer. Cover loosely with wax paper. MICROWAVE 7 MINUTES on '8', turning livers over after 4 minutes.

Gently stir in onion, catsup and wine. Cover with wax paper. MICROWAVE 5 MINUTES on '8', or until livers are tender. Stir. Serve hot on bed of rice.

Roast Cornish Hens

Casserole Cookery

Microwave cooking produces superior casseroles. Vegetables cook tender while retaining character, color and crispness. Precooked meatballs taste fresh cooked. Many casseroles can be made ahead and reheated, or divided into single portions for split-shift dining.

When a recipe makes more servings than you need, freeze single portions in boil-in-bags for a variety of homemade entrees.

LASAGNA

10 servings
4-quart casserole
10x12-inch baking dish

1 *pound lean ground beef*
½ *pound sausage*
1 *clove garlic, pressed or finely chopped*
1 *medium onion, finely chopped*
1 *teaspoon fennel*
1 *can (16-ounces) plum or Italian tomatoes*
1 *can (16-ounces) stewed tomatoes*
1 *can (12-ounces) tomato paste*
1 *teaspoon salt*
½ *teaspoon seasoned pepper*
½ *teaspoon thyme*
½ *teaspoon oregano*
½ *teaspoon basil*
2 *bay leaves*

1½ *cups ricotta cheese, drained*
1½ *cups cottage cheese*
¼ *cup chopped fresh parsley*
¾ *cup Parmesan cheese*
2 *eggs, beaten*
1 *teaspoon salt*
1 *pound lasagna noodles, cooked and drained*
12 *ounces sliced mozzarella cheese*

Combine beef, sausage, garlic, onion and fennel in 4-quart casserole. MICROWAVE 15 MINUTES on HIGH. Drain.

Add tomatoes, tomato paste, salt, pepper and seasonings. MICROWAVE 20 MINUTES on HIGH or until sauce thickens, stirring after 10 minutes.

Combine ricotta cheese, cottage cheese, parsley, Parmesan cheese, eggs and salt.

Layer ½ of noodles, cheese filling, meat sauce and mozzarella in (10x12-inch) baking dish. Repeat. MICROWAVE 15 MINUTES on '8', or until cheese melts and center is hot.

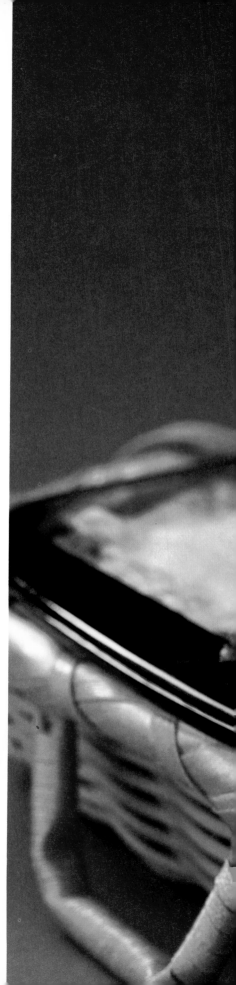

CASSEROLE BASICS

Casseroles may require occasional stirring to distribute heat. They cook more evenly when made with ingredients of similar size and shape. And because of their shorter cooking time, casseroles cooked in the microwave oven generally need less liquid. Casseroles with cream and cheese sauces, or meats which need slower cooking to tenderize, cook best on lower heat control settings.

A number of these casserole recipes call for leftover meats, because leftovers remain flavorful and fresh tasting when reheated in the microwave oven. Any casserole leftovers can be frozen in individual servings.

When cooking a favorite casserole, make two and freeze the second for future use. Line a casserole or baking dish with plastic wrap. Transfer the cooked food to the lined container and freeze. As soon as the food is frozen in the shape of the dish, remove it and wrap with freezer paper. Later it can be unwrapped and returned to the container for defrosting and heating. See the chart for reheating frozen casseroles at the end of the Convenience Food Guide.

DRIED BEEF BAKE

6 to 8 servings
3-quart casserole

2 *cups macaroni, uncooked*
4 *cups hot water*
1 *teaspoon salad oil*
¼ *pound dried beef*
½ *pound Colby cheese, cubed*
1 *small onion, chopped*
4 *hard-cooked eggs, chopped*
1 *can (10¾-ounces) condensed cream of mushroom soup, undiluted*
1 *can (10½-ounces) condensed cream of chicken soup, undiluted*
2 *cups milk*

Combine macaroni, water and oil in 3-quart casserole. MICROWAVE 10 to 12 MINUTES on HIGH, or until macaroni is beginning to soften. Drain.

Add dried beef, cheese, onion, eggs, soups and milk. Mix together carefully. Cover. MICROWAVE 10 MINUTES on HIGH, or until mixture is bubbly and noodles fully cooked, stirring twice.

COUNTRY PIE

6 servings
10-inch pie plate

2 *cans (8-ounces each) tomato sauce*
½ *cup soft bread crumbs*
1 *small green pepper, chopped*
1 *medium onion, chopped*
1 *pound lean ground beef*
1⅓ *cups instant rice*
1 *cup water*
1 *cup grated Cheddar cheese*
1 *teaspoon salt*
⅛ *teaspoon oregano*
⅛ *teaspoon pepper*

Combine ½ can tomato sauce, bread crumbs, green pepper, onion and ground beef in medium mixing bowl. Mix well. Pat mixture onto bottom and sides of 10-inch pie plate.

Combine rice, water, ¼ cup cheese, remaining tomato sauce, salt, oregano and pepper. Spoon into pie plate. Cover with plastic wrap. MICROWAVE 20 to 25 MINUTES on '8', or until rice is fluffed and tender.

Sprinkle with remaining cheese. MICROWAVE 3 to 4 MINUTES on '8', or until cheese is melted. Cut into wedges to serve.

EASY BEEF STEW SUPREME

6 to 8 servings
4-quart casserole

2 *pounds beef round steak, cut in ½-inch cubes*
1 *bottle (8-ounces) Italian dressing*
2 *medium onions, quartered*
4 *potatoes, quartered*
4 *carrots, quartered*
2 *cans (10½-ounces each) condensed tomato soup, undiluted*
4 *bay leaves*
½ *teaspoon salt*
⅛ *teaspoon pepper*

Marinate beef overnight in Italian dressing. Drain meat. Combine with onions, potatoes and carrots in 4-quart casserole. Cover with soup. Add bay leaves, salt and pepper. Cover. MICROWAVE 60 MINUTES on '6', or until meat and vegetables are tender, stirring twice. Remove bay leaves before serving.

Oven Stew

SATURDAY SPECIAL

6 servings
2-quart casserole

1 *pound lean ground beef*
½ *cup chopped onion*
1 *cup dairy sour cream*
1 *can (10¾-ounces) condensed cream of mushroom*
  soup, undiluted
1 *can (16-ounces) whole kernel corn, drained*
1 *jar (2-ounces) chopped pimiento*
1 *teaspoon salt*
⅛ *teaspoon pepper*
1 *large tomato, thinly sliced*

Crumble ground beef into 2-quart casserole. Add onion. MICROWAVE 5 MINUTES on HIGH until beef is set and onion is transparent.

Add sour cream, soup, corn, pimiento, salt and pepper. Cover with wax paper. MICROWAVE 5 MINUTES on HIGH.

Top with tomato slices. MICROWAVE 3 MINUTES on HIGH, or until tomatoes are slightly softened. Garnish with canned French fried onion rings, if desired. Let stand 3 minutes, uncovered.

OVEN STEW

4 to 6 servings
3-quart casserole

2 *pounds beef bottom round steak, cut in ¾-*
  inch cubes
½ *cup flour*
2 *cups carrots, cut in ½-inch slices*
6 *to 8 small onions*
2 *medium boiling potatoes, quartered*
2 *bay leaves*
½ *teaspoon marjoram*
1 *teaspoon salt*
¼ *teaspoon pepper*
1 *can (10½-ounces) condensed tomato soup,*
  undiluted
1 *can (10¼-ounces) consomme, undiluted*
1½ *cups water*
1 *package (10-ounces) frozen peas*

Coat beef cubes with flour. Combine beef, carrots, onions, potatoes, bay leaves, marjoram, salt and pepper in 3-quart casserole. Stir in soups and water until well mixed. Cover. MICROWAVE 5 MINUTES on HIGH. Stir.

Reduce setting. MICROWAVE 50 to 60 MINUTES on '6', or until meat and vegetables are tender, stirring 2 or 3 times. Add peas during last 10 minutes of cooking.

Let stand 10 minutes, covered. Remove bay leaves. Serve over biscuits, if desired.

GOULASH

8 servings
4-quart casserole

2 tablespoons salad oil
2 chopped onions
1 clove garlic, pressed or finely chopped
1 teaspoon paprika
2 pounds beef stew meat, cut in ¾-inch cubes
4 medium boiling potatoes, peeled and cut in small
    cubes
4 medium tomatoes, peeled and chopped, or 1 can
    (14-ounces) stewed tomatoes
1 green pepper, chopped
½ teaspoon caraway seeds
4 cups beef broth, or ¼ cup instant beef bouillon
    dissolved in 4 cups hot water
    Salt and pepper
    Dairy sour cream

Combine oil, onion and garlic in 4-quart casserole.
MICROWAVE 2 to 3 MINUTES on HIGH, or until
onion is transparent. Stir in paprika.

Add beef, potatoes, tomatoes, green pepper,
caraway seeds and beef broth. Cover. MICRO-
WAVE 5 MINUTES on HIGH.

Reduce setting. MICROWAVE 45 to 60 MINUTES
on '6', or until meat is fork tender, stirring once.
Season with salt and pepper. Let stand 5 minutes,
covered.

Serve in bowls with sour cream spooned on top.

GROUND BEEF "ADD MEAT" DINNER

4 servings
Browning dish
3-quart casserole

1 tablespoon salad oil
1 pound ground beef
1 package (7-ounces) "add meat" dinner mix
    for hamburger

To preheat browning dish, MICROWAVE 4 MIN-
UTES on HIGH. Add oil. Crumble beef into browning dish. MICROWAVE 3 to 5 MINUTES on HIGH,
or until meat is set.

Remove meat from browning dish to 3-quart casserole. Add mix and hot tap water as directed on package. Cover. MICROWAVE 20 to 22 MINUTES on
HIGH. Stir well. Let stand 5 minutes, covered.

QUICK BEEF CHIP CASSEROLE

3 to 4 servings
1-quart mixing bowl
2-quart casserole

1 pound lean ground beef
1 large onion, chopped
2 cups corn chips
1 can (15-ounces) chili with beans
1 can (8-ounces) tomato sauce
¼ cup grated Cheddar cheese

Crumble meat into 1-quart mixing bowl. Add onion.
MICROWAVE 4 MINUTES on HIGH, or until meat
is set.

In 2-quart casserole, layer half the corn chips, half
the meat, half the chili and half the tomato sauce.
Repeat layers. Cover. MICROWAVE 6 MINUTES
on HIGH. Sprinkle grated cheese on top. MICRO-
WAVE 30 SECONDS on HIGH, or until cheese
melts.

GARBANZO CASSEROLE

6 to 8 servings
2½-quart casserole

1 pound lean ground beef
1 large onion, chopped
1 can (15-ounces) garbanzo beans, drained
1 can (15-ounces) chili without beans
1 can (16-ounces) corn, drained
½ cup sharp Cheddar cheese, cubed

Crumble ground beef in 2½-quart casserole. Add
onion. MICROWAVE 4 to 5 MINUTES on HIGH,
or until meat is set. Drain excess fat.

Mix in beans, chili and corn. Carefully stir in cheese
cubes. Cover. MICROWAVE 10 to 12 MINUTES
on '8', or until mixture is heated through and cheese
cubes have started to melt. Let stand 10 minutes,
covered.

ONE DISH SPAGHETTI ❄

4 to 6 servings
2-quart casserole

1 *tablespoon butter or margarine*
1 *large onion, sliced*
1 *clove garlic, pressed or finely chopped*
1 *pound lean ground beef*
1 *teaspoon parsley flakes*
½ *teaspoon salt*
¼ *teaspoon pepper*
½ *teaspoon oregano*
2 *cans (8-ounces each) tomato sauce*
1½ *cups water*
¼ *pound uncooked spaghetti*
   Grated Parmesan cheese

Combine butter, onion and garlic in 2-quart casserole. MICROWAVE 2 to 3 MINUTES on HIGH, or until onion is transparent.

Crumble ground beef into casserole. MICROWAVE 3 MINUTES, 30 SECONDS to 4 MINUTES, 30 SECONDS on HIGH, or until beef is set.

Add parsley flakes, salt, pepper and oregano. Stir in tomato sauce and water. Cover. MICROWAVE 4 MINUTES on HIGH.

Break spaghetti in half. Mix into sauce. Cover. MICROWAVE 10 to 12 MINUTES on HIGH, or until spaghetti is tender, stirring twice. Let stand 5 to 10 minutes, covered. Serve with grated Parmesan cheese.

MOM'S TATER TOT HOT DISH ⚓

4 to 6 servings
10 x 8-inch utility dish

1 *pound lean ground beef*
1 *envelope dry onion soup mix*
1 *can (10½-ounces) condensed cream of chicken soup, undiluted*
1 *package (10-ounces) Tater Tots*

Lightly spread ground beef in bottom of (10 x 8-inch) utility dish. Sprinkle soup mix on top. Mask with soup. Top with Tater Tots. MICROWAVE 10 to 11 MINUTES on HIGH, or until soup is bubbly and ground beef firm. Let stand 3 to 5 minutes.

JOHNNY MARZETTI

6 servings
3-quart casserole

1 *package (10-ounces) wide egg noodles, cooked and drained*
1 *pound lean ground beef*
½ *cup chopped onion*
¼ *cup chopped green pepper*
1 *jar (2½-ounces) mushroom stems and pieces, drained*
1 *clove garlic, pressed or finely chopped*
⅛ *teaspoon pepper*
1 *can (10¾-ounces) condensed cream of mushroom soup, undiluted*
1 *can (8-ounces) tomato sauce*
1 *cup finely diced American process cheese*

Crumble ground beef into 3-quart casserole. Add onion, green pepper, mushrooms, garlic and pepper. MICROWAVE 5 MINUTES on HIGH, or until meat is set and onion is transparent.

Add cooked noodles and mushroom soup. Mix well. Pour tomato sauce over mixture. Sprinkle with cheese. Cover. MICROWAVE 5 MINUTES on HIGH, or until cheese is melted and bubbly. Let stand 3 minutes. Garnish with parsley, if desired.

TOP THE TATERS DINNER ⚓

4 servings
1½-quart casserole

1 *pound lean ground beef*
2 *tablespoons chopped onion*
1 *can (10¾-ounces) condensed tomato soup, undiluted*
1 *can (15¾-ounces) French-cut green beans with juice*
   Instant mashed potatoes, prepared for 4

Crumble ground beef into 1½-quart casserole. Mix in onions. MICROWAVE 3 to 4 MINUTES on HIGH, or until meat is set.

Stir in soup and beans. MICROWAVE 5 to 6 MINUTES on HIGH, or until hot and bubbly.

Serve over mashed potatoes.

NOODLES BOLOGNESE

6 to 8 servings
2-quart casserole
3-quart casserole

  3 *cups noodles, cooked and drained*
1½ *pounds lean ground beef*
  4 *green onions, including tops, chopped*
  1 *can (8-ounces) tomato sauce*
  1 *teaspoon salt*
¼ *teaspoon garlic salt*
   Pepper to taste
  1 *cup dairy sour cream*
  1 *cup small curd cottage cheese*
  1 *cup grated Cheddar or finely diced American*
    process cheese

Crumble beef into 2-quart casserole. Mix in onion. MICROWAVE 5 MINUTES on HIGH.

Add tomato sauce, salts and pepper. MICROWAVE 2 MINUTES on HIGH.

Combine noodles, sour cream and cottage cheese. Layer one third noodle mixture and one third sauce in 3-quart casserole. Repeat layers. Cover. MICROWAVE 12 MINUTES on '8'.

Sprinkle with cheese. Let stand 3 minutes, or until cheese melts. Garnish with parsley springs.

LAZY BEEF CASSEROLE

3 to 4 servings
2-quart casserole

¼ *cup flour*
  1 *pound beef top round steak, cut in ½ to ¾-inch*
    cubes
  1 *can (10½-ounces) condensed beef bouillon,*
    diluted with water to make 2 cups
  1 *can (6-ounces) tomato paste*
  1 *small onion, thinly sliced*
¾ *teaspoon salt*
⅛ *teaspoon pepper*

Measure flour into paper bag. Add meat cubes and shake to coat thoroughly.

Combine meat, bouillon, tomato paste, onion, salt and pepper in 2-quart casserole. Stir until tomato paste is mixed with broth. Cover. MICROWAVE 5 MINUTES on HIGH.

Reduce setting. MICROWAVE 25 MINUTES on '6', or until meat is fork tender, stirring after 15 minutes.

CHILI ✺

4 to 5 servings
2-quart casserole

  1 *pound ground beef*
½ *cup chopped onion*
  1 *can (16-ounces) stewed tomatoes*
  1 *can (8-ounces) tomato sauce*
  1 *can (15¼-ounces) kidney beans, drained*
  1 *small green pepper, chopped*
1½ *teaspoons parsley flakes*
  1 *teaspoon salt*
¼ *teaspoon dried oregano*
¼ *teaspoon chili powder*
⅛ *teaspoon pepper*

Crumble ground beef into 2-quart bowl. Add onion. MICROWAVE 4 to 5 MINUTES on HIGH, or until meat is set, stirring once. Drain fat.

Add remaining ingredients. Mix well. Cover with wax paper or paper towel. MICROWAVE 10 MINUTES on '8', or until hot, stirring once.

NOTE: Recipe can be doubled easily, using a 4-quart bowl. First cooking period MICROWAVE 10 to 12 MINUTES on HIGH. Second cooking period MICROWAVE 15 MINUTES on HIGH, stirring twice.

CHOW MEIN

4 servings
2-quart casserole

  1 *pound chow mein meat (½ pork, ½ veal)*
  2 *cups diagonally sliced celery (½-inch slices)*
  1 *medium onion, sliced*
  1 *can (4-ounces) mushroom stems and pieces,*
    drained
  3 *tablespoons cornstarch*
  3 *tablespoons soy sauce*
  1 *can (16-ounces) chow mein vegetables, rinsed and*
    drained
  1 *can (8½-ounces) water chestnuts, drained*
    and sliced
½ *teaspoon ginger*

Combine chow mein meat, celery, onion and mushrooms in 2-quart casserole. Cover. MICROWAVE 4 to 6 MINUTES on HIGH, or until meat is set.

Dissolve cornstarch in soy sauce. Stir into meat mixture. Mix in chow mein vegetables, water chestnuts, water and ginger. Cover. MICROWAVE 4 to 6 MINUTES on HIGH, or until vegetables are tender-crisp.

PORK AND BEAN CASSEROLE

4 servings
2-quart casserole

1 *pound lean ground beef*
1 *small onion, chopped*
1 *can (16-ounces) pork and beans*
1 *can (8-ounces) tomato sauce*
2 *tablespoons prepared mustard*
2 *teaspoons Worcestershire sauce*
½ *teaspoon salt*
¼ *teaspoon pepper*

Crumble ground beef into 2-quart casserole. Add onion, MICROWAVE 4 to 5 MINUTES on HIGH, or until meat is set.

Stir in pork and beans, tomato sauce, mustard, Worcestershire sauce, salt and pepper. Cover. MICROWAVE 8 to 10 MINUTES on '8', or until hot.

OYSTERS AND MACARONI AU GRATIN

6 servings
1-quart measure
1½-quart casserole

3 *tablespoons butter or margarine*
3 *tablespoons flour*
1½ *cups milk*
1 *cup macaroni, cooked and drained*
2 *cans (8-ounces) oysters, drained*
  Salt and pepper
1 *cup grated Cheddar cheese*

Place butter in 1-quart measure. MICROWAVE on HIGH until butter melts. Blend in flour to make a smooth paste. Gradually stir in milk. MICROWAVE 2 MINUTES, 30 SECONDS to 3 MINUTES, 30 SECONDS on HIGH, or until thickened, stirring once with wire whisk.

Layer half the macaroni and half the oysters in 1½-quart casserole. Season with salt and pepper. Sprinkle with one-third of the cheese. Repeat layers. Pour sauce over and top with remaining cheese. MICROWAVE 10 MINUTES on '8', or until heated through. Garnish with parsley, if desired.

Scalloped Bologna Bake

SCALLOPED BOLOGNA BAKE

4 to 6 servings
2-quart casserole

1 *package (15½-ounces) scalloped potato mix*
1 *ring (1-pound) coarse ground bologna, skinned and cut in ¾-inch slices*

Use ¼ cup less water then amount recommended in mix. Pour water over potatoes in 2-quart casserole. Let stand 20 minutes.

Add bologna slices, sauce mix and milk, omit butter or margarine. Cover. MICROWAVE 10 to 15 MINUTES on '6', or until potatoes are tender.

JAMBALAYA

6 servings
4-quart casserole dish

1 tablespoon butter or margarine
1 medium onion, thinly sliced
2 bell peppers, coarsely chopped
⅛ teaspoon garlic
2 tablespoons flour
1 package (6-ounces) boiled cooked ham, cubed
1 package (12-ounces) shrimp, cooked and drained
5 diced tomatoes
1 can (14-ounces) pear shaped tomatoes
2 tablespoons parsley
2 tablespoons Worcestershire sauce
1 teaspoon salt
½ teaspoon thyme
2 dried red peppers

Melt butter. Add onions, pepper and garlic. MICROWAVE 2 to 3 MINUTES, or until onions are transparent. Stir in flour.

Slowly add water, stirring to keep smooth. Add remaining ingredients. MICROWAVE 12 MINUTES on HIGH. Reduce 45 MINUTES on '5', or until rice is tender.

ARROZ CON POLLO

6 servings
3 or 4-quart casserole dish

1 chicken, cut up (2 pounds)
2 cups converted rice
3 dried red peppers
2 teaspoons garlic salt
¼ teaspoon saffron
2 medium onions, chopped
1 can (16-ounces) tomatoes
1 jalepeno peppers, chopped
8 ounces green peas
1 jar pimientos, chopped
½ cup olives with pimientos, chopped
1 can (10-ounces) chicken broth

Combine rice, red peppers, garlic salt, onion and saffron. MICROWAVE 5 MINUTES on HIGH, or until onion is transparent and rice is lightly browned.

Add tomatoes, jalepeno peppers, peas, pimientos, olives and chicken broth. Stir well.

Place chicken on top of rice mixture. Cover. MICROWAVE 20 to 25 MINUTES on HIGH, or until rice is tender. Let stand for 10 minutes, covered.

ATHENIAN MOUSSAKA

4 to 6 servings
Browning dish
2-quart casserole
3-quart casserole

1 medium eggplant
¼ cup olive oil or salad oil
  Meat sauce
2 teaspoons fine dry bread crumbs
½ teaspoon Parmesan cheese
  Custard topping
¼ cup Parmesan cheese
  Ground nutmeg

Meat Sauce:
1 tablespoon oil
1¼ pounds lean ground lamb or beef
1 medium onion, chopped
1 clove garlic, pressed or finely chopped
1 teaspoon salt
1 can (6-ounces) tomato paste
2 tablespoons finely chopped parsley
½ teaspoon ground cinnamon

Custard Topping:
3 tablespoons butter or margarine
¼ cup all-purpose flour
2 cups milk
3 eggs, beaten
½ teaspoon salt
⅛ teaspoon ground nutmeg
½ cup Parmesan cheese

Preheat browning dish 5 minutes. Add ¼ cup oil. Stir to coat bottom of dish. Add eggplant slices. MICROWAVE 3 MINUTES on HIGH, or until soft. Set aside.

Meat Sauce:
Add 1 tablespoon oil to browning dish. Crumble meat into dish and add onion and garlic. MICROWAVE 3 to 5 MINUTES on HIGH, or until meat is set and onion is transparent. Drain excess fat. Add salt, tomato paste, parsley and cinnamon. Set aside.

Custard Topping:
Place butter in 2-quart casserole. MICROWAVE 30 SECONDS on HIGH, or until melted. Add flour, stir. Slowly add milk, stirring to prevent lumping. Add remaining ingredients. Set aside.

To assemble Moussaka:
Line bottom of 3-quart casserole with half of the eggplant. Top with half of the meat sauce. Sprinkle with 2 teaspoons bread crumbs and ½ teaspoon Parmesan cheese. Repeat layers. Pour custard over layers. Sprinkle with ¼ cup Parmesan cheese and nutmeg. MICROWAVE 16 to 18 MINUTES on '8', or until custard is set.

ENCHILADA CASSEROLE

6 servings
3-quart casserole
6 x 10-inch baking dish

1 *can tortillas*
1 *pound lean ground beef*
1 *medium onion, chopped*
1 *cup refried beans*
1 *package taco sauce mix*
½ *cup water*
¼ *cup chopped pitted ripe olives*
1 *jalepeno pepper, chopped*
1 *can (10-ounces) mild enchilada sauce*
1 *can (15-ounces) tomato sauce*
1 *cup grated cheese*

Soften tortillas by placing between damp paper towels, placing in a plastic bag and microwaving for 45 SECONDS. Allow to rest in sealed plastic bag while preparing remainder of ingredients. Crumble beef into casserole. Add onion. MICROWAVE 3 MINUTES on HIGH, or until meat is set and onion transparent. Add beans, taco sauce, water, olives and pepper. Place 1 to 2 tablespoons meat mixture inside tortilla, roll. Place seam side down in baking dish.

Combine enchilada and tomato sauces, mix well. Pour over filled tortillas. MICROWAVE 3 to 5 MINUTES on HIGH, or until warmed through.

CASHEW CHICKEN

6 servings
10½-inch browning dish

2 *pounds boneless chicken breasts, cut in*
   1½-inch chunks
1 *tablespoon cooking oil*
¼ *cup cornstarch*
⅓ *cup water*
2 *tablespoons soy sauce*
2 *teaspoons salt*
1½ *teaspoons sugar*
   Dash pepper
1 *can (5-ounces) water chestnuts, drained*
   and chopped
½ *cup frozen peas, thawed*
1 *cup thinly sliced celery*
1 *can (4-ounces) whole mushrooms, drained*
½ *cup cashews*

Preheat browning dish 7 minutes. Place oil and chicken in dish and MICROWAVE 5 MINUTES on HIGH, stirring once halfway through. Combine cornstarch and water in small bowl, stir until smooth. Stir into chicken mixture, along with soy sauce, seasonings, water chestnuts, peas, celery, mushrooms and cashews. Cover. MICROWAVE 10 to 15 MINUTES on HIGH, or until vegetables are tender-crisp.

Enchilada Casserole

Stir-Fry The Microwave Way

Oriental techniques for quickly cooking meats, poultry and vegetables to a tender-crisp state are easily duplicated in the microwave. Use a preheated browning dish to stir-fry with a minimum of fuss and bother.

Try our combinations or make up some of your own.

Stir-fry shrimp

SUKIYAKI

4 to 6 servings
10-inch browning dish

2 teaspoons instant beef bouillon
¼ cup water
1 tablespoon oil
1½ pound sirloin steak, thinly sliced strips
2 stems celery, sliced
1 bunch green onions, 1-inch pieces
1 tablespoon chopped, fresh parsley
3 cups coarsely shredded Chinese cabbage
3 onions, halved and quartered
1 green pepper, cut into chunks
1 can (15-ounces) bamboo shoots, drained

Combine instant beef bouillon and water in 1-cup measure. Set aside. Preheat browning dish 5 MINUTES on HIGH. Add oil. Brown beef in oil 5 to 7 MINUTES on HIGH. Stir after 3 minutes. Add remaining ingredients to beef. Pour bouillon over mixture. Stir. MICROWAVE 12 MINUTES on HIGH.

STIR-FRY SHRIMP

4 servings
10-inch browning dish

2 tablespoons peanut oil
1 pound shrimp, peeled and deveined
4 green onions, 1-inch slices
2 cups yellow squash, ¼-inch slices
2 cups Chinese cabbage, shredded
1 cup sliced fresh mushrooms
1 cup yellow summer squash, ¼-inch slices
1 cup sliced zucchini squash, ¼-inch slices
1 tablespoon soy sauce

Preheat browning dish 5 MINUTES on HIGH. Add oil.

Add all ingredients, except soy sauce, to browning dish. Stir. MICROWAVE 8 MINUTES on HIGH, stirring at 4 MINUTES. Add soy sauce and stir.

GROUND BEEF STIR-FRY

4 to 6 servings
10-inch browning dish

1 pound ground beef
1 can (8½-ounces) water chestnuts, sliced
1 can (16-ounces) bean sprouts
1 package (6-ounces) frozen snow pea pods, defrosted and drained
2 tablespoons fresh ground ginger
2 tablespoons soy sauce

Preheat browning dish for 5 minutes. Crumble ground beef into browning dish. Stir. MICROWAVE 3 MINUTES on HIGH. Stir. Drain. Add remaining ingredients. Cover. MICROWAVE 5 MINUTES on HIGH.

SWEET AND SOUR CHICKEN

4 servings
10-inch browning dish

1 pound boneless chicken breast, cut into bite-size pieces
2 tablespoons peanut oil
2 cups bite-size broccoli pieces
4 green onions, 1-inch pieces
1 cup carrots, ½-inch slices
2 cups cauliflowerets
2 tablespoons freshly ground ginger
1 cup sliced, fresh mushrooms
2 tablespoons peanut oil

Pineapple Sauce:
1 can (8¼-ounces) crushed pineapple, drained, reserve liquid
2 tablespoons soy sauce
2 tablespoons cornstarch

Preheat browning dish 6 MINUTES on HIGH. Add oil.

Add chicken immediately, stirring to prevent sticking. Add other ingredients, except mushrooms. Toss until sizzling stops. Cover. MICROWAVE 10 MINUTES on HIGH. Stir after 5 minutes.

Sauce:
Combine reserved pineapple juice, soy sauce and cornstarch in 1-cup measure.

Add pineapple and mushrooms to chicken mixture. Stir. Pour in pineapple sauce mixture. Cover. MICROWAVE 3 MINUTES on HIGH.

TUNA CHOW MEIN

4 servings
1½-quart casserole

2 tablespoons butter or margarine
½ cup finely chopped onion
1 cup finely chopped celery
2 tablespoons finely chopped green pepper
1 can (10¾-ounces) condensed cream of
    mushroom soup, undiluted
1 can (3-ounces) chow mein noodles, ⅓ cup
    reserved
1 can (6½-ounces) tuna, drained and flaked
    Salt and pepper to taste

Combine butter, onion, celery and green pepper in
1½-quart casserole. MICROWAVE 4 MINUTES on
HIGH, or until onion is transparent.

Add soup, noodles, tuna, salt and pepper. Mix well.
Cover. MICROWAVE 5 MINUTES on HIGH. Let
stand 3 minutes, covered. Top with reserved chow
mein noodles before serving.

CRAB GUMBO

4 servings
2½-quart casserole

½ cup chopped onion
½ cup chopped celery
2 tablespoons finely chopped green pepper
1 clove garlic, pressed or finely chopped
2 tablespoons butter or margarine
1 package (10-ounces) frozen okra, partially
    defrosted and sliced
1 can (14½-ounces) stewed tomatoes
¼ teaspoon sugar
1 bay leaf
¼ teaspoon thyme
1 teaspoon salt
1 can (6½-ounces) crab meat, drained and broken
    up with fork
1½ cups cooked rice

Combine onion, celery, green pepper, garlic and
butter in 2-quart casserole. MICROWAVE 3 to 4
MINUTES on HIGH, or until onion is transparent.

Add okra, tomatoes and seasonings. Cover tightly.
MICROWAVE 12 MINUTES on HIGH, or until
okra is tender and mixture is bubbly.

Remove bay leaf. Add crab meat. Cover and let stand
5 minutes. Serve over rice.

TASTY TUNA BAKE

6 to 8 servings
2-quart casserole

1 can (3-ounces) French fried onion rings
1 package (7-ounces) macaroni, cooked and
    drained
2 cans (6½-ounces each) tuna, flaked and
    drained
1 can (13-ounces) evaporated milk
1 can (10¾-ounces) condensed cream of
    mushroom soup, undiluted
1 jar (2½-ounces) mushroom pieces and stems,
    drained
1 jar (4-ounces) chopped pimiento

Reserve ½ French fried onion rings. Combine remaining onion rings, macaroni, tuna, milk, soup,
mushrooms and pimiento in 2-quart casserole. Mix
well. MICROWAVE 10 MINUTES on HIGH, or
until center is hot, stirring once.

Spread reserved onion rings over casserole. Let
stand 3 to 5 minutes.

Variation:
Substitute 1 can (16-ounces) salmon for tuna.

ORIENTAL TUNA

6 servings
2-quart casserole

1 can (3-ounces) chow mein noodles
1 can (10¾-ounces) condensed cream of
    mushroom soup, undiluted
¼ cup water
1 can (6½-ounces) tuna, drained and flaked
1 package (4-ounces) salted cashews, chopped
½ cup finely chopped celery
¼ cup finely chopped onion
1 tablespoon soy sauce

Reserve ½ can chow mein noodles. Combine remaining noodles with soup, water, tuna, cashews,
celery, onion and soy sauce. Mix well. MICRO-
WAVE 8 to 10 MINUTES on HIGH, or until hot,
stirring once. Top with reserved noodles and let
stand 3 to 5 minutes.

WEENIE-MAC

4 to 6 servings
3-quart casserole

1 *jar (8-ounces) process cheese spread*
1 *package (6-ounces) elbow macaroni, cooked and drained*
1 *pound wieners, cut in ½-inch pieces*
½ *cup chopped green onions, including green tops*
1 *tablespoon prepared mustard*

Remove lid from jar of process cheese spread. MI-CROWAVE on HIGH, until cheese melts.

Combine all ingredients in 3-quart casserole. MI-CROWAVE 4 MINUTES on HIGH, or until bubbly.

NOTE: An excellent dish for children to cook as well as eat.

SAUSAGE NOODLE CASSEROLE

4 servings
1½-quart casserole

1 *pound pork sausage roll, cut into ½-inch chunks*
1 *large onion, sliced*
1 *small green pepper, diced*
½ *cup diced celery*
1 *package (1½-ounces) dry chicken noodle soup mix*
1 *can (10¾-ounces) condensed cream of mushroom soup, undiluted*
1 *cup cooked rice*
½ *cup water*

Combine sausage and onion in 1½-quart casserole. Cover. MICROWAVE 4 to 5 MINUTES on HIGH, or until sausage is set. Drain fat.

Add green pepper, celery, soup mix, soup, rice and water. Cover. MICROWAVE 6 to 8 MINUTES on HIGH, or until bubbly.

TUNA "ADD MEAT" DINNER

4 servings
3-quart casserole

1 *package (8¾-ounces) "add meat" dinner mix for tuna*
1 *can (6½-ounces) tuna*

In 3-quart casserole, prepare dinner as directed on package. Cover. MICROWAVE 20 to 22 MIN-UTES on HIGH, stirring twice. Let stand 5 minutes, covered.

SUMMER VEGETABLE CASSEROLE

6 servings
2-quart casserole

3 to 4 *medium yellow summer squash, sliced*
3 *medium tomatoes, sliced*
1 *medium onion, thinly sliced*
⅓ *cup grated Parmesan cheese*
1 *teaspoon basil*
½ *teaspoon thyme*
1 *teaspoon seasoned salt*

In 2-quart casserole layer ½ of the squash, onions and tomatoes. Sprinkle with ½ of cheese, basil, thyme and salt. Repeat with remaining ingredients. Cover. MICROWAVE 10 to 12 MINUTES on HIGH, or until vegetables are tender.

SAN FRANCISCO CASSEROLE

4 to 6 servings
8x8-inch baking dish

1 *pound lean ground beef*
1 *medium onion, chopped*
10 *ounce package frozen spinach, cooked and drained*
¼ *cup sliced, fresh mushrooms*
½ *teaspoon salt*
½ *teaspoon pepper*
¼ *cup grated Cheddar cheese*
6 *beaten eggs*

Crumble beef into baking dish. Add onion. MICRO-WAVE 3 MINUTES on HIGH. Stir. MICROWAVE 1½ MINUTES. Drain. Add spinach, mushrooms, salt, pepper and cheese. Stir in beaten eggs. MICRO-WAVE 4 MINUTES on '8'. Stir partially cooked areas to center. MICROWAVE 4 MINUTES on '8'. Stir again. MICROWAVE 5 to 6 MINUTES on '8', or until set.

Speedy Macaroni and Cheese

SPEEDY MACARONI AND CHEESE

4 servings
1½-quart casserole

1 *cup finely diced American process cheese*
1 *cup white sauce, (page* 201)
1 *cup macaroni, cooked*

Stir cheese into hot white sauce until melted. Combine cheese sauce and cooked macaroni in 1½-quart casserole. Toss lightly to mix. Cover. MICROWAVE 5 MINUTES on '8', until bubbly, stirring after 3 minutes. Let stand 3 minutes, covered. Garnish with parsley, if desired.

Variation:
Substitute 1 jar (16-ounces) process cheese spread for cheese sauce.

Add one of the following:
½ *cup ham cubes*
½ *cup tuna, drained*
 1 *cup wieners, cut into* ¼-*inch slices*
¼ *cup onion*

MOSTACCIOLI ROMANOFF

4 to 6 servings
2-quart casserole

4 *cups Mostaccioli macaroni*
1 *teaspoon salt*
1 *teaspoon oil*
2 *tablespoons butter or margarine*
2 *tablespoons flour*
  Salt
3 *green onions, sliced*
1 *clove garlic, pressed or finely chopped*
1 *cup milk*
½ *cup dairy sour cream*
½ *cup Parmesan cheese*
  Tomato slices
  Green pepper rings

Cook macaroni as directed on package or in a 3-quart casserole or glass bowl. Bring 1½ quarts of hot water to a boil. MICROWAVE 5 to 7 MINUTES on HIGH, covered. Add macaroni, 1 teaspoon salt and 1 teaspoon oil. Reduce setting to '5' and MICROWAVE 8 to 10 MINUTES, uncovered. Drain.

In a 2-quart casserole dish melt butter in microwave oven. Stir in flour, salt, onions, garlic and milk. MICROWAVE 5 to 6 MINUTES on '8', or until mixture boils and thickens, stirring once during last half of cooking time.

Stir in cooked macaroni, sour cream and half of cheese.

Top with sliced tomato and green pepper rings. Sprinkle with remaining cheese. MICROWAVE 4 to 6 MINUTES on '8', or until hot and bubbly.

BOLOGNA-CHEESE BAKE

4 to 5 servings
1½-quart casserole

1 *to* 1½ *cups diced raw potatoes*
½ *pound bologna, diced*
3 *tablespoons finely chopped green pepper*
1 *tablespoon finely chopped onion*
1 *can* (10¾-*ounces) condensed cream of celery soup, undiluted*
1 *cup grated sharp Cheddar cheese*

Combine potatoes, bologna, green pepper, onion and soup in 1½-quart casserole. Cover. MICROWAVE 15 MINUTES on HIGH, or until potatoes are tender. Top with grated cheese. Let stand, uncovered, until cheese begins to melt.

POTATO-CHEESE CASSEROLE

4 to 6 servings
8 x 8-inch baking dish
2-cup measure

4 *cups sliced cooked potatoes*
1 *tablespoon butter or margarine*
1 *small onion, finely chopped*
1 *tablespoon flour*
¼ *teaspoon salt*
   Dash pepper
¼ *teaspoon dry mustard*
½ *teaspoon Worcestershire sauce*
½ *cup shredded American process cheese*
¾ *cup milk*
4 *slices American process cheese*

Arrange potato slices in (8 x 8-inch) baking dish. Set aside.

Combine butter and onion in 2-quart measure. MICROWAVE 3 MINUTES on HIGH, or until onion is transparent. Stir in flour, salt, pepper, mustard, Worcestershire sauce, shredded cheese and milk. MICROWAVE 3 to 4 MINUTES on HIGH, or until mixture is hot and cheese is melted. Stir.

Pour over potatoes. Top with cheese slices. MICROWAVE 6 to 8 MINUTES on '6', or until potatoes are heated through and cheese is melted.

MUSHROOM-BARLEY CASSEROLE

6 to 8 servings
3-quart casserole

1 *can (4-ounces) mushrooms, drained*
¼ *cup butter or margarine*
1 *cup chopped onion*
1 *cup medium barley*
4 *cups chicken broth*
½ *teaspoon salt*
⅛ *teaspoon pepper*

Combine all ingredients in 3-quart casserole. Cover with waxed paper. MICROWAVE 35 MINUTES on HIGH, or until barley is tender, stirring after 15 minutes.

Let stand 3 minutes, covered with wax paper.

Serve with chicken, duck or Cornish hens.

NOODLES ALMONDINE

6 to 8 servings
1-quart casserole
1-cup measure

1 *package (7-ounces) egg noodles, cooked and drained (page 199)*
3 *tablespoons butter or margarine*
¼ *cup slivered almonds*

Place noodles in 1-quart casserole.

Combine butter with almonds in 1-cup measure. MICROWAVE 5 MINUTES on HIGH, or until almonds are golden, stirring once.

Pour over noodles. MICROWAVE 3 MINUTES on HIGH, or until butter is bubbly and noodles are hot.

NOODLES ROMANO

4 servings
2-cup measure

1 *package (8-ounces) medium noodles, cooked and drained (page 199)*
¼ *cup butter or margarine*
½ *cup whipping cream*
1 *egg yolk, slightly beaten*
½ *cup freshly grated Romano or Parmesan cheese*
1 *tablespoon snipped parsley*

Place butter in 2-cup measure. MICROWAVE on HIGH until butter melts. Stir in cream. MICROWAVE 1 MINUTE on HIGH, or until cream is warm.

Stir a little of the cream mixture into egg yolk. Add warmed egg yolk to cream mixture, stirring with fork. Pour sauce over steaming hot noodles. Sprinkle with cheese. Toss gently to coat well. Garnish with parsley.

MACARONI AND CHEESE DINNER MIX

3 to 4 servings
3-quart casserole

2 *cups water*
1 *teaspoon salt*
1 *tablespoon oil*
1 *package (7½-ounces) macaroni and cheese mix*

Combine water, salt, oil and macaroni in 3-quart casserole. Cover. MICROWAVE 18 to 20 MINUTES on HIGH, or until tender, stirring twice.

Stir in cheese mixture thoroughly. Let stand 5 minutes, covered.

All-In-One Beef Dinner

ALL-IN-ONE BEEF DINNER

4 servings
2-quart casserole

1½ to 2 cups cut up, cooked roast beef
1 large onion, thinly sliced
2 cups frozen cut green beans, defrosted
1 can (6-ounces) tomato paste
1 package (¾-ounce) brown gravy mix
1 cup hot water
2½ cups mashed potatoes
  Paprika

Combine roast beef, onion, green beans, tomato paste, gravy mix and water in 2-quart casserole. MICROWAVE 6 to 8 MINUTES on HIGH, or until mixture is bubbly.

Spoon mounds of mashed potatoes on top of dish, or pipe with pastry tube. Sprinkle with paprika. MICROWAVE 4 to 6 MINUTES on '8', or until potatoes are heated through and well set.

NOTE: Any leftover vegetables or gravy can be added to this dish.

COOKED BEEF STROGANOFF

4 to 6 servings
2-quart casserole

3 tablespoons butter or margarine
1 clove garlic, pressed or chopped
1 onion, finely chopped
1 green pepper, cut in thin strips
4 ounces mushrooms, sliced
1 tablespoon tomato paste
2 tablespoons flour
1½ to 2 cups julienned cooked beef
½ cup beef stock, or 1 teaspoon beef bouillon dissolved in 1 to 2 cups boiling water
½ cup dry red wine (or 1 cup beef stock)
½ teaspoon paprika
  Salt and pepper to taste
1 carton (8-ounces) dairy sour cream

Combine butter, garlic, onion, green pepper and mushrooms in 2-quart casserole dish. MICROWAVE 3 MINUTES on HIGH, or until onion is transparent.

Stir in tomato paste. Sprinkle flour over contents of dish. Blend until smooth. Add beef, toss. Add beef stock and wine gradually, stirring until mixture is smooth. MICROWAVE 3 MINUTES on HIGH, or until mixture thickens, stirring after 1 minute, 30 seconds.

Add paprika, salt and pepper. Stir in sour cream. MICROWAVE 1 MINUTE on HIGH. Serve with buttered noodles.

ROAST BEEF STEW

4 to 5 servings
2-quart casserole

2 cups diced roast beef
1 cup chopped onion
1 cup thinly sliced carrots
1 cup diced potatoes
1 package (¾-ounce) brown gravy mix
½ teaspoon salt
½ teaspoon celery salt
2 teaspoons instant beef bouillon dissolved in
    1½ cups hot water
1 bay leaf

Combine all ingredients in 2-quart casserole. Cover. MICROWAVE 20 MINUTES on HIGH, or until vegetables are tender-crisp, stirring twice. Remove bay leaf.

CHICKEN-TUNA BAKE

3 to 4 servings
2-quart casserole

2 cans (10¾-ounces) condensed cream of mushroom or chicken soup, undiluted
½ cup milk
3 cups cooked chopped chicken
1 can (6½-ounces) tuna, drained and flaked
1⅓ cups finely chopped celery
¼ cup finely chopped onion
1 can (3-ounces) chow mein noodles
⅓ cup slivered almonds, toasted if desired

Combine soup and milk in 2-quart casserole. Blend
well. Stir in chicken, tuna, celery, onion and chow
mein noodles. Cover. MICROWAVE 8 to 10
MINUTES on HIGH, or until hot in the center.
Sprinkle with almonds. Let stand 3 minutes,
covered.

SAUCY BEEF HASH

4 to 5 servings
1½-quart casserole

2 cups cooked rice
2 cups diced cooked beef
1 small onion, chopped
½ cup snipped parsley
1 can (10½-ounces) condensed cream of tomato
soup, undiluted
2 teaspoons Worcestershire sauce
⅛ teaspoon pepper
4 to 5 thin slices cheddar cheese

Combine rice, beef, onion, parsely, soup, Worcestershire sauce and pepper in 1½-quart casserole.
Cover. MICROWAVE 8 to 10 MINUTES on
HIGH, or until hot and bubbly. Let stand 3 minutes,
covered. When serving, top each serving with thin
slice of cheese. Serve with dinner rolls and Whipped
Herb Butter.

SAUCY TURKEY AND RICE

4 servings
2-quart casserole
1½-quart casserole

Rice:
½ cup uncooked rice
¼ cup chopped onion
¼ cup chopped celery
¼ cup chopped green pepper
1½ cups chicken broth
¼ teaspoon seasoned salt

Turkey Sauce:
2 tablespoons butter or margarine
¼ cup flour
2 cups milk
½ teaspoon salt
Dash paprika
1 teaspoon instant chicken bouillon
2 cups cubed cooked turkey

Combine rice, onion celery and green pepper in
2-quart casserole. Add chicken broth and salt.
Cover. MICROWAVE 13 MINUTES on HIGH.
Let stand, covered, while preparing sauce.

Place butter in 1½-quart casserole. MICROWAVE
on HIGH, until melted. Stir in flour to make a
smooth paste. Gradually add milk, stirring until
blended. MICROWAVE 6 MINUTES on '8', or
until thickened, stirring after 4 minutes.

Beat in salt, paprika and bouillon with a wire whip
until bouillon is dissolved and sauce is smooth. Stir
in turkey. Cover. MICROWAVE 5 MINUTES on
'8', or until hot.

BUSY DAY CASSEROLE

6 servings
2-quart casserole

1 can (10½-ounces) cream of onion soup,
undiluted
1 can (10¾-ounces) chicken gumbo soup,
undiluted
2½ to 3 cups large chunks cooked turkey or
chicken
½ cup seasoned croutons

Combine soups in 2-quart casserole. Stir until well
blended. Stir in turkey. Sprinkle with croutons.
MICROWAVE 8 to 10 MINUTES on HIGH, or until
hot.

CHICKEN AND WILD RICE CASSEROLE

6 to 8 servings
3-quart casserole

4 cups diced, cooked chicken or turkey
4 cups cooked wild rice
1 medium onion, chopped
½ cup chopped celery
¼ cup chopped pimientos
½ cup slivered almonds
2 tablespoons butter or margarine
2 eggs, well beaten
1 cup chicken broth, or 1 teaspoon instant chicken bouillon dissolved in 1 cup hot water
½ cup milk
½ cup dry white wine
1 teaspoon salt

Mix all ingredients in 3-quart casserole. Cover. MICROWAVE 8 to 10 MINUTES on HIGH, or until center is hot, stirring twice.

TURKEY SPECIAL

4 to 6 servings
3-quart casserole

1 can (10¾-ounces) condensed cream of mushroom soup, undiluted
1 can (10½-ounces) condensed turkey vegetable soup, undiluted
1½ soup cans milk or water
1 cup chopped fresh spinach
1 cup chopped cooked turkey

Combine all ingredients in 3-quart casserole. Stir until well blended. Cover. MICROWAVE 7 to 8 MINUTES on HIGH, or until hot.

COOKED PORK AND SAUERKRAUT

6 servings
2-quart casserole or baking dish

2 tablespoons butter or margarine or bacon drippings
3 cups sauerkraut, drained
6 sliced cooked pork roast, cut ¼-inch thick
¼ teaspoon salt
Pepper
½ cup water

Place butter or bacon drippings in 2-quart casserole. MICROWAVE on HIGH until melted. Stir in sauerkraut and spread evenly.

Arrange pork slices on sauerkraut. Season with salt and pepper. Pour water over all. MICROWAVE 8 MINUTES on HIGH, or until hot. Let stand 3 minutes covered.

CONFETTI CASSEROLE

4 to 6 servings
12 x 8-inch baking dish

1 tablespoon butter or margarine
1 large onion, chopped
½ green pepper, chopped
1½ cups cubed, cooked ham
1 can (10¾-ounces) condensed cream of mushroom soup, undiluted
1 can (4-ounces) sliced mushrooms, drained
1 can (2-ounces) chopped pimiento, drained
8 pitted black olives, quartered
⅓ cup broken cashews
2 cans (15-ounces each) macaroni and cheese

Combine butter, onion and pepper in (12 x 8-inch) baking dish. MICROWAVE 3 MINUTES on HIGH, or until onion is transparent.

Mix in ham, soup, mushrooms, pimiento, olives, cashews and macaroni and cheese. Cover with plastic wrap. MICROWAVE 10 to 12 MINUTES on HIGH, or until hot and bubbly.

HEAVENLY HAM LOAF

4 to 6 servings
9 x 5-inch glass loaf dish

2 eggs
¾ pound lean ground ham
½ pound lean ground veal
¼ pound lean ground pork
¾ cup bread crumbs
¾ cup milk
2 tablespoons finely chopped onion
¼ teaspoon pepper
¼ cup firmly packed brown sugar
1 tablespoon prepared mustard
⅓ cup pineapple juice

Break eggs into large mixing bowl. Beat lightly with fork. Add ham, veal and pork. Mix to combine meats. Add bread crumbs, milk, onion, and pepper. Mix thoroughly. Spread in (9 x 5-inch) loaf dish.

Mix sugar and mustard together. Spread on top of loaf. Pour pineapple juice over all. Cover with waxed paper. MICROWAVE 5 MINUTES on HIGH.

Reduce setting. MICROWAVE 15 MINUTES on '6', until firm, or meat thermometer registers 160°. Let stand 5 minutes uncovered. Garnish with parsley, if desired.

NOTE: Do not use meat thermometer in oven while cooking.

HAWAIIAN SWEET-SOUR HAM

4 to 6 servings
1½-quart casserole

2 cups cubed, cooked ham
2 tablespoons firmly packed brown sugar
1½ tablespoons corn starch
1 cup pineapple tidbits
2 teaspoons prepared mustard
3 to 4 teaspoons vinegar
¾ cup water
½ teaspoon salt
2 cups hot, cooked rice

Place ham in 1½-quart casserole. Combine sugar and corn starch in 1-quart measure. Drain juice from pineapple tidbits into sugar mixture. Stir in mustard, vinegar and water. Pour over ham. MICROWAVE 4 to 6 MINUTES on HIGH, or until sauce is thickened.

Stir in pineapple. MICROWAVE 1 MINUTE on HIGH. Stir in salt. Serve over cooked rice.

ASPARAGUS HAM BIRDS

4 servings
1-quart measure
Shallow dish

12 spears fresh or frozen asparagus, cooked and drained, (page 190)
2 tablespoons butter or margarine
2 tablespoons flour
½ teaspoon salt
½ teaspoon dry mustard
1 cup milk
2 egg yolks, slightly beaten
4 slices leftover or boiled ham
½ cup grated sharp cheddar cheese

Place butter in 1-quart measure. MICROWAVE on HIGH until butter melts. Stir in flour, salt and mustard to make a smooth paste. Gradually stir in milk. MICROWAVE 2½ MINUTES to 3 MINUTES on HIGH, or until thickened, stirring once with a wire whip.

Stir a little of the hot mixture into egg yolks. Blend warmed yolks into hot sauce.

Wrap each slice of ham around three asparagus spears, secure with wooden pick. Arrange roll-ups in shallow dish. Pour white sauce over them. MICRO-WAVE 4 to 5 MINUTES on '5', or until heated through. Sprinkle with cheese. MICROWAVE 20 SECONDS on '5', or until cheese melts.

Serve on buttered toast triangle, if desired.

ORIENTAL HASH

6 servings
Browning dish

2 tablespoons salad oil
1½ cups cubed pork, cooked
2 cups rice, cooked
3 tablespoons soy sauce
Dash garlic powder
2 eggs, well beaten
2 cups shredded lettuce

Place empty browning dish in oven. MICROWAVE 4 to 5 MINUTES on HIGH. Add oil and cooked pork. MICROWAVE 2 to 3 MINUTES on HIGH, or until lightly browned, stirring once.

Mix in rice, soy sauce and garlic powder. Cover. MICROWAVE 3 to 4 MINUTES on HIGH, or until steaming.

Stir in beaten eggs. MICROWAVE 1 MINUTE on HIGH, or until eggs are set.

Add shredded lettuce and toss to combine. Serve immediately.

Asparagus Ham Birds

Eggs & Cheese

High and handsome cheese souffles, creamy quiches, puffy omelets are just a few of the egg and cheese dishes you can prepare in heat control microwave ovens. Eggs scrambled by microwave are not only faster and easier, they're better. You get greater volume, fluffier eggs and no crusty pan to clean. Cheese melts rapidly, making it an attractive finish for casseroles and sandwiches.

FAMILY QUICHE

8 servings
Large quiche dish or 10-inch pie pan

1 10-*inch baked quiche or pastry shell*
5 *or 6 slices bacon*
5 *eggs*
1 *cup milk*
1 *teaspoon seasoned salt*
1 *medium onion sliced*
1 *medium green pepper, cut in ¼-inch strips*
4 *ounces fresh mushrooms, sliced*
2 *tablespoons butter or margarine*
1 *tablespoon flour*

On roasting rack or layers of paper towels, MICROWAVE bacon 5 to 6 MINUTES on HIGH, or until crisp. Crumble into bottom of cooked pie shell.

In medium mixing bowl, combine eggs, milk and seasoned salt. Mix well. Set aside.

In 1-quart measure, combine onion, green pepper, mushrooms and butter. MICROWAVE 3 to 5 MINUTES on HIGH, or until onions are transparent. Add flour. Mix well. Add to egg mixture. Stir until blended. Pour into pie shell. MICROWAVE 14 to 16 MINUTES on '6', or until metal knife inserted in center comes out clean.

EGGS BASICS

Eggs cook differently by microwave. The high fat content of egg yolks absorbs energy, so yolks cook faster than whites. It's easy to poach eggs in a microwave oven, but if you want soft yolks, remove eggs from the oven before whites are completely cooked. A brief standing time allows whites to set without over-cooking yolks. Check eggs for doneness early, they toughen when over-cooked.

When eggs and yolks are mixed together for omelets, scrambled eggs or custards, they cook evenly and need less stirring than with the conventionally cooking methods.

Do not try to cook eggs in the shell. Steam can build up inside the shells, causing them to burst.

QUICHE

4 to 6 servings
9-inch quiche or pie dish

1 *recipe plain pastry, (page* 117)
Filling, below

On a lightly floured cloth or board, roll out pastry ⅛-inch thick. Lift pastry over rolling pin and unroll into 9-inch quiche or pie dish. Press pastry into dish from center to edges, using the back of the fingers. Prick pastry lightly but thoroughly with fork. MICROWAVE 4 MINUTES on '8'.

Fill quiche shell according to one of the variations below. MICROWAVE 12 MINUTES on '6', or until a metal knife inserted in center comes out clean.

SHRIMP AND ASPARAGUS QUICHE

5 to 6 servings
Baked quiche shell

Baked quiche shell
½ *cup cooked shrimp or* 1 *can (6½-ounces) drained*
1 *can (8-ounces) asparagus, drained and cut in* 1*-inch lengths*
1 *egg*
¾ *cup evaporated milk or light cream*
¼ *teaspoon salt*
Pinch white pepper
1½ *tablespoons grated parmesan cheese*

Flake shrimp and mix with asparagus. Spread over bottom of baked quiche shell. Beat egg lightly with wire whip. Stir in evaporated milk, salt and pepper. Sprinkle with parmesan cheese. MICROWAVE 12 MINUTES on '6'.

QUICHE LORRAINE

4 to 6 servings
9-inch quiche or pie dish

Baked quiche shell
6 *slices bacon cooked crisp and crumbled*
2 *eggs, beaten*
½ *cup evaporated milk*
6 *shallots, thinly sliced or* 1 *small onion, thinly sliced*
¼ *cup grated Swiss cheese*
Pinch pepper

Sprinkle cooked bacon over bottom of baked shell. Beat eggs with wire whip. Stir in evaporated milk, shallots, cheese and pepper. Pour into shell, MICROWAVE 12 MINUTES on '6', or until metal knife inserted comes out clean.

MUSHROOM QUICHE

5 to 6 servings
2-cup measure

Baked quiche shell
1 *onion, sliced*
1 *cup sliced mushrooms*
2 *tablespoons butter or margarine*
3 *tablespoons flour*
¾ *cup milk*
1 *egg, beaten*
¼ *cup evaporated milk or cream*
¼ *teaspoon salt*
Pinch pepper

Combine onion, mushrooms and butter in 2-quart measure. MICROWAVE 2 to 3 MINUTES on HIGH.

Add flour and mix well. Stir in milk. MICROWAVE 1 to 2 MINUTES on '8', or until mixture boils.

Stir a little of the hot liquid into beaten egg. Stir egg mixture, evaporated milk, salt and pepper into hot mushroom sauce. Pour into baked quiche shell. MICROWAVE 12 MINUTES on '6', or until metal knife inserted in center comes out clean.

OMELET DELUXE

2 to 4 servings
9-inch pie plate

4 *eggs, separated*
¼ *cup milk*
½ *teaspoon salt*
   Dash pepper
¼ *teaspoon baking powder*
1 *tablespoon butter or margarine*

In 1-quart bowl, beat egg whites until stiff peaks form. In small bowl, beat egg yolks with milk, salt, pepper and baking powder until lemon-colored. Gently fold into beaten egg whites.

Place butter in 9-inch pie plate. MICROWAVE on '6' until butter melts. Pour egg mixture into hot butter and spread evenly in pie plate. MICRO-WAVE 6 to 8 MINUTES on '6', or until center is almost set. Fold in half and serve.

NOTE: Omelet should be removed from oven before it is completely set, since it will continue to cook.

Variations:
FILLED OMELETS

Before folding omelet, fill with one of the following combinations:

Crumbled cooked bacon
Finely chopped green onion
Grated cheddar cheese
Chopped ham
Finely chopped green pepper
Finely chopped onion
Chopped tomato

SAUCED OMELETS

Top omelet with one of the following sauces:

Spanish sauce (page 92)
Fluffy hollandaise (page 200)
Mornay sauce (page 201)
Newburg sauce (page 201)

WESTERN OMELET

Fold into omelet before cooking:

¼ *cup finely chopped ham*
1 *tablespoon chopped onion*
1 *tablespoon finely chopped green pepper*

SOUR CREAM OMELET MELBA

4 to 6 servings
9-inch pie plate

1 *10 oz. package whole frozen raspberries*
2 *teaspoons cornstarch*
1 *teaspoon Cointreau or Grand Marnier*

Drain the juices into a small mixing bowl, and set berries aside. Add cornstarch to the juice and stir to dissolve. MICROWAVE 3 MINUTES on HIGH, or until thick, stirring once.

Stir in Cointreau or Grand Marnier, and whole berries. Cover. MICROWAVE 1½ MINUTES on HIGH, or until hot. Let stand covered while making the omelet.

OMELET:

3 *eggs, separated*
3 *tablespoons commercial sour cream*
½ *teaspoon salt*
   Dash pepper
2 *teaspoons butter*

Beat egg whites until stiff but not dry. Beat egg yolks slightly and stir in sour cream, salt, and pepper. Mix well. Fold egg yolk mixture into stiffy beaten egg whites.

In 9-inch pie plate, melt the butter. Pour in egg mixture.

MICROWAVE 1 MINUTE on HIGH then 7 MINUTES on '5'.

TO SERVE:

Slide omelet onto a serving dish and top with hot melba sauce.

Beat egg whites until stiff but not dry.

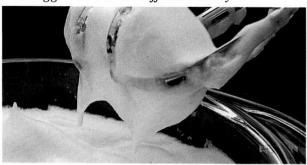

Fold egg yolk mixture into beaten egg whites.

Cheese Souffle

CHEESE SOUFFLE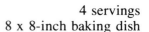

6 servings
1½-quart casserole
2-quart souffle dish

¼ cup all-purpose flour
¾ teaspoon salt
½ teaspoon dry mustard
⅛ teaspoon paprika
1⅔ cup evaporated milk, undiluted
¼ teaspoon hot pepper sauce
4 ounces sharp cheddar cheese, grated
6 eggs, separated
1 teaspoon cream of tartar

Blend flour, salt, mustard and paprika in 1½-quart casserole. Add evaporated milk and pepper sauce. Stir. MICROWAVE 3 to 4 MINUTES on HIGH, or until thickened, stirring after 2 minutes, then every 30 seconds.

Add cheese. Stir until melted. If necessary, MICROWAVE 1 to 2 MINUTES on HIGH until cheese melts, stirring every minute.

Beat egg whites with cream of tartar until stiff but not dry. Set aside. Beat egg yolks until thick and lemon colored. Slowly pour cheese mixture over beaten egg yolks, beating constantly until well combined. Spoon mixture over egg whites. Fold gently until just blended. Turn into ungreased 2-quart souffle dish. MICROWAVE 20 to 30 MINUTES on '3', or until top is dry, rotating dish every 10 minutes. Serve immediately.

NOTE: This recipe is not suitable for ovens without variable heat control.

POACHED EGGS

4 servings
4 individual custard cups
4 teaspoons water (1 teaspoon per cup)
4 eggs

Place 1 teaspoon water in each cup. Carefully break eggs into water. Cover tightly with plastic wrap. MICROWAVE 2 to 2½ MINUTES on '8', depending on doneness desired.

Let stand 1 to 2 minutes, or until whites coagulate, tightly covered.

EGGS BENEDICT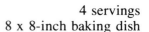

4 servings
8 x 8-inch baking dish

2 English muffins, split, toasted and buttered
4 slices ham, approximately 3-inches square
4 eggs poached
  Mock Hollandaise Sauce, below, or Fluffy
    Hollandaise (page 200)

Arrange muffin halves in (8 x 8-inch) baking dish. Place ham slice on buttered side of each muffin. Top with poached egg. Spoon Hollandaise sauce over eggs. Sprinkle with paprika, if desired. MICRO-WAVE 1 MINUTE, 30 SECONDS to 2 MINUTES on '5', or until heated through.

MOCK HOLLANDAISE SAUCE

About 1 cup
2-cup measure

2 tablespoons butter or margarine
1 cup mayonnaise or salad dressing
2 to 4 tablespoons lemon juice

Place butter in 2-cup measure. MICROWAVE on HIGH until butter melts. Stir in mayonnaise and lemon juice. MICROWAVE 2 MINUTES on '6', or just until hot.

SCRAMBLED EGGS

2 servings
1-quart casserole

1 *tablespoon butter or margarine*
4 *eggs*
¼ *cup milk*
¼ *teaspoon salt*
⅛ *teaspoon pepper*

Place butter in 1-quart casserole. MICROWAVE on HIGH until butter is melted. Add eggs, milk, salt and pepper. Beat with fork to scramble. MICROWAVE 2 MINUTES, 30 SECONDS to 3 MINUTES, or until eggs are almost set, stirring after 2 minutes.

Stir and let stand to complete cooking.

NOTE: For 6 to 8 eggs, use 2 tablespoons butter, ⅓ to ½ cup milk. Cover casserole. MICROWAVE 3 MINUTES, 30 SECONDS to 4 MINUTES, 30 SECONDS, stirring after 2 minutes, 45 seconds.

Variations:
Add one or two of the following:
½ *cup grated cheese*
1 *can (4-ounces) mushroom stems and pieces, drained*
1 *can (6½-ounces) minced clams, drained*
¼ *cup finely chopped onion or green pepper*
1 *tablespoon parsley flakes*

PREPARATION INSTRUCTIONS FOR SCRAMBLED EGGS

EGGS	MILK	BUTTER	SETTING	TIME
2	2 Tbsp.	1 Tbsp.	High	1-2 Min.
4	¼ Cup	1 Tbsp.	High	2-3 Min.
6	⅓ Cup	2 Tbsp.	High	3-4½ Min.
8	½ Cup	2 Tbsp.	High	4-5½ Min.

Salt and pepper to taste.

Stir half-way through cooking time.

CHEESE SCRAMBLED EGGS

4 servings
Shallow 2-quart casserole

2 *tablespoons butter or margarine*
8 *eggs*
½ *cup milk*
   Salt and pepper
4 *thin slices Swiss or cheddar cheese*

Place butter in shallow 2-quart casserole. MICROWAVE on HIGH until butter is melted.

Add eggs, milk, salt and pepper. Beat with fork to scramble. MICROWAVE 4 to 5 MINUTES on HIGH, or until eggs are almost set but very soft, stirring once.

Top with cheese. MICROWAVE 30 SECONDS to 1 MINUTE on HIGH, or until cheese is softened.

EGG FOO YUNG

4 servings
9-inch browning dish

1 *tablespoon butter or margarine*
6 *eggs*
1 *medium onion chopped*
1 *small green pepper, diced*
1 *can (10-ounces) bean sprouts, drained*
½ *teaspoon salt*

Preheat browning dish 4 MINUTES, add butter. Beat eggs until thick and lemon colored. Fold in remaining ingredients. MICROWAVE 7 to 9 MINUTES on '6', or until eggs are nearly set. Let stand 1 to 2 minutes, covered.

EGG FOO YUNG GRAVY

1-quart measure

1½ *cups chicken broth*
2 *teaspoons corn starch*
½ *teaspoon sugar*
½ *teaspoon salt*
   Dash pepper
1½ *to 2 teaspoons soy sauce*

Blend chicken broth and corn starch in 1-quart measure. Stir in remaining ingredients. MICROWAVE 4 to 5 MINUTES on HIGH, or until mixture thickens. Stir once with wire whip. Pour over Egg Foo Yung before serving.

Variation:

SEAFOOD EGG FOO YUNG

Add 1 cup diced, cooked shrimp or flaked crabmeat to egg mixture.

CHEESE BASICS

Because of its high fat content, cheese melts rapidly and can become tough or stringy when overcooked. When cheese is combined with eggs, cream or milk, use a lower heat control setting to produce a smooth and creamy dish without excessive stirring.

SPINACH QUICHE

5 to 6 servings
1-quart bowl

    Baked quiche shell
1 *cup cooked and well drained spinach*
2 *eggs, beaten*
½ *cup evaporated milk or light cream*
½ *teaspoon nutmeg*
¼ *teaspoon salt*
    Pinch pepper
1½ *tablespoons greated parmesan cheese*

Combine spinach, eggs, evaporated milk, nutmeg, salt and pepper. Pour into baked quiche shell. Sprinkle with parmesan cheese. MICROWAVE 8 to 10 MINUTES on '6', or until metal knife inserted in center comes out clean.

WELSH RAREBIT

4 servings
1-quart casserole

½ *cup beer*
1 *teaspoon dry mustard*
½ *teaspoon paprika*
    Dash cayenne
1 *teaspoon Worcestershire sauce*
1 *pound cheddar cheese, shredded*
1 *egg, slightly beaten*
4 *slices toast, cut in triangles*

Combine beer, mustard, paprika, cayenne and Worcestershire sauce in 1-quart casserole. MICRO-WAVE 2 MINUTES on HIGH, or until mixture is warm.

Stir in cheese. MICROWAVE 4 MINUTES on '6', or until cheese melts, stirring twice. Stir a little of the hot mixture into egg. Add warmed egg to cheese mixture. Stir until smooth. MICROWAVE 2 MINUTES on '6'. Stir and serve over toast triangles.

RICOTTA CHEESE BAKE

6 servings
8 x 8-inch baking dish

1 *pound seasoned bulk pork sausage*
6 *eggs*
2 *tablespoons fresh parsley, chopped*
1 *teaspoon seasoned salt*
1 *teaspoon sweet basil*
¼ *teaspoon pepper*
¼ *cup ricotta cheese*

Cut sausage into 1½-inch chunks and place on roasting rack. MICROWAVE 4 to 5 MINUTES on HIGH, or until no longer pink.

In a medium mixing bowl beat eggs well with a fork. Add other seasonings (parsley, salt, sweet basil, pepper) and mix well. Add ricotta cheese to egg mixture by the spoonful, mix gently. Do not stir until smooth.

Place sausage evenly in 8 x 8-inch baking dish. Pour egg and cheese mixture evenly over the sausage.

MICROWAVE 3 MINUTES on HIGH and 14 MIN-UTES on '6', or until metal knife inserted in center comes out clean. Rotate once if needed.

CHEESE TOPPERS

To add variety to casseroles or vegetables, top with one of the following combinations. Add topping and MICROWAVE 20 SECONDS to 1 MINUTE on HIGH, or until cheese melts.

¼ *cup parmesan cheese*
½ *cup fine bread crumbs*
½ *teaspoon favorite herbs*
¼ *cup process cheese spread, softened*
1 *teaspoon seasoned salt*

Grated cheddar or Swiss cheese
Snipped parsley or chives

Grated cheddar or Swiss cheese
Snipped parsley or chives

Slices or triangles of Swiss, cheddar, Monterey jack, mozzarella or colby

Cubes of seasoned cheese, such as onion, salami, garlic, pepper or spice

MUSHROOM-CHEESE FONDUE DIP

2-cups
1-quart casserole or ceramic fondue pot

1 *roll (5½-ounces) garlic cold pack club cheese, softened*
1 *can (10¾-ounces) condensed cream of mushroom soup, undiluted*
½ *cup water*
½ *teaspoon instant beef bouillon*
1 *teaspoon sherry*
Crisp raw vegetables, such as cauliflowerets, green pepper strips, celery sticks, zucchini sticks

Combine cheese, soup, water, bouillon and sherry in casserole or fondue pot. Mix well. MICROWAVE 4 MINUTES on HIGH, or until creamy, stirring after 2 minutes.

Keep warm over warming candle. Serve with assorted raw vegetables or crisp crackers.

NOTE: Can be reheated if necessary.

HAM AND EGGS AU GRATIN

4 to 6 servings
1½-quart casserole

4 *tablespoons butter or margarine*
¼ *cup flour*
2 *cups milk*
1½ *teaspoons prepared mustard*
2 *teaspoons Worcestershire sauce*
1 *cup shredded sharp cheddar cheese*
1 *cup cubed, cooked ham (½-inch cubes)*
6 *hard cooked eggs, halved*

Place butter in 1½-quart casserole. MICROWAVE on HIGH until butter melts. Blend in flour. Stir in milk. MICROWAVE 4 to 6 MINUTES on HIGH, or until thickened. Beat with wire whip.

Add mustard, Worcestershire sauce and cheese. MICROWAVE 1 MINUTE on HIGH, or until cheese melts.

Mix in ham and eggs. MICROWAVE 1½ MINUTES to 2 MINUTES on HIGH, or until bubbly. Serve over toast.

CHEESE FONDUE

6 cups
2-quart casserole or ceramic fondue dish

3 *cups shredded natural Swiss cheese*
1 *cup finely diced gruyere cheese*
1½ *tablespoons flour*
¼ *teaspoon nutmeg*
¼ *teaspoon pepper*
1 *clove garlic, pressed or finely chopped*
2 *cups dry white wine*
3 *tablespoons dry sherry.*

Lightly toss cheese, flour, nutmeg, pepper and garlic together in 2-quart bowl. Set aside.

Pour wine into 2-quart casserole or fondue dish. MICROWAVE 5 to 6 MINUTES on '6', or until wine is hot. Stir in cheese mixture. MICROWAVE 2 to 4 MINUTES on '6', or until cheese melts. Stir well.

Stir in sherry, serve immediately. Can be kept hot or reheated as needed.

NOTE: Serve with crusty French bread cut into 1 to 1½-inch squares. For variety experiment with other breads, such as rye, whole wheat or herb breads, bread sticks or pretzels.

Cheese Fondue

Vegetables

If you've never tasted vegetables cooked in a microwave oven, you don't really know how delicious vegetables can be. Flavors are more distinct, colors are brighter, and maximum nutrients are retained. Some vegetables, such as corn, onions or peas, cook in their own natural moisture. Others need only a few tablespoons of butter, margarine or water to cook tender-crisp.

To prepare this bouquet of vegetables see the Vegetable Chart beginning on page 190. The recipe for Stuffed Tomatoes is found on page 189.

VEGETABLE BASICS

Most vegetables cook on the HIGH setting, unless they are sauced or cheesed. For best results, cover vegetables tightly. If your casserole does not have a tight-fitting cover, substitute plastic wrap. Be careful when uncovering vegetables, as steam burns.

This cookbook recommends that vegetables be cooked tender-crisp. This means that a vegetable is tender to bite but retains its texture. If you prefer softer vegetables, microwave a little longer.

For vegetable cooking times and methods, see chart beginning on page 190.

ASPARANUTS

6 to 8 servings
1½-quart casserole

2 *packages (10-ounces each) frozen asparagus*
2 *tablespoons butter or margarine*
¼ *cup finely chopped or slivered almonds*
1 *teaspoon tarragon vinegar*

Place asparagus in 1½-quart casserole. Cover tightly. MICROWAVE 10 to 12 MINUTES on HIGH, or until asparagus is tender-crisp. Rearrange asparagus after 6 minutes.

Combine butter, almonds and vinegar in small mixing bowl. MICROWAVE 30 to 45 SECONDS on HIGH, or until butter is melted.

Pour almond butter sauce over asparagus. Serve immediately.

GREEN BEAN AND BACON CASSEROLE

4 servings
1-quart casserole

4 *slices bacon*
¼ *cup bread crumbs*
1 *package (9 to 10-ounces) frozen green beans, cooked and drained, (page 191)*
⅓ *cup condensed cream of mushroom soup, undiluted*

Place bacon in 1-quart casserole. MICROWAVE 2 to 3 MINUTES on HIGH. Remove bacon, crumble and set aside.

Add bread cubes to bacon drippings. Stir. MICROWAVE 2 MINUTES on HIGH, stirring once. Drain and set aside.

Combine beans, bacon and soup in 1-quart casserole. Mix well. Top with bread cubes. MICROWAVE 4 to 5 MINUTES on HIGH, or until hot.

MUSHROOM CREAMED BEANS

4 servings
1-quart casserole

1 *can (15-ounces) green beans, drained*
¾ *cup condensed cream of mushroom soup, undiluted*
¾ *cup canned French fried onion rings*

Combine beans and soup in 1-quart casserole. Cover. MICROWAVE 3 MINUTES on HIGH. Stir in onion rings. MICROWAVE 2 MINUTES on HIGH or until bubbly. Garnish with additional onion rings.

ASPARAGUS CASSEROLE

1 *large can asparagus*
1 *can condensed cream of mushroom soup*
3 *or 4 hard-cooked eggs (sliced thin)*
½ *cup grated cheese*
  Slivered almonds
½ *cup cracker crumbs (optional)*
  Salt and pepper to taste

Mix soup with ¼ cup liquid from asparagus. Beginning with asparagus, make layers of asparagus, eggs and soup mixture in a buttered casserole dish. MICROWAVE 6 to 8 MINUTES on '8'. Then top with cracker crumbs, grated cheese and almonds, MICROWAVE 1 to 2 MINUTES on HIGH.

BAKED BEANS

10 to 12 servings
3-quart casserole

6 *slices bacon, in 1-inch pieces*
1 *large onion, chopped*
3 *jars baked beans (16 to 18-ounces) with brown sugar-based sauce*
1 *can (16-ounces) crushed pineapple, drained*
⅔ *cup catsup*
2 *tablespoons molasses*
2 *tablespoons mustard*
1 *teaspoon salt*

MICROWAVE bacon 4 to 5 MINUTES on HIGH, stirring occasionally until bacon is crisp. Add onion. MICROWAVE 3 MINUTES on HIGH.

Add remaining ingredients. Mix well. MICROWAVE 12 to 14 MINUTES on HIGH, or until hot. Stir several times, and on removal from oven.

MAPLE GLAZED LIMA BEANS

4 to 6 servings
1-quart casserole

1 *package (10-ounces) frozen lima beans*
2 *tablespoons hot water*
¼ *cup maple syrup*
¼ *cup firmly packed brown sugar*
1 *tablespoon catsup*
1 *teaspoon prepared mustard*
2 *tablespoons butter or margarine, cut in bits*

Place frozen beans in 1-quart casserole. Add 2 tablespoons hot water. Cover. MICROWAVE 4 MINUTES on HIGH. Stir with fork after 2 minutes.

Drain beans. Add maple syrup, sugar, catsup and mustard. Mix well. Cover. MICROWAVE 3 MINUTES on HIGH. Stir.

Dot with butter. Cover. MICROWAVE 2 to 3 MINUTES on HIGH, or until beans are tender-crisp. Let stand 3 to 5 minutes, covered.

COLOSSAL BAKED LIMAS

8 servings
2 to 3-quart casserole or bowl

1 *pound dried lima beans*
1 *teaspoon salt*
½ *cup butter or margarine, cut in chunks*
½ *cup firmly packed brown sugar*
2 *tablespoons molasses*
1 *teaspoon prepared mustard*
1 *teaspoon salt*
1 *cup dairy sour cream*

In 2 to 3-quart casserole, soak lima beans overnight in water to cover.

Drain beans. Cover with fresh water. Add salt. Cover. MICROWAVE 30 to 35 MINUTES on '8', or until beans are tender. Drain.

Add butter chunks to hot beans. Stir in sugar, molasses, mustard and salt. Gently fold in sour cream. MICROWAVE 5 MINUTES on '6', or until hot.

CHEESY TOMATO BEANS

4 servings
1-quart casserole

1 *package (4-ounces) green beans, cooked and drained (page 191)*
1 *tablespoon butter or margarine, melted*
½ *teaspoon salt*
   Dash pepper
2 *tomatoes, peeled and quartered*
⅛ *teaspoon oregano*
½ *cup shredded Cheddar cheese*

Place hot cooked beans in 1-quart casserole. Drizzle with butter. Season with salt and pepper. Spread tomato quarters on top. Sprinkle with oregano and cheese. MICROWAVE 2 to 4 MINUTES on '6', or until tomatoes are hot and cheese has melted.

Cheesy Tomato Beans

HARVARD BEETS

4 servings
1-quart casserole

¼ cup sugar
1 tablespoon corn starch
½ teaspoon salt
   Dash white pepper
1 can (16-ounces) sliced beets
   Liquid drained from beets
¼ cup vinegar
¼ cup orange juice
1 teaspoon grated orange rind

Combine sugar, corn starch, salt and pepper in 1-quart casserole.

Drain beet liquid into 1-cup measure. If necessary, add water to make ¾ cup. Set beets aside.

Stir beet liquid, vinegar and orange juice into sugar mixture. Cover. MICROWAVE 5 to 7 MINUTES on HIGH, or until mixture is glossy and slightly thickened, stirring twice. Sprinkle with orange rind before serving.

FOOD FOR THE GODS WITH GREEN BEANS

4 to 6 servings
1½-quart casserole

2 cups green beans, cooked and drained
3 tablespoons vinegar
2 tablespoons butter or margarine
1 tablespoon sugar
1 tablespoon chicken broth, or 1 tablespoon hot
   water and ⅛ teaspoon instant chicken bouillon
   Dash dill seed
   Dash pepper
1 tablespoon corn starch
1 tablespoon water
2 packed cups chopped cabbage

Combine vinegar, butter, sugar, chicken broth, dill seed and pepper in 1½-quart casserole. MICRO-WAVE 1 to 2 MINUTES on HIGH, or until mixture begins to boil.

Mix corn starch and water together. Stir into boiling liquid. MICROWAVE 2 MINUTES on HIGH, or until mixture thickens.

Stir in cabbage. Cover. MICROWAVE 3 to 4 MINUTES on HIGH, or until cabbage is tender. Stir in cooked green beans. Let stand 3 minutes, covered.

TANGY CREAMED BEETS

4 servings
1-quart casserole

1 can (16-ounces) sliced or diced beets, drained
4 tablespoons dairy sour cream
1 tablespoon vinegar
1 teaspoon sugar
⅛ teaspoon garlic powder
⅛ teaspoon onion powder
2 teaspoons snipped fresh chives

Combine beets, sour cream, vinegar, sugar, salt, garlic and onion powders in 1-quart casserole. Mix well. MICROWAVE 3 MINUTES on HIGH, or until hot. Sprinkle with chives before serving.

BROCCOLI PUFF PIE

6 servings
9-inch pie dish

9-inch pie shell, prebaked and cooled
2 cups cooked chopped broccoli, fresh or
   frozen
2 tablespoons butter
2 eggs, separated
1½ cups commercial sour cream
2 tablespoons flour
2 tablespoons chopped chives, optional
1 teaspoon salt
⅛ teaspoon pepper
¼ teaspoon cream of tartar
2 tablespoons grated parmesan cheese
2 tablespoons seasoned bread crumbs

Place butter in custard cup. MICROWAVE on HIGH until butter melts. Stir warm butter into broccoli, to coat.

In another bowl beat egg yolks slightly, add sour cream, salt, flour, chives, and pepper.

In a large mixing bowl beat egg whites with cream of tartar until stiff but not dry. Fold sour cream mixture into the beaten egg whites.

Place half the cooked broccoli in the pie shell; spoon half of the sour cream mixture over the broccoli. Top with remaining broccoli, then with remaining sour cream mixture.

Combine parmesan cheese and bread crumbs, sprinkle over the pie.

PROGRAM TO MICROWAVE on '4' for 14 MINUTES, or until a knife inserted in the center comes out clean.

BROCCOLI & MUSHROOMS IN SOUR CREAM

6 to 8 servings
2-quart casserole
2-cup measure

2 *packages (10-ounces each) frozen whole broccoli spears, cooked and drained, (page 192)*
1½ *tablespoons butter or margarine*
1 *package (8-ounces) fresh mushrooms, stems removed, or 2 jars (4-ounces each) mushroom caps drained*
½ *teaspoon onion salt*
Dash pepper
1 *tablespoon white wine*
1 *tablespoon dry sherry*
½ *cup dairy sour cream*
1 *teaspoon snipped chives*
3 *tablespoons chopped cucumber (optional)*

Place hot, cooked broccoli in 2-quart casserole. Cover. Set aside.

Combine butter and mushroom caps in 2-cup measure. MICROWAVE 3 to 4 MINUTES on '6', or until mushroom caps are almost tender.

Stir in onion salt, pepper, wine, sherry, sour cream, chives and cucumber, if desired. MICROWAVE 3 to 4 MINUTES on '6', or until heated through.

Pour over broccoli. MICROWAVE 1 to 2 MINUTES on '6', or until dish is bubbly hot.

Variation:
Substitute asparagus or green beans for broccoli.

BROCCOLI ITALIAN STYLE

4 servings
2-cup measure

1 *pound fresh broccoli, or 1 package (10-ounces) frozen broccoli spears, cooked and drained*
2 *tablespoons butter or margarine*
¼ *cup sliced green onions, including tops*
1 *jar (4-ounces) chopped pimiento*
2 *teaspoons lemon juice*
½ *teaspoon salt*
⅛ *teaspoon pepper*
¼ *teaspoon oregano*

Combine butter and onions in 2-cup measure. MICROWAVE 2 MINUTES on HIGH, or until onions are transparent. Stir in pimiento, lemon juice, salt, pepper and oregano. Pour over cooked and drained broccoli. Reheat if necessary.

Broccoli-Rice Quiche

BROCCOLI-RICE QUICHE

6 servings
10-inch quiche dish

2 *cups hot cooked rice (⅔-cup uncooked)*
4 *to 5 ounces grated cheddar cheese*
3 *eggs*
1 *teaspoon salt*
½ *cup chopped onions*
1 *package (10-ounces) frozen chopped broccoli*
2 *tablespoons milk*
½ *teaspoon pepper*
1 *can (4-ounces) sliced mushrooms, drained*

Cook rice according to package directions, (or page 199)

Combine 2 cups cooked rice, ¾ cup grated cheddar cheese, 2 eggs, slightly beaten, ½ teaspoon salt. Press mixture firmly into greased dish. Set aside. Defrost broccoli in package. MICROWAVE 4 MINUTES on HIGH. Place broccoli in 1½-quart casserole, add onions to broccoli. MICROWAVE 6 to 8 MINUTES on HIGH, let stand 3 minutes covered. Drain broccoli thoroughly, return to casserole.

Beat remaining egg slightly. Stir in milk, pepper, mushrooms and remaining salt, add to broccoli and mix well. Spoon into rice quiche shell.

MICROWAVE 8 to 10 MINUTES on '6'. Rotate if necessary. Sprinkle with remaining cheese. MICROWAVE 20 SECONDS on HIGH if necessary to melt cheese.

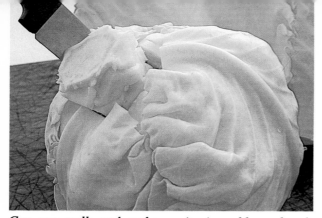

Cut out stalk and make cavity in cabbage head.

Loosley pack meat and cheese mixture in cavity.

HAM AND CHEESE FILLED CABBAGE

6 servings
2-quart mixing bowl

  1 *large cabbage*
  2 *cups precooked or chopped ham*
  ½ *cup seasoned bread crumbs*
  ½ *cup onion, chopped*
  1 *tablespoon butter or margarine, melted*
1¾ *cups grated American cheese*
  ½ *teaspoon paprika*
  ½ *teaspoon salt*
  ¼ *teaspoon dry mustard*
    Dash hot pepper sauce

Remove and save outer leaves of cabbage head. Cut out the stalk and make a cavity large enough to hold the meat and cheese filling, without cutting through the top. Set aside.

Mix the remaining ingredients in a large bowl. Loosely pack the meat and cheese mixture in the cabbage. Some filling may be left over. Cover with a moist cabbage leaf.

Place stuffed cabbage on a small trivet in a large mixing bowl.

Insert temperature probe in center of the filling. Cover with plastic wrap. Place in the oven and connect the temperature probe.

PROGRAM TO MICROWAVE on HIGH until the internal temperature reaches 110°, and'then on '6' until 140°.

Remove top cabbage leaf. Slice and serve.

BRUSSEL SPROUTS AU GRATIN

6 to 8 servings
1½-quart casserole
1-cup measure

2 *packages (10-ounces each) frozen brussel*
  sprouts, cooked and drained, (page 192)
½ *cup process sharp cheese spread*
¼ *cup butter or margarine*
¼ *cup crushed dry bread crumbs*
⅓ *cup chopped walnuts*

Place hot cooked brussel sprouts in 1½-quart casserole. Dot with cheese spread. Set aside.

Place butter in 1-cup measure. MICROWAVE on HIGH until butter melts. Stir in bread crumbs and walnuts. Toss to coat. Scatter crumb mixture over brussel sprouts. MICROWAVE 30 SECONDS to 1 MINUTE on HIGH, or until cheese melts.

WINE BRAISED CELERY AND MUSHROOMS

4 to 6 servings
2-quart casserole

1 *pound fresh mushrooms, cut in thick slices*
4 *cups diagonally sliced celery, 1 to 1½-inches*
  thick
½ *cup burgundy wine*
1 *teaspoon instant beef bouillon*
3 *tablespoons lemon juice*
2 *tablespoons butter or margarine, melted*
1 *teaspoon salt*
¼ *teaspoon pepper*
1 *tablespoon parsley flakes*

Spread half the mushrooms in bottom of 2-quart casserole. Cover with celery. Top with remaining mushrooms. Pour wine over vegetables. Sprinkle with instant bouillon, lemon juice, butter, salt, pepper and parsley flakes. Cover. MICROWAVE 6 to 8 MINUTES on HIGH, or until celery is tender-crisp.

GLAZED CARROT COINS

2 to 3 servings
1-quart casserole

¼ cup water
¼ teaspoon salt
3 to 4 medium carrots, thinly sliced in rounds
1½ tablespoons butter or margarine
⅓ cup firmly packed brown sugar
1 tablespoon grated lemon rind

Combine water, salt and carrots in 1-quart casserole. Cover tightly with plastic wrap. MICROWAVE 5 MINUTES on HIGH, or until carrots are tender-crisp.

Stir in butter, sugar and lemon rind. Cover. MICROWAVE 4 MINUTES on HIGH, or until hot and glazed.

SPICY CARROTS

4 servings
1-quart casserole

4 or 5 large, fresh carrots, cut in julienne strips
½ cup sugar
1 teaspoon salt
¼ teaspoon cinnamon
2 tablespoons butter or margarine, cut in pieces

Place carrots, sugar and cinnamon in 1-quart casserole. Toss to combine. Dot with butter. Cover tightly. MICROWAVE 7 to 8 MINUTES on HIGH, or until carrots are tender-crisp.

GRAPE GLAZED CARROTS

4 servings
1-quart casserole

2 tablespoons butter or margarine
2 tablespoons honey
1 cup red grapes, halved and seeded
2 cups small carrots, cooked and drained, (page 192)
1 tablespoon snipped parsley

Combine butter and honey in 1-quart casserole. MICROWAVE 1 to 2 MINUTES on HIGH, or until mixture is bubbling.

Stir in grapes and carrots. MICROWAVE 2 MINUTES on HIGH, or until hot. Garnish with parsley.

DEVILED CAULIFLOWER

4 servings
1-quart measure

1 pound fresh cauliflower, broken into flowerets, or 1 package (10-ounces) frozen cauliflower, cooked and drained, (page 192)
1 can (4½-ounces) deviled ham
1 teaspoon basil
1 teaspoon pepper
1 teaspoon prepared mustard
1 cup white sauce, (page 201)

Stir ham, basil, pepper and mustard into white sauce. MICROWAVE 2 MINUTES on '8', or until heated through.

Pour deviled ham sauce over cooked and drained cauliflower. MICROWAVE 1 to 2 MINUTES on '8', or until sauce begins to bubble.

BRAISED CELERY

4 servings
1-quart casserole

2 cups celery, cut diagonally in ½-inch pieces
½ teaspoon basil
¼ teaspoon thyme
¼ cup red wine, or ¼ teaspoon instant beef bouillon dissolved in ¼ cup hot water

Place celery in 1-quart casserole. Season with basil and thyme. Pour wine over celery. Cover. MICROWAVE 5 to 7 MINUTES until celery is tender crisp.

GERMAN RED CABBAGE

8 to 10 servings
2-quart casserole

4 cups shredded red cabbage
⅓ cup white wine
⅓ cup cider vinegar
1 medium tart apple, peeled and diced
1 tablespoon sugar
1 teaspoon salt
½ teaspoon caraway seed

Mix ingredients well in dish. Cover. MICROWAVE 8 to 10 MINUTES on HIGH, or until cabbage is tender, stirring twice during cooking time. Let stand covered for 10 minutes before serving.

Corn On The Cob

CORN ON THE COB cooked in the microwave oven comes to the table tender, sweet and piping hot. You can prepare it in several ways. With fresh corn, strip back the husk, remove silk, bring the husk back up over the corn and microwave. Husked corn may be arranged in a baking dish with a small amount of water and covered with plastic wrap. Individual ears may be wrapped in waxed paper and arranged on the oven floor. For cooking times, see the Vegetable Chart.

CORN BUBBLE

4 to 6 servings
1-quart casserole

2 *tablespoons butter or margarine*
1 *small onion, finely chopped*
2 *tablespoons flour*
1 *teaspoon salt*
½ *teaspoon paprika*
¼ *teaspoon dry mustard*
  Pepper to taste
¾ *cup milk*
1 *egg, slightly beaten with milk*
1 *can (16-ounces) whole kernel corn, drained*

Place butter and onion in 1-quart casserole. MICROWAVE 1 to 2 MINUTES on HIGH, or until onion is transparent.

Add flour, salt, paprika, mustard and pepper. Blend well.

Add milk and egg mixture slowly, stirring until smooth. Stir in corn. Cover. MICROWAVE 8 to 10 MINUTES on '8', or until bubbly. Let stand 3 to 5 minutes, covered.

ESCALLOPED CORN

4 to 6 servings
1-quart casserole

1 *can (8-ounces) cream-style corn*
1 *can (8-ounces) whole kernel corn, drained*
1 *cup cracker crumbs*
1 *can (5.33-ounces) evaporated milk*
1 *egg, slightly beaten*
2 *tablespoons butter or margarine, cut in pieces*

Combine cream-style and whole kernel corn, cracker crumbs and evaporated milk in 1-quart casserole. Mix well.

Stir in egg. Dot with butter. Cover. MICROWAVE 7 MINUTES, 30 SECONDS on '8', or until set. Let stand 3 to 5 minutes, covered. Garnish with paprika if desired.

ENGLISH PEA CASSEROLE

4 servings
1-quart casserole

12 *ounces frozen English Peas*
1 *cup small whole onions (frozen)*
1 *can (4-ounces) sliced mushrooms*
¼ *cup slivered almonds*

Combine ingredients in 1-quart casserole. MICROWAVE 10 to 12 MINUTES on HIGH.

SENSATIONAL ONION BAKE

4 servings
8x8-inch baking dish

4 *large white onions, peeled*
1 *can (5-ounces) boned chicken*
2 *tablespoons mayonnaise*
  Salt and pepper
¼ *cup butter or margarine*
2 *cups catsup*

With a grapefruit knife, hollow out the center of each onion leaving a half-inch thick shell. Set aside.

Finely chop center portions. Combine onion, chicken and mayonnaise in medium bowl. Season with salt and pepper. Mix well.

Fill onion shells with stuffing and place in (8x8-inch) baking dish. Dot each onion with 1 tablespoon butter.

Pour catsup around onions. Cover with plastic wrap. MICROWAVE 9 MINUTES on HIGH, or until onions are tender-crisp.

For variety: substitute 1 *can (10¾-ounces) double-strength chicken broth, undiluted, for catsup.*

Can be prepared in advance and cooked later.

MINTED PEAS

3 to 4 servings
1-cup measure
1-quart casserole

2 *tablespoons butter or margarine*
1 *tablespoon chopped fresh mint leaves*
1 *teaspoon sugar*
1 *package (10-ounces) frozen peas*
½ *teaspoon salt*

Place butter in 1-cup measure. MICROWAVE on HIGH until butter melts.

Stir in mint leaves and sugar. Place frozen peas in 1-quart casserole. Sprinkle with salt. Pour minted butter over peas. Cover. MICROWAVE 3 to 5 MINUTES on HIGH, or until peas are tender. Stir well to coat with sauce.

RATATOUILLE ✴

6 to 8 servings
3-quart casserole

¼ *cup olive or salad oil*
2 *medium onions, thickly sliced*
1 *clove garlic, pressed or finely chopped*
1 *large green pepper, cut in strips*
1 *medium eggplant, peeled and cut into ½-inch*
  cubes (about 1½-pounds)
2 *medium zucchini, cut into ¼-inch slices (about*
  1½-pounds)
3 *to 4 large tomatoes, peeled and cut in wedges, or*
  1 *can (16-ounces) tomatoes*
2 *teaspoons basil*
2 *teaspoons parsley flakes*
1 *teaspoon marjoram*
1 *teaspoon salt*
⅛ *teaspoon pepper*

Combine olive oil, onion, garlic and green pepper in 3-quart casserole. MICROWAVE 4 to 5 MINUTES on HIGH, or until onions are transparent.

Mix in eggplant and zucchini. Cover. MICROWAVE 4 to 5 MINUTES on HIGH, or until eggplant softens.

Gently stir in tomatoes, basil, parsley, marjoram, salt and pepper. MICROWAVE 10 MINUTES on '6', or until vegetables are tender.

MASHED POTATOES

6 to 8 servings
Paper towel
2-cup measure

6 *medium baking potatoes, baked (page 194)*
¾ *cup milk*
¼ *cup butter or margarine*
  Salt and pepper to taste

Bake potatoes and let stand 5 minutes.

Combine milk and butter in 2-cup measure. MICROWAVE 1 MINUTE on HIGH to warm milk.

Cut potatoes in half. Scoop out cooked potato into medium bowl. Add milk and butter mixture. Season with salt and pepper. Beat with rotary or electric beater until fluffy.

NOTE: Potatoes may be prepared in advance. Omit heating milk and butter. To reheat mashed potatoes, MICROWAVE 3 MINUTES on HIGH, or until hot.

GERMAN POTATO SALAD

4 servings
1½-quart casserole

6 *slices bacon*
¾ *cup finely chopped onion*
2 *tablespoons flour*
⅓ *cup sugar*
1 *teaspoon salt*
  Pepper to taste
½ *teaspoon celery seed*
⅔ *cup water*
5 *tablespoons cider vinegar*
4 *medium boiling potatoes, cooked, peeled and sliced*

Place bacon in 1½-quart casserole. MICROWAVE 3 to 4 MINUTES on HIGH, or until crisp. Remove bacon. Crumble and set aside.

Add onion to bacon drippings. MICROWAVE 2 to 3 MINUTES on HIGH, or until onion is transparent.

Stir in flour, sugar, salt, pepper and celery seed. MICROWAVE 1 MINUTE on HIGH. Stir in water and vinegar. MICROWAVE 3 to 4 MINUTES on HIGH, or until mixture boils. Add potatoes and bacon, stirring gently to coat with sauce.

SOUR CREAM MASHED POTATO PUFF

6 servings
2-quart souffle dish

6 *servings (3 cups) prepared instant mashed potatoes*
3 *eggs, separated*
1 *teaspoon cream of tartar*
1 *cup commercial sour cream*
1 *teaspoon salt*
¼ *teaspoon pepper*

Prepare 6 servings of instant mashed potatoes according to directions on the package. Stir in slightly beaten egg yolks, mix well and set aside to cool to lukewarm.

Beat egg whites with cream of tartar until stiff but not dry. Set aside.

To mashed potato mixture add sour cream, salt, and pepper. Blend well and fold gently into stiffly beaten egg whites. Pour mixture into a 6 to 8-cup souffle dish.

PROGRAM TO MICROWAVE on HIGH for 2 MINUTES, on '6' for 5 MINUTES and then on '4' for 10 to 12 MINUTES. Serve immediately. The center will be slightly creamy.

CHEESE STUFFED POTATOES

8 servings
Paper towels
Serving plate

4 *medium baking potatoes, baked (page 150)*
¼ *cup butter or margarine*
½ *cup milk*
  Salt and pepper to taste
1 *cup grated cheddar cheese or finely diced American process cheese, ¼ cup reserved*
1 *tablespoon finely chopped onion*

Bake potatoes. After standing time, halve potatoes lengthwise and carefully scoop out inside. Set shells aside. Combine potato, butter, milk, salt and pepper in medium mixing bowl. Mash until fluffy.

Stir in ¾ cup cheese and onion. Spoon mashed potato mixture into potato shells. Sprinkle remaining ¼ cup cheese on top.

Place stuffed potatoes on serving plate. MICROWAVE 1 MINUTE, 30 SECONDS to 2 MINUTES on HIGH, or until cheese melts and potatoes are hot. Garnish with paprika if desired.

NOTE: Potatoes may be prepared in advance and refrigerated without cheese topping. To reheat, MICROWAVE 4 to 5 MINUTES on HIGH, or until potatoes are hot. Top with reserved cheese. MICROWAVE 1 MINUTE on HIGH, until cheese melts.

AU GRATIN POTATOES

6 servings
2-quart casserole

1 *box (5½-ounces) au gratin potatoes*
2¼ *cups boiling water*
⅔ *cup milk*
2 *tablespoons butter or margarine*

Mix ingredients in order directed on box, using quantities and casserole size given here. Cover. MICROWAVE 18 to 20 MINUTES on '6', or until potatoes are tender and most of liquid is absorbed.

NOTE: Larger casserole is necessary to prevent over boiling. If drier potatoes are desired, use liquid as directed on box, a 2-quart casserole, and cook uncovered.

SWEET POTATO CUPS

6 servings
1 large microwave safe dinner plate

3 *medium sweet potatoes*
½ *cup orange juice*
½ *cup brown sugar*
½ *teaspoon salt*
½ *teaspoon nutmeg*
¼ *teaspoon cinnamon*
¼ *teaspoon vanilla*
6 *tablespoons cranberry orange relish*
1 *cup chopped pecans*
¼ *cup brown sugar*

Cook sweet potatoes in jackets. MICROWAVE 10 to 12 MINUTES on HIGH or until tender. Peel potatoes and mash. Add juice, sugar, salt, nutmeg, cinnamon and vanilla. Beat with mixer until well blended. Divide mixture evenly into six "cups" on dinner plate, forming cups with a spoon leaving a well in the center of each.

Fill each well with 1 tablespoon of Cranberry-Orange Relish. Mix together pecans and brown sugar. Top each cup with mixture. MICROWAVE 5 to 8 MINUTES on HIGH or until heated through.

SWEET POTATO MARSHAROLE

4 to 6 servings
1½-quart casserole

2 *tablespoons butter or margarine*
1 *can (23-ounces) sweet potatoes, drained and mashed*
2 *tablespoons milk*
2 *tablespoons raisins*
2 *tablespoons orange marmalade*
¼ *teaspoon salt*
¼ *teaspoon cinnamon*
¼ *teaspoon nutmeg*
½ *cup miniature marshmallows*

Place butter in 1½-quart casserole. MICROWAVE on HIGH until melted.

Add sweet potatoes, milk, raisins, marmalade, salt and spices. Mix well. Cover. MICROWAVE 7 MINUTES on HIGH, or until hot.

Top with marshmallows. Cover. MICROWAVE 1 MINUTE, 30 SECONDS to 2 MINUTES on HIGH until marshmallows begin to soften.

Let stand 5 minutes, covered.

Orange-Potato Shells

ORANGE-POTATO SHELLS

4 servings
2-quart bowl

2 *oranges, reserve 2 tablespoons juice*
1 *can (23-ounces) vacuum packed sweet potatoes*
4 *portions instant mashed potatoes, prepared according to package directions*
1 *marshmallow, cut in quarters*

Cut oranges in half with sharp paring knife, making a saw-tooth pattern. Using a grapefruit knife, free fruit from shell carefully. Save juice.

With a fork, mash sweet potatoes in 2-quart bowl. Stir in 2 tablespoons reserved orange juice. Blend in mashed potatoes. Mix well.

Fill orange shells with potato mixture, using a pastry tube or spoon. Top with marshmallow quarters. MICROWAVE 1 MINUTE on HIGH, or until marshmallow softens.

SCALLOPED POTATOES

4 servings
1-quart casserole

2 *medium baking potatoes, peeled and thinly sliced*
1 *cup medium white sauce*
1 *teaspoon butter or margarine, cut in pieces*

Layer half of potato slices in 1-quart casserole. Mask with half of sauce. Repeat with potatoes and sauce. Dot with butter. MICROWAVE 25 to 30 MINUTES on '4', or until potatoes are fork tender. Let stand 5 minutes before serving.

LEMON POTATO WEDGES

6 to 8 servings
shallow dish

3 *medium baking potatoes, do not peel*
3 *tablespoons butter or margarine*
2 *tablespoons fresh lemon juice*
2 *tablespoons fresh grated lemon peel*
½ *teaspoon paprika*
3 *tablespoons grated parmesan cheese*

Cut potatoes in wedges by cutting in quarters lengthwise. Set aside.

In 1 cup measure, MICROWAVE butter 1 MINUTE on HIGH, or until melted. Add lemon juice. Place potatoes in shallow baking dish, brush cut edges with butter mixture.

Combine lemon peel, paprika, and cheese in small cup. Sprinkle over potatoes. MICROWAVE, uncovered, 10 to 12 MINUTES on HIGH, or until potatoes are tender. Let stand, loosely covered with wax paper, for 4 minutes before serving.

SWEET-SOUR SPINACH

4 servings
1-quart casserole

4 *slices bacon*
1 *tablespoon flour*
1 *teaspoon sugar*
¼ *cup whipping cream*
1 *tablespoon cider vinegar*
1 *pound fresh spinach, or 1 package (10-ounces) frozen leaf spinach cooked and drained, (page 195)*

Place bacon in 1-quart casserole. MICROWAVE 2 to 3 MINUTES on HIGH, or until crisp. Remove bacon. Crumble and set aside.

Drain all but 1 tablespoon bacon drippings from casserole. Add flour and mix until smooth. Stir in sugar and cream. MICROWAVE 1 MINUTE on HIGH, stirring once after 30 seconds. Stir in vinegar.

Add spinach and toss lightly to coat with sauce. MICROWAVE 1 MINUTE on HIGH, or until spinach is hot. Garnish with crumbled bacon.

SPINACH SOUFFLE

8 servings
2-quart souffle dish

¼ *cup butter*
¼ *cup flour*
1 *cup milk*
1 *teaspoon salt*
¼ *teaspoon dry mustard*
⅛ *teaspoon pepper*
4 *eggs, separated*
1 *package (10-ounces) chopped spinach, defrosted and drained*
1 *teaspoon cream of tartar*

In a 1½-quart bowl MICROWAVE butter on HIGH until melted. Stir in dry ingredients to make smooth paste. Gradually stir in milk. MICROWAVE 3 to 4 MINUTES on HIGH, or until thick, stirring twice. Add slightly beaten egg yolks, blend well. Stir in the spinach.

In a large mixing bowl, beat egg whites with cream tarter until stiff but not dry.

Fold thickened sauce into beaten egg whites and pour gently into a 6 to 8-cup souffle dish PROGRAM TO MICROWAVE on '6' for 2 minutes, then on '3' for 25 to 30 MINUTES.

Serve immediately.

STUFFED ZUCCHINI

4-servings
8 x 8-inch baking dish

4 *to 6 small zucchini, cut in half lengthwise*
1 *tablespoon olive oil or salad oil*
1 *medium onion, finely chopped*
1 *clove garlic, pressed or finely diced*
1 *cup bread crumbs*
¾ *cup grated parmesan cheese*
4 *tablespoons snipped parsley*
1 *teaspoon basil*
1 *chopped tomato*

Scoop out and discard seeds from zucchini. Set aside. In 2-cup measure, combine oil, onions and garlic. MICROWAVE 2 to 3 MINUTES on HIGH, or until onions are transparent.

Mix in bread crumbs, cheese, 2 tablespoons parsley and basil. Spoon filling into zucchini shells. Arrange in baking dish. Top with remaining parsley and chopped tomatoes. Cover with plastic wrap. MICROWAVE 6 to 8 MINUTES on HIGH, or until zucchini is tender.

CARIBBEAN BAKED SQUASH

2 to 4 servings
1-quart casserole
2-cup measure

1 *pound winter squash (hubbard, acorn) peeled*
    and cut in 1-inch cubes
¼ *cup butter or margarine*
1 *can (8-ounces) crushed pineapple*
1 *teaspoon grated orange rind*
    Dash nutmeg

Place squash in 1-quart casserole. Cover. MICRO-WAVE 8 to 10 MINUTES on HIGH, or until almost tender, stirring once. Set aside.

Place butter in 2-cup measure. MICROWAVE 30 SECONDS on HIGH, or until butter is melted. Add pineapple, orange rind and nutmeg. Mix well.

Spoon mixture over cooked squash. Cover. MICROWAVE 2 MINUTES on HIGH, or until hot.

Let stand 5 minutes to finish cooking and blend flavors. Garnish with parsley if desired.

MATTERHORN VEGETABLE BAKE

6 servings
1½-quart casserole

¼ *cup butter or margarine*
1½ *cups sliced summer squash*
1 *package (10-ounces) frozen, chopped*
    broccoli, defrosted
1 *egg*
½ *cup shredded Swiss cheese*
¼ *cup milk*
1 *teaspoon salt*
¼ *teaspoon dry mustard*
3 *tablespoons grated parmesan cheese*

Place butter in 1½-quart casserole. MICROWAVE on HIGH until butter melts. Stir in squash and broccoli to coat with butter. Cover. MICROWAVE 6 to 8 MINUTES on HIGH, or until tender.

Beat egg lightly in small mixing bowl. Mix in cheese, milk, salt and mustard. Pour mixture over vegetables. Sprinkle with parmesan cheese. MICROWAVE 4 MINUTES on '6', or until cheese melts and is bubbly.

STUFFED TOMATOES

4 servings
8 x 8-inch square baking dish
1-quart casserole

4 *large ripe tomatoes*
2 *tablespoons butter or margarine*
2 *tablespoons finely chopped onion*
1 *cup crushed dry bread crumbs*
½ *teaspoon salt*
¼ *teaspoon poultry seasoning*
⅛ *teaspoon pepper*
2 *tablespoons butter or margarine, cut in*
    small pieces
    Paprika

Remove stem ends of tomatoes and scoop out center pulp and seeds. Place tomatoes in (8 x 8-inch) square baking dish. Set aside.

Combine butter and onion in a 1-quart casserole. Cover. MICROWAVE 4 MINUTES on HIGH, or until onion is transparent. Stir in bread crumbs, salt, poultry seasoning and pepper. Mix well.

Spoon stuffing mixture into tomatoes. Dot with remaining butter. Sprinkle with paprika. Cover. MICROWAVE 3 to 4 MINUTES on HIGH, or until skins begin to break and tomatoes are heated through.

ZUCCHINI PARMESAN

4 servings
1-quart casserole
Custard cup

1½ *pounds zucchini, sliced ¼-inch thick*
¼ *cup parmesan cheese*
½ *teaspoon basil*
¼ *teaspoon salt*
1 *tablespoon butter or margarine*

Arrange zucchini slices in the bottom of a 1-quart casserole. Mix parmesan cheese, basil and salt together. Sprinkle over zucchini.

Place butter in custard cup. MICROWAVE on HIGH until butter melts. Drizzle over top of zucchini. Cover. MICROWAVE 4 to 5 MINUTES on HIGH, or until zucchini is tender crisp.

Vegetable Cooking Chart

Blue areas indicate frozen items

VEGETABLE	AMOUNT	COOKING PROCEDURE	TIME	SETTING	STANDING TIME
Artichokes (fresh)	1 medium	1 tablespoon water in 8 x 8-inch dish, covered.	4-6 minutes	High	3 minutes, covered
	2 medium	¼ cup water, 1 teaspoon salt, in cake dish, covered.	5-7 minutes	High	3 minutes, covered
	3 medium	½ cup water, ½ teaspoon salt in a round cake dish, covered.	7-9 minutes	High	3 minutes, covered
Asparagus (fresh)	15 4-inch pieces	¼ cup water, ½ teaspoon salt in 1½-quart covered casserole.	5-7 minutes	High	3 minutes, covered
Asparagus (frozen)	10 ounces	Use 1-quart covered casserole. Separate after 3 minutes.	5-7 minutes	High	3 minutes, covered
Beans, Butter (fresh)	1 pound (2 cups shelled)	½ cup water in 1-quart covered casserole. Stir.	6-8 minutes	High	3 minutes, covered
	2 pounds (4 cups shelled)	½ cup water in 1½-quart covered casserole. Stir.	9-11 minutes	High	3 minutes, covered

Fresh Vegetables *when they are available, may be used for many of the recipes in this book which call for frozen vegetables. If you have favorite fresh vegetable dishes, prepare a double portion. Remove the extra amount when half cooked, chill and freeze for future use. When sweet corn is in season, buy it freshly picked. Husk it and blanch briefly. Chill, then seal individual ears in plastic pouches. Microwave frozen corn right in the pouch and you'll have fresh-tasting corn all winter long.*

If you are a home gardener, pick vegetables right at the peak of flavor, even if you have only one serving. Blanch by microwave and freeze. It's easier and better to freeze vegetables as they ripen than to harvest everything at once, the unripe, the ripe and the over ripe. If you must do large lot canning or freezing, your conventional range will handle the large quantities better than the microwave oven.

TO BLANCH small quantities (up to 4 cups), use ½ cup water for each cup of vegetables. Bring water to a boil in the microwave oven. Add vegetables and MICROWAVE 30 SECONDS to 1 MINUTE on HIGH, depending upon the quantity of vegetables. Stir until vegetables lose their raw appearance. Chill and freeze.

VEGETABLE	AMOUNT	COOKING PROCEDURE	TIME	SETTING	STANDING TIME
Beans, Green or Wax (fresh)	1 pound snapped or French cut	¼ cup water, ½ teaspoon salt in 1½-quart covered casserole.	7-9 minutes	High	3 minutes, covered
Beans, Green cut or wax French cut (frozen)	10 ounces	Use 1-quart covered casserole. Add 2 teaspoons hot water and stir.	6-8 minutes	High	3 minutes, covered
Beans, Lima (fresh)	1 pound (2 cups shelled)	½ cup water in 1-quart covered casserole. Stir.	6-8 minutes	High	3 minutes, covered
	2 pounds (4 cups shelled)	½ cup water in 1½-quart covered casserole. Stir.	9-11 minutes	High	3 minutes, covered
Beans, Pinto (fresh)	2 cups (1 pound)	Soak overnight. 3 cups water in 2-quart covered casserole. Stir.	20-25 minutes	High	3-5 minutes, covered
Beets (fresh)	4 whole, medium size	Barely cover with water. add ¼ teaspoon salt. Cook in 2-quart covered casserole.	15-17 minutes	High	3 minutes, covered
	4 medium, sliced	½ cup water, ¼ teaspoon salt in 1-quart covered casserole.	12 minutes	High	3 minutes, covered

Vegetable Cooking Chart continued

VEGETABLE	AMOUNT	COOKING PROCEDURE	TIME	SETTING	STANDING TIME
Broccoli (fresh)	1 small bunch (1½ pounds)	Cut away tough part of stalk, split tender ends. ½ cup water, ½ teaspoon salt in 1½-quart covered casserole.	7 - 9 minutes	High	3 minutes, covered
Broccoli (frozen)	10 ounces	Use 1-quart covered casserole. Separate after 4 minutes.	7 - 9 minutes	High	3 minutes, covered
Brussel Sprouts (fresh)	½ pound (2 cups)	2 tablespoons water in 1-quart covered casserole.	4 - 6 minutes	High	3 minutes, covered
	1 pound (4 cups)	3 tablespoons water in 1½-quart covered casserole.	5 - 7 minutes	High	3 minutes, covered
Brussel Sprouts (frozen)	10 ounce package	2 tablespoons water.	4 - 6 minutes	High	3 minutes, covered
	10 ounce pouch	Slit pouch with knife.	4½ - 5 minutes	High	3 minutes, covered
Cabbage (fresh)	1 small head chopped	Fill 1½-quart casserole with chopped cabbage, add ½ teaspoon salt, 2 tablespoons water. Cover.	10 - 12 minutes	High	3 minutes, covered
	1 medium head, whole	½ teaspoon salt, 2 tablespoons water in 2-quart covered casserole.	12 - 15 minutes	High	3 minutes, covered
Carrots (fresh)	4 medium sliced	2 tablespoons water in 1-quart covered casserole.	4 - 6 minutes	High	3 minutes, covered
	6 medium sliced	2 tablespoons water in 1½-quart covered casserole.	6 - 8 minutes	High	3 minutes, covered
Carrots (frozen)	10 ounce package	2 tablespoons water in 1-quart covered casserole.	5 - 7 minutes	High	3 minutes, covered
	10 ounce pouch	Slit pouch with knife.	4 - 6 minutes	High	3 minutes, covered
Cauliflower (fresh)	1 small head	½ cup water, ¼ teaspoon salt in 1½-quart covered casserole	5 - 7 minutes	High	3 minutes, covered
	1 medium head	½ cup water, ¼ teaspoon salt in 2-quart covered casserole	9 - 11 minutes	High	3 minutes, covered
Cauliflower (frozen)	10 ounces	2 tablespoons hot water in 1-quart covered casserole	4 - 6 minutes	High	3 minutes, covered

VEGETABLE	AMOUNT	COOKING PROCEDURE	TIME	SETTING	STANDING TIME
Celery (fresh)	4 cups coarsely chopped	¼ cup water, ½ teaspoon salt in 1½-quart covered casserole	6 - 8 minutes	High	3 minutes, covered
	6 cups coarsely chopped	¼ cup water, ½ teaspoon salt in 2-quart covered casserole	10 - 12 minutes	High	3 minutes, covered
Corn, cut off the cob (fresh)	1½ cups	¼ cup water, ½ teaspoon salt in 1-quart covered casserole	3 - 5 minutes	High	3 minutes, covered
Corn, cut off the cob (frozen)	10 ounces	¼ cup hot water in 1-quart covered casserole	4 - 6 minutes	High	3 minutes, covered
Corn on the cob (fresh)	2 ears	Put ears in open glass dish. Pour melted butter over corn. Turn ears 2 or 3 times during cooking.	4 - 6 minutes	High	3 minutes, covered
	4 ears	Same as above	8 - 10 minutes	High	3 minutes, covered
Corn on the cob (frozen)	2 ears	¼ cup hot water in 1-quart covered casserole. Turn ears after 3 minutes	6 - 8 minutes	High	3 minutes, covered
Eggplant (fresh) Not available for frozen	1 medium (4 cups, cubed)	Peel and dice eggplant. Put in 2-quart covered casserole. Add 2 table-spoons water, ¼ teaspoon salt	4 - 6 minutes	High	3 minutes, covered
Okra (frozen)	10 ounces	2 tablespoons hot water in 1-quart covered casserole	5 - 7 minutes	High	3 minutes, covered
Onions (fresh)	2 large, cut in quarters or eighths	½ cup water, ½ teaspoon salt in 1-quart covered casserole	5 - 7 minutes	High	3 minutes, covered
	4 large, cut in quarters or eighths	½ cup water, ½ teaspoon salt in 2-quart covered casserole	7 - 9 minutes	High	3 minutes, covered
Parsnips (fresh)	2 medium	2 tablespoons water in 1-quart covered casserole	5 - 7 minutes	High	3 minutes, covered
	4 medium	¼ cup water in 2-quart covered casserole	7 - 9 minutes	High	3 minutes, covered

VEGETABLE	AMOUNT	COOKING PROCEDURE	TIME	SETTING	STANDING TIME
Peas, Black Eyed (frozen)	10 ounce package	¼ cup water in 1-quart covered casserole	8 - 10 minutes	High	3 minutes, covered
Peas and Carrots (frozen)	10 ounces	2 tablespoons hot water in 1-quart covered casserole. Stir after 4 minutes	4 - 6 minutes	High	3 minutes, covered
Peas, Green (fresh)	2 cups shelled	2 tablespoons water in 1-quart covered casserole	4 - 6 minutes	High	3 minutes, covered
	3 cups shelled	2 tablespoons water in 1-quart covered casserole	5 - 7 minutes	High	3 minutes, covered
Peas, Tiny Green (frozen)	10 ounces	2 tablespoons hot water in 1-quart covered casserole	4 - 6 minutes	High	3 minutes, covered
Potatoes, baked (Irish) Idaho (fresh)	All medium size 1 2 3 4	Scrub potatoes and dry. Spread paper towel on oven shelf. Put potatoes on paper towel about 1-inch apart. Times are approximate and vary with size and variety. When baking more than 4 potatoes, rearrange after half the cooking time has expired	5 - 6 minutes 7 - 9 minutes 10 - 12 minutes 14 - 16 minutes	High High High High	Wrap in foil, let stand 5 - 10 minutes
Potatoes, boiled (fresh)	6 medium, cut in half, peeled	¼ cup water, ½ teaspoon salt in 2-quart covered casserole. Stir once after 6 minutes	12 - 16 minutes	High	3 - 5 minutes, covered
Potatoes, buttered (Irish) (fresh)	4 medium, sliced	2 tablespoons butter in 1½-quart glass casserole. Sprinkle potatoes with ½ teaspoon salt, dot with butter	12 - 14 minutes	High	5 minutes,
	6 medium, sliced	2 tablespoons butter in 2-quart glass casserole. Stir after 5 minutes	17 - 19 minutes	High	5 minutes,
Rutabaga (fresh)	One (1 lb.)	Wash, peel and cube rutabaga. ½ cup water, 3 tablespoons butter, salt and pepper to taste. Use 1-quart covered casserole	7 - 9 minutes	High	3 minutes, covered
Spinach (fresh)	4 cups (1 lb.)	Wash. Cook in water that clings to the leaves. 2-quart covered casserole.	3 - 5 minutes	High	3 minutes, covered

VEGETABLE	AMOUNT	COOKING PROCEDURE	TIME	SETTING	STANDING TIME
Spinach, leaf or chopped (frozen)	10 ounces	Use 1-quart covered casserole	4 - 6 minutes	High	3 minutes, covered
	10 ounce package	2 tablespoons water in 1-quart covered casserole	4 - 6 minutes	High	3 minutes, covered
Squash, Acorn or Butternut (fresh)	One (1 lb.)	Cook whole. Pierce skin with sharp knife in several places. Cook on paper towel.	4 - 6 minutes	High	5 minutes,
Squash, Hubbard (frozen)	10 ounce package	2 tablespoons water in 1-quart casserole	4 - 6 minutes	High	3 minutes, covered
Sweet Potatoes (fresh)	4 medium, cut in half lengthwise, peeled	¼ cup water, ½ teaspoon salt in 1½-quart covered casserole	8 - 10 minutes	High	3 minutes, covered
	6 medium, cut in half lengthwise, peeled	¼ cup water, ½ teaspoon salt in 2-quart covered casserole. Stir after 5 minutes	12 - 14 minutes	High	3 minutes, covered
Sweet Potatoes, baked whole (fresh)	All medium size 1 2 4	Scrub and dry potatoes. Cover oven shelf with paper towel, put potatoes on towel about 1-inch apart	5 - 7 minutes 7 - 9 minutes 14 - 16 minutes	High High High	Wrap in foil after cooking, let stand 5 - 10 minutes
Zucchini (fresh)	One (1 lb.)	Wash, remove stems. Cut into thin slices. Add ¼ cup water in 1-quart covered casserole	5 - 5½ minutes	High	3 minutes, covered
Tomatoes (fresh)	4 large 2½ - 3-inch dia. (1 lb.)	Clean, peel and halve tomatoes. Place in 1½-quart covered casserole. Add 2 tablespoons water	4 - 6 minutes	High	3 minutes, covered Add ½ teaspoon salt
Turnips (fresh)	2 or 3 medium (1 lb.)	Peel and cube. Add 3 tablespoons water, ¼ teaspoon salt in 1½-quart covered casserole	7 - 9 minutes	High	3 minutes, covered
Vegetables, Mixed (frozen)	10 ounce package	Add ¼ cup hot water in 1-quart covered casserole	4 - 6 minutes	High	3 minutes, covered
	10 ounce pouch	Split pouch with knife	4 - 6 minutes	High	3 minutes,

Rice Pilaf

Rice, Pasta & Cereals

Rice and pasta are dry foods, and need time to absorb moisture. Since only a little time is saved by microwave cooking, you may prefer to cook rice and pasta conventionally while you prepare the sauce or main dish in the microwave oven. Rice and pasta reheat easily in a covered casserole and need no additional water. If they have been refrigerated, stir once or twice during heating.

Use rice and pasta to create your own quick-and-easy dinners. Add chopped onion, green pepper or celery, canned shrimp, chopped luncheon meat or leftover roast. For variety, add 1 teaspoon instant chicken or beef bouillon for each cup of water when cooking rice.

Hot cooked cereals are so easy by microwave that children can cook their own breakfast right in the cereal bowl, and there won't be a messy pan left to soak in the sink.

RICE PILAF

6 to 8 servings
2-quart casserole

¼ cup butter or margarine
1 medium onion, finely chopped
½ cup finely chopped celery
1½ cups uncooked regular rice
¼ cup snipped parsley
¼ teaspoon salt
  Dash pepper
⅓ bay leaf
⅛ teaspoon thyme
1 can (10½-ounces) condensed chicken broth
1⅓ cups water

Combine butter, onion and celery in 2-quart casserole. MICROWAVE 3 to 4 MINUTES on HIGH, or until onion is transparent.

Add rice, parsley, salt, pepper, bay leaf, thyme, broth and water. Cover. MICROWAVE 5 to 6 MINUTES on HIGH, or until mixture begins to boil.

Reduce setting. MICROWAVE 16 to 18 MINUTES on '5', or until rice is tender. Let stand 3 to 5 minutes, covered. Remove bay leaf before serving.

Variations:

ITALIAN RICE

Substitute ⅓ cup dry white wine for ⅓ cup water. Add ⅛ teaspoon powdered or crushed saffron threads to water. Just before serving, stir in 2 tablespoons soft butter and ⅓ cup grated parmesan cheese.

RICE PUDDING

4 servings
1-quart measure
2-quart casserole

2 cups cooked rice
1¼ cups milk
2 eggs, beaten
½ cup sugar
⅛ teaspoon salt
½ cup raisins
¼ teaspoon cinnamon
½ teaspoon vanilla

Measure milk in 1-quart measure. MICROWAVE 3 MINUTES on HIGH, stir, MICROWAVE 3 MINUTES on HIGH, or until almost boiling.

Combine eggs, sugar and salt in 2-quart casserole. Stir in scalded milk. Mix in rice, raisins, cinnamon and vanillia thoroughly. MICROWAVE 3 MINUTES on HIGH, stir. MICROWAVE on HIGH 3 MINUTES, stir again. Let stand 5 to 10 minutes until set.

RICE VERDE

3 to 4 servings
1½-quart casserole

¼ cup butter or margarine
1 small onion, finely chopped
1 cup hot cooked rice
1 package (10-ounces) chopped spinach,
    defrosted
1 cup milk
1 egg, slightly beaten
½ teaspoon salt
1 cup grated sharp cheddar cheese

Combine butter and onion in 1½-quart casserole. MICROWAVE 2 to 3 MINUTES on HIGH, or until onion is transparent. Stir in rice, spinach, milk, beaten egg, salt and cheddar cheese, mixing well with fork. Cover. MICROWAVE 4 to 6 MINUTES on HIGH, or until mixture is hot and cheese is melted.

NOTE: If using cold leftover rice, microwave 1 to 2 minutes longer.

QUICK SHRIMP RICE

4 to 6 servings
1½-quart casserole

3 cups hot cooked rice
1 can (8-ounces) small cooked shrimp, drained
1 can (6-ounces) water chestnuts, drained
    and sliced
½ cup finely chopped onion
½ cup finely chopped celery
⅓ cup butter, cut in bits
¼ cup dry sherry
1 clove garlic, pressed or finely chopped
½ teaspoon salt

Combine all ingredients in a 1½-quart casserole. Mix well. Cover. MICROWAVE 4 MINUTES on HIGH, or until heated through, stirring after 2 minutes.

MINNESOTA WILD RICE CASSEROLE

4 to 6 servings
1-quart casserole

1 package (12-ounces) frozen white and wild rice
4 ounces fresh mushrooms, chopped
1 medium onion, chopped
2 tablespoons butter or margarine

Place pouch of rice in oven. MICROWAVE 5 MINUTES on HIGH, or until hot, flexing pouch after 3 minutes. Set aside.

Combine mushrooms, onions and butter in casserole with butter on top. MICROWAVE 2 MINUTES, 30 SECONDS to 3 MINUTES on HIGH, stirring after 1 minute.

Add rice to mushroom mixture. If necessary, MICROWAVE 30 SECONDS to warm.

SPANISH RICE

6 servings
1-quart casserole

1 package (7-ounces) instant rice
1¾ cups water
1 can (8-ounces) tomato sauce
¼ cup finely chopped green peppers
1 tablespoon onion flakes
2 tablespoons chili powder
2 tablespoons bacon drippings
¾ teaspoon salt

Combine all ingredients in 1-quart casserole. Cover. MICROWAVE 10 to 12 MINUTES on HIGH, or until water is absorbed. Fluff rice with fork.

YELLOW RICE STUFFING

8 to 10 servings
3-quart casserole

2 5-ounce packages yellow rice mix
½ cup butter or margarine
1 medium onion, chopped
1½ cups minced celery
½ cup celery leaves
1 pound mushrooms, chopped
¼ teaspoon rubbed sage
¼ teaspoon thyme
½ teaspoon marjoram
1 teaspoon salt
4-5 cups herb seasoned croutons (optional)

Cook rice in 3-quart casserole, adding water, salt, and butter as directed on package. Cover. MICROWAVE 7 MINUTES on HIGH, then 12 to 14 MINUTES on '5' stirring once. Let stand 5 minutes covered.

Add butter, onion, celery, celery leaves and mushrooms. Mix well. MICROWAVE 6 to 8 MINUTES on HIGH, or until hot. Add sage, thyme, marjoram, and salt, and mix well. Let stand 5 minutes.

Serve as a side dish or add 4 to 5 cups herb seasoned croutons and use to stuff an 8 to 12 pound bird.

LONG GRAIN RICE

4 to 6 servings
2-quart casserole

2½ cups water
1 teaspoon salt
1 teaspoon salad oil, butter or margarine
1 cup long grain rice.

Combine all ingredients in 2-quart casserole. Stir. Cover. MICROWAVE 5 MINUTES on HIGH.

Reduce setting. MICROWAVE 10 to 12 MINUTES on '5', or until rice is tender and water is absorbed.

QUICK CREAM OF WHEAT

1 serving
Cereal bowl

2 tablespoons cream of wheat
¾ cup water
Dash salt

Stir cream of wheat, water and salt together in cereal bowl. MICROWAVE 1 MINUTE, 30 SECONDS on HIGH, stirring once. Let stand 3 minutes.

GRITS ROYALE

4 servings
1½-quart casserole

⅔ cup grits
3 cups water
¾ teaspoon salt

Stir grits and water together in 1½-quart casserole. MICROWAVE 5 MINUTES to 5 MINUTES, 30 SECONDS on HIGH, or until desired doneness. Stir in salt. Serve with butter or margarine, or with milk and sugar as a hot cereal. Grits may be substituted for rice as a side dish.

For fried grits, make as above. Preheat micro-browner 3 to 4 MINUTES on HIGH, add butter or margarine and grits. MICROWAVE 30 SECONDS on HIGH. Turn if desired.

One serving of grits may be made in 1-quart casserole following method above. Use 3 tablespoons grits, 1 cup water, dash salt. MICROWAVE 3 MINUTES to 3 MINUTES, 30 SECONDS on HIGH.

FAMILY OATMEAL

4 to 6 servings
1½ to 2-quart casserole

1½ cups regular oatmeal
3 cups water
¾ teaspoon salt

Stir oatmeal, water and salt together in 1½-quart casserole. MICROWAVE 6 to 8 MINUTES on HIGH, or until creamy, stirring once. Let stand 3 to 5 minutes, covered. Serve with milk and granulated or brown sugar.

ONE MAN OATMEAL

1 serving
Cereal bowl

¼ cup quick-cooking oats
½ cup water
Dash salt

Stir oats, water and salt together in cereal bowl. MICROWAVE 1 MINUTE, 15 SECONDS on HIGH. Stir. Let stand 3 minutes, covered. Serve with milk and sugar.

PREPARATION INSTRUCTIONS FOR RICE

ITEM	COOKING DISH	HOT WATER	ADD RICE TO WATER PLUS:	HEAT ON HIGH	REDUCE SETTING TO '5'	SPECIAL INSTRUCTIONS
Brown Rice 1 cup	2-quart casserole	3 cups	1 tsp. salt	6 min. covered	11-13 min. covered	Let stand if necessary.
Long Grain 1 cup	2-quart casserole	2 cups	1 tsp. oil or butter	5 min. covered	10-12 min. covered	Let stand
Quick Cooking 1½ cups	1-quart casserole	1½ cups	1 tsp. salt	2-4 min. covered		Let stand 3-5 min. fluff with fork.
Wild Rice 1 cup	2-quart casserole	2½ cups	1 tsp. salt, 2 tsp. butter	6 min. covered	16-18 min. covered	Let stand if necessary.
Wild and White Rice Mix 6 oz. package	2-quart casserole	2 cups	1 tsp. salt, 1 tsp. butter	5 min. covered	12-14 min. covered	Let stand if necessary.

PREPARATION INSTRUCTIONS FOR PASTA

ITEM	COOKING DISH	HOT WATER	BRING WATER TO BOIL ON HIGH	Add Pasta, 1 teaspoon salt, 1 teaspoon oil.	REDUCE SETTING TO '5' AND HEAT	SPECIAL INSTRUCTIONS
Egg Noodles 8 oz. (4 cups)	3-quart casserole	1½-quart	5-7 minutes covered		6-8 minutes uncovered	Drain and rinse if desired
Lasagna 8 oz.	2-quart utility dish	1-quart	4-6 minutes covered		8-10 minutes uncovered	Drain and rinse if desired
Macaroni 7 oz. (2 cups)	3-quart casserole	1½-quart	5-7 minutes covered		8-10 minutes uncovered	Drain and rinse if desired
Spaghetti 7 oz.	2-quart utility dish	1-quart	4-6 minutes covered		6-8 minutes uncovered	Drain and rinse if desired

White Clam Sauce

Sauces & Toppings

Sauces are easy to make in the microwave oven. Add variety to meals with sauced meats, fish or vegetables. Make old-fashioned cooked salad dressing with modern ease. Create a quick dessert with sauce and fruit, cake or ice cream.

With microwave cooking, sauces heat more evenly, so they require less attention. An occasional stir with a wire whisk is all they need to prevent scorching and lumping.

Make sauces right in the cup you use to measure. For small quantities, halve the recipe and cook for the same amount of time on '5'. Small amounts do better on the lower setting.

SALSA DI VONGOLE (White Clam Sauce)

3 cups
1-quart measure

2 *tablespoons butter or margarine*
1 *clove garlic, pressed or finely chopped*
1 *tablespoon flour*
1 *egg, beaten*
1 *cup milk*
1 *can (6½-ounces) minced clams, drained*
¼ *cup snipped fresh parsley*
¾ *teaspoon thyme*
¾ *teaspoon basil*
¼ *teaspoon salt*
⅛ *teaspoon pepper*

Combine butter and garlic in 1-quart measure. MICROWAVE on HIGH until butter melts. Blend in flour to make a smooth paste. Stir in remaining ingredients. MICROWAVE 4 MINUTES on '8', or until slightly thickened. Stir half way through.

Serve with pasta or fish.

FLUFFY HOLLANDAISE

⅔ cup
1-quart mixing bowl

¼ *cup butter or margarine*
¼ *cup whipping cream*
2 *egg yolks, well beaten*
1 *tablespoon lemon juice*
½ *teaspoon dry mustard*
¼ *teaspoon salt*

Place butter in 1-quart bowl. MICROWAVE on HIGH until melted. Add remaining ingredients. Mix well. MICROWAVE 1 MINUTE to 1 MINUTE, 30 SECONDS on '5', or until thickened, stirring halfway through. Beat with wire whisk or rotary beater until light and fluffy.

Serve with eggs, fish or vegetables.

NOTE: Over-cooking will curdle sauce.

BECHAMEL SAUCE

1 cup
Glass custard cup
1-quart measure or bowl

2 tablespoons butter or margarine
1 tablespoon flour
½ cup light cream
½ cup chicken broth, or ½ teaspoon instant chicken bouillon dissolved in ½ cup water
2 teaspoons grated onion, or ½ teaspoon instant minced onion
½ teaspoon salt
Pepper
Pinch thyme

Place butter in custard cup. MICROWAVE on HIGH until butter is melted. Blend in flour to make a smooth paste. Set aside.

Combine cream, chicken broth and onion in 1-quart measure or bowl. MICROWAVE 2 MINUTES, 30 SECONDS on HIGH, or until mixture is about to boil.

Beat in butter-flour paste, using a wire whisk. MICROWAVE 2 MINUTES on '8', or until thickened, stirring after 1 minute. Stir in salt, pepper and thyme.

MORNAY SAUCE

Stir in ¼ to ½ cup grated Swiss cheese. Serve with eggs, fish, poultry, pasta or vegetables.

NEWBURG SAUCE

Follow directions for Bechamel Sauce, substitute fish stock for chicken broth. After cooking, add ¼ cup chopped cooked shrimp and a pinch of cayenne. Serve with eggs, fish, rice or toast.

GRAVY

2 cups
1-quart measure

½ cup all-purpose flour
1½ cups water
½ cup pan drippings
Salt and pepper

Combine flour and water in 1-quart measure. Beat with wire whisk until smooth. Beat in drippings. MICROWAVE 3 to 4 MINUTES on HIGH, or until mixture boils, stirring once. Season with salt and pepper.

WHITE SAUCE

1 cup
Glass custard cup
1-quart measure or bowl

2 tablespoons butter or margarine
2 tablespoons flour
½ teaspoon salt
1 cup milk

Place butter in custard cup. MICROWAVE on HIGH until butter is melted. Blend in flour and salt to make a smooth paste. Set aside.

Place milk in 1-quart measure or bowl. MICROWAVE 2 MINUTES, 30 SECONDS on HIGH, or until milk is about to boil.

Beat in butter-flour paste, using a wire whisk. MICROWAVE 2 MINUTES on '8', or until thickened, stir after 1 minute. Mix well before using.

NOTE: To double recipe, heat 2 cups milk 4 to 5 minutes on HIGH.

CHEDDAR CHEESE SAUCE

Add ½ cup grated sharp Cheddar cheese and pinch of cayenne to white sauce. Stir until melted.

CURRY SAUCE

Add 1 teaspoon or more curry powder to white sauce.

TERIYAKI SAUCE

2¼ cups
1-quart bowl or casserole

2 tablespoons cornstarch
¼ cup soy sauce
1 can (10½-ounces) beef broth, diluted with water to make 2 cups, or 2 teaspoons instant beef bouillon dissolved in 2 cups water
2 tablespoons dry white wine
2 teaspoons finely chopped fresh ginger, or ⅛ teaspoon ground ginger
1 clove garlic, pressed or finely chopped

Blend cornstarch with soy sauce in a 1-quart bowl to make a smooth paste. Add beef broth, wine, ginger and garlic. Mix well. MICROWAVE on HIGH 4 to 5 MINUTES, or until clear, stirring after 3 minutes. Serve with pork, poultry or as a rumaki dip.

Currant-Raisin Sauce

BARBECUE SAUCE

1½ cups
1-quart measure or bowl

1 cup catsup
¼ cup cider vinegar
1 tablespoon Worcestershire sauce
2 tablespoons finely chopped onion
2 tablespoons firmly packed brown sugar
1 tablespoon paprika
1 teaspoon sugar
1 teaspoon salt
  Pepper to taste

Combine all ingredients in a 1-quart measure or bowl. Mix well. MICROWAVE 5 MINUTES on HIGH, or until sauce is hot and thick enough to coat a spoon, stirring after 3 minutes.

FRUIT SALAD DRESSING

2 cups
1-quart bowl

¼ cup lemon juice
¼ cup pineapple juice
½ cup sugar
2 eggs, well beaten
1 cup whipping cream, whipped

Combine lemon and pineapple juices in 1-quart bowl. MICROWAVE 1 to 2 MINUTES on HIGH, or until hot.

Fold sugar into beaten eggs. Slowly add egg mixture to hot fruit juice, beating well after each addition. MICROWAVE 1 MINUTE on HIGH, or until thickened. Stir.

Chill at least 20 minutes in refrigerator. Before serving, fold in whipped cream.

CURRANT-RAISIN SAUCE

2 cups
1-quart measure or casserole

½ cup orange juice
½ cup water
⅓ cup currant jelly
⅓ cup raisins
½ teaspoon grated orange rind
1 tablespoon corn starch
1 tablespoon water
2 tablespoons firmly packed brown sugar
  Dash of allspice
  Dash of salt

Combine orange juice, water, jelly, raisins and orange rind in 1-quart measure or casserole. MICROWAVE 3 to 4 MINUTES on HIGH, or until boiling.

Blend corn starch with water in a small bowl to make a smooth paste. Add brown sugar, allspice and salt. Mix well. Stir into hot mixture. MICRO-WAVE 4 MINUTES on HIGH, or until thick and clear, stirring after 2 minutes. Serve with ham or duck.

OLD-FASHIONED COOKED SALAD DRESSING

3 cups
1½-quart bowl

1½ cups water
1 cup cider vinegar
½ cup sugar
3 tablespoons flour
1 teaspoon salt
1 teaspoon dry mustard
6 egg yolks, well beaten

Combine 1 cup water, vinegar and sugar in 1½-quart bowl. MICROWAVE 3 to 4 MINUTES on HIGH, or until sugar is dissolved.

Blend flour, salt and mustard with remaining ½ cup water in 1-cup measure. Stir into hot vinegar mixture. Mix well. MICROWAVE 4 MINUTES on HIGH, or until slightly thickened. Stir.

Pour ¼ cup hot sauce into beaten egg yolks. Mix well. Pour into remaining sauce and stir until well blended. MICROWAVE 5 MINUTES on HIGH, or until thickened, beating well after 3 minutes.

NOTE: Keeps well in refrigerator.

Peanut Butter Honey Sauce, Hot Fudge Sauce and Tipsy Fruit Sauce

HOT FUDGE SAUCE

1 cup
1-quart measure or bowl

2 *squares unsweetened chocolate*
¼ *cup butter or margarine*
¼ *cup evaporated milk*
½ *cup powdered sugar*
1 *teaspoon vanilla*

Place chocolate and butter in 1-quart measure or bowl. MICROWAVE 2 MINUTES on HIGH, or until chocolate and butter are melted. Stir.

Stir in milk. Add sugar and beat until smooth and creamy. Add vanilla.

NOTE: Can be reheated easily. Excellent over ice cream, cake or fruits.

PEANUT BUTTER AND HONEY TOPPING

Makes 1 cup
2-cup measure

½ *cup chunk style peanut butter*
2 *tablespoons honey*
½ *cup milk*

Combine peanut butter and honey in 2-cup measure. MICROWAVE 2 MINUTES on HIGH. Stir. MICROWAVE 30 SECONDS on HIGH. Slowly add milk, stirring constantly.

TIPSY FRUIT SAUCE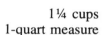

1¼ cups
1-quart measure

1 *package (10-ounces) frozen berries or peaches, defrosted*
2 *tablespoons liqueur or sweet wine*

Pour berries and their juice into 1-quart measure. MICROWAVE 1 MINUTE, 30 SECONDS on HIGH, or until berries are warm. Stir in liqueur.

Serve warm over ice cream, cake or sherbet.

LEMON DESSERT SAUCE

1½ cups
2-cup measure

1 *cup water*
½ *cup sugar*
1 *tablespoon corn starch*
2 *tablespoons butter or margarine*
1½ *teaspoons lemon juice*
½ *teaspoon lemon rind*
⅛ *teaspoon salt*

Measure water into 2-cup measure. Stir in sugar and corn starch until dissolved. MICROWAVE 4 MINUTES on HIGH, or until slightly thickened.

Add butter, lemon juice, rind and salt. Stir until butter is melted. Serve warm or cold over pudding or cake.

NOTE: Sauce will be the consistency of light cream.

Baking

With microwave's short cooking times you can have fresh hot muffins and coffeecakes whenever you want them, as a surprise for breakfast or an impromptu coffee break with a neighbor. Save time by proofing fresh or frozen yeast breads in the microwave oven. Warm rolls. Treat yourself to dressed-up French breads for a party touch at a family meal. Use the microwave oven set at '5' to dry bread crumbs and toast croutons. To make seasoned croutons, spread butter and seasonings on bread slices, cut in cubes and dry on a microwave roasting rack.

Clockwise from top left: Casserole Bread, Apple Cheddar Bread, Garlic Bread

BAKING BASICS

With microwave cooking, muffins, and coffeecakes will be ready in one-sixth to one-third the time needed conventionally. As they will not brown in this time, they need toppings, frostings or ingredients which supply color, such as spices, brown sugar or corn meal.

Baked goods rise more in the microwave oven, so fill muffin cups half full. Use an 8x8-inch baking dish for coffeecakes. If you want a round coffeecake, use the extra batter for muffins.

Use the microwave oven for proofing fresh or frozen yeast breads. If you wish to bake yeast breads in the microwave oven, use a recipe with corn meal, whole wheat or rye flour for color.

Breads and rolls should be heated only until warm to the touch. A few seconds is sufficient. Overheating makes bread tough or rubbery.

Heat breads on a paper napkin or towel to absorb excess moisture, or use the microwave roasting rack.

CASSEROLE BREAD

1 loaf
2½-quart casserole

  4 *cups all-purpose flour*
⅓ *cup sugar*
  1 *tablespoon baking powder*
  1 *teaspoon soda*
  1 *teaspoon salt*
½ *cup butter or margarine*
1½ *cups raisins*
½ *cup chopped nuts*
1⅓ *cups sour milk (add 1 teaspoon vinegar to regular milk)*
  1 *egg*
  1 *tablespoon water*
  1 *egg yolk*

Stir together flour, sugar, baking powder, soda and salt in large mixing bowl. Cut in butter with a pastry blender until mixture is well blended to a coarse grainy texture. Stir in raisins and nuts. Thoroughly mix in milk and egg.

Set into lightly greased 2½-quart casserole. With a sharp knife, cut an X in top. Mix water and egg yolk together. Brush surface of bread. MICROWAVE 14 to 16 MINUTES on '8', or until center is firm.

Turn out of pan on rack. Cool completely before serving.

WHOLE WHEAT BREAD

1 loaf
Medium mixing bowl
9 x 5-inch loaf dish

¾ *cup milk*
¼ *cup sugar*
  1 *teaspoon salt*
  2 *tablespoons shortening*
  1 *package active dry yeast*
¼ *cup warm water (105° to 115°)*
  1 *egg, slightly beaten*
1½ *cups all-purpose flour*
  2 *cups whole wheat flour*
    Soft butter or margarine

Measure milk into large mixing bowl. MICROWAVE 3 to 4 MINUTES on HIGH, or until bubbles form around edge. Stir in sugar, salt and shortening. Let stand until lukewarm.

Dissolve yeast in warm water. Stir yeast into lukewarm milk mixture. Add egg, all-purpose flour and ½ cup whole wheat flour. Beat until smooth. Mix in remaining flour. Turn dough out onto well-floured board. Knead until smooth and elastic (about 5 minutes). Place in greased bowl. Turn greased side up. Cover with plastic wrap. Let rise until double in bulk. (See note.)

Punch dough down. Knead lightly on floured board. Shape into loaf. Place in greased (9 x 5-inch) loaf dish. Brush with butter. Let rise until double. (See note.) MICROWAVE 6 to 8 MINUTES on '5'.

NOTE: To proof bread in microwave ovens with variable or solid state heat control, MICROWAVE 15 to 20 MINUTES on '1'.

PROOFING FROZEN BREAD

1 pound loaf
9x5-inch loaf dish

1 *loaf (1-pound) frozen white bread dough*

Place dough in greased (9 x 5-inch) loaf dish. Cover loosely with plastic wrap. MICROWAVE 55 to 60 MINUTES on '1' (low), or until double.

Heat conventional oven to 425°. Bake loaf 20 to 25 minutes, or until golden brown and loaf sounds hollow when tapped.

Remove from loaf dish. Brush with soft butter. Cool on wire rack.

NOTE: This recipe is not suitable for ovens without variable heat control.

GARLIC BREAD 🕐 🍞

24 ½-inch slices
Custard cup
Wax paper

1 loaf (1-pound) French or Vienna bread
⅓ cup butter or margarine
1 teaspoon Parmesan cheese
½ teaspoon garlic salt

Cut bread in ½-inch slices, leaving bottom crust intact. Set aside on piece of wax paper large enough to wrap bread.

Place butter in custard cup. MICROWAVE 30 SECONDS on High, or until butter melts. Stir in cheese and garlic salt. Pour between bread slices.

Bring sides of wax paper up over top of loaf. Twist ends to close loosely. MICROWAVE 45 SECONDS on HIGH, or until bread is warm. Cut slices free. Serve.

Variation:
ONION HERB BREAD

Substitute for cheese-garlic butter:

½ cup butter
2 teaspoons snipped parsley
½ teaspoon salt
¼ teaspoon onion salt
¼ teaspoon thyme
¼ teaspoon paprika

CORN BREAD

9 to 12 pieces
8 x 8-inch baking dish

1 cup corn meal
1 cup flour
¼ cup sugar
1 teaspoon baking powder
1 teaspoon salt
½ teaspoon soda
1 cup sour milk
1 egg, well beaten
2 tablespoons melted shortening

Blend all ingredients in mixing bowl. Beat thoroughly. Pour into (8 x 8-inch) baking dish. MICROWAVE 5 to 6 MINUTES on HIGH, or until wooden pick inserted in center comes out clean.

Variation:
Spoon batter into doubled paper baking cups or custard cups with paper liners. Fill cups ½ full. Bake according to muffin chart, page 209.

APPLE CHEDDAR BREAD

1 loaf
1½-quart casserole dish

2 cups self-rising flour, sifted
⅔ cup sugar
½ teaspoon cinnamon
½ cup coarsely broken walnuts or pecans
2 eggs, slightly beaten
½ cup butter or margarine, melted
1½ cups finely chopped, peeled apples
½ cup shredded sharp Cheddar cheese
¼ cup milk

Combine flour, sugar, cinnamon and nuts in a large bowl. Mix remaining ingredients and add to flour mixture. Stir just until blended, batter will be lumpy.

Spoon batter into 1½-quart casserole dish and MICROWAVE 10 to 12 MINUTES on '8', or until center is firm. Sprinkle with shredded sharp Cheddar cheese and let stand for 5 minutes. Remove onto serving plate.

Variation:
Substitute 1 teaspoon celery seed for cinnamon, omit nuts. Substitute ½ cup finely chopped onions for apples.

BUTTERMILK BRAN MUFFINS

20 to 24 pieces
Medium mixing bowl
Doubled paper baking cups

½ cup hot water
1½ cups all bran cereal
¼ cup butter or margarine
¾ cup sugar
¼ cup brown sugar
2 eggs
2 cups all-purpose flour
3 teaspoons baking powder
¼ teaspoon salt
1 cup buttermilk

Measure water into medium mixing bowl. MICROWAVE 2 MINUTES on HIGH, or until water boils. Stir in cereal. Add butter. Let stand until butter is softened. Beat in sugars and egg. Blend in flour, baking powder, salt and buttermilk until well mixed. Spoon into baking cups, filling them half full. See chart, page 209, for cooking times.

NOTE: This recipe can be doubled, stored in refrigerator for 1 month to 6 weeks and used as needed. Add 12 to 15 seconds additional time when using chilled batter.

Clockwise, starting from basket, Corn Muffins, Sticky Buns, Date Bread, Onion-Cheese Sticks. Recipes on following pages.

ONION-CHEESE STICKS

16 pieces
Microwave roasting rack in
12 x 8-inch utility dish or,
Paper towels

1 *cup quick biscuit mix*
⅓ *cup milk*
⅓ *cup grated American cheese*
1 *package (1¼-ounces) dry onion soup mix*

Measure biscuit mix into 1-quart bowl. Stir in milk to make soft dough. Mix in cheese. Turn out on lightly floured pastry cloth. Knead lightly several times.

Pinch off 1-inch balls of dough. Roll into sticks. Roll sticks in soup mix to coat. Arrange 6 to 8 at a time on microwave roasting rack in (12 x 8-inch) utility dish, or paper towels. MICROWAVE 3 to 4 MINUTES on '8', or until firm to touch.

STICKY BUNS

8 pieces
8-inch cake dish

1 *cup quick biscuit mix*
⅓ *cup milk*
2 *tablespoons butter or margarine, melted*
¼ *cup sugar*
1 *teaspoon cinnamon*
2 *tablespoons butter or margarine, softened*
2 *tablespoons firmly packed brown sugar*
¼ *cup walnut or pecan pieces*

Measure biscuit mix into 1-quart bowl. Stir in milk to make a soft dough. Turn out on lightly floured pastry cloth. Knead lightly several times. Roll out in 8-inch square. Brush with melted butter. Mix together sugar and cinnamon. Sprinkle on dough. Roll up. Cut in 1-inch pieces.

Combine softened butter and brown sugar in 8-inch cake dish. Spread to cover bottom. Scatter nuts over sugar mixture. Arrange rolls in dish. MICRO-WAVE 5 to 6 MINUTES on HIGH, or until wooden pick inserted in center comes out clean. Let stand 5 minutes. Invert onto serving plate.

DOWN HOME STREUSEL COFFEE CAKE

9 to 12 servings
8 x 8-inch baking dish

⅓ cup butter or margarine
¾ cup sugar
2 eggs
1 teaspoon almond or vanilla extract
1½ cups all-purpose flour
2½ teaspoons baking powder
½ teaspoon salt
½ cup milk
   Streusel, below

Place butter in large mixing bowl. If necessary, MICROWAVE 20 SECONDS on '5' to soften. Cream sugar with butter until fluffy. Beat in eggs and almond extract. Stir in flour, baking powder, salt and milk.

Pour all coffee cake mixture in pan. MICROWAVE 6 MINUTES on '8'. Then sprinkle on streusel topping and MICROWAVE 4 to 5 MINUTES on '8' or until wooden pick inserted in center comes out clean.

STREUSEL TOPPING

1 cup firmly packed brown sugar
¼ cup flour
¼ cup granulated sugar
½ teaspoon cinnamon
½ cup chopped nuts
2 tablespoons butter or margarine, melted

Blend all ingredients in small bowl.

Down Home Streusel Coffee Cake

EVERLASTING APPLE MUFFINS

40 to 50 muffins
Microwave muffin pan

1 cup butter or margarine
2 cups sugar
2 eggs
2 cup chopped nuts
3 teaspoons cinnamon
2 teaspoons baking soda
1 teaspoon allspice
½ teaspoon salt
4 cups flour
2 cups applesauce

Cream butter with electric mixer. Blend in sugar and eggs. Add nuts, cinnamon, soda, allspice and salt. Mix well. Add flour and applesauce, mix thoroughly.

Using greased muffin pan, or pan lined with paper baking cups, fill each cup ½ full. MICROWAVE 2 MINUTES on HIGH, rotating pan if necessary.

NOTE: The batter will keep for 6 weeks in refrigerator and can be used as needed, or all muffins may be baked and frozen.

DEPENDABLE DUMPLINGS

8 servings
1½ to 2-quart casserole

2½ cups stock or lightly salted water
1 cup flour
1½ teaspoons baking powder
½ teaspoon salt
3 tablespoons shortening
⅔ cup milk

Pour stock into 1½-quart casserole. MICROWAVE 6 to 8 MINUTES on HIGH, or until boiling.

Measure flour, baking powder and salt into mixing bowl. Cut in shortening until mixture looks like corn meal. Stir in milk until mixture is moistened but not smooth. Drop dough by rounded teaspoonfuls onto boiling stock. Do not cover. MICROWAVE 6 MINUTES on HIGH.

Cover. MICROWAVE 5 MINUTES on HIGH, or until dumplings are firm. Remove dumplings to serving dish with slotted spoon.

APRICOT BISCUIT RING

4 to 5 servings
8-inch round cake dish or
ceramic ring mold

¼ *cup firmly packed brown sugar*
½ *cup chopped dried apricots*
1 *tablespoon water*
3 *tablespoons butter*
⅓ *cup chopped walnuts*
10 *refrigerator biscuits*

Combine sugar, apricots, water and butter in cake dish. MICROWAVE 1 MINUTE on HIGH or until butter melts. Stir in nuts.

Cut each biscuit into quarters. Stir biscuits and apricot mixture together in cake pan until biscuit pieces are coated. MICROWAVE 3 to 4 MINUTES on HIGH, rotating once or twice as needed, until biscuits are firm to touch. Remove from oven. Let stand 2 minutes in pan, turn out on plate.

VARIATIONS:
Instead of apricots and walnuts substitute one of the following:

1 *small can (8-ounces) crushed pineapple, thoroughly drained, and ⅓ cup chopped peanuts*
⅓ *cup candied cherries and ⅓ cup chopped pecans*
⅓ *cup raisins, ½ teaspoon cinnamon and ⅓ cup walnuts*
⅓ *cup mixed candied fruit, finely chopped and ⅓ cup slivered almonds*

DRESSED UP GINGERBREAD

9 servings
8 x 8-inch baking dish

1 *package gingerbread mix*
Sweetened whipped cream or ice cream
¼ *cup crushed peppermint candy*

Prepare gingerbread as directed on package. Pour into (8 x 8-inch) baking dish. MICROWAVE 5 to 7 MINUTES on '8', or until top is slightly firm to touch.

Cool slightly. Serve warm topped with whipped cream or ice cream. Sprinkle with crushed candy.

PREPARATION INSTRUCTIONS FOR MUFFINS

NUMBER OF MUFFINS	SETTING	TIME
1	High	35 - 40 sec.
2	High	45 - 60 sec.
4	High	45 sec. - 1½ min.
6	High	1½ - 2 min.

Prepare mix according to package directions. Microwave in paper muffin cups (double thickness).

DATE NUT BREAD

1 loaf
9 x 5-inch loaf dish

1 *package (17-ounces) Date Nut Bread mix*

Prepare bread as directed on package. Grease loaf dish and line bottom with waxed paper. Pour batter into loaf dish. MICROWAVE 8 to 9 MINUTES on '8', or until top is slightly moist and wooden pick inserted in center comes out clean, rotating dish once. Let stand 10 minutes. Remove from loaf dish.

NOTE: Top will be slightly irregular.

STREUSEL COFFEE CAKE

9 servings
8 x 8-inch baking dish

1 *package (14½-ounces) streusel coffee cake mix*

Prepare coffee cake as directed on package. Pour all the batter into (8 x 8-inch) baking dish. Sprinkle all streusel topping on top. MICROWAVE 7 to 9 MINUTES on '6', or until wooden pick inserted in center comes out clean, rotating dish once. Let stand 5 minutes.

Desserts

Glamorous party desserts, traditional family favorites, spur-of-the-moment treats, all become quick and easy with your microwave oven. Desserts make even a simple meal something special.

Use the microwave oven to soften toppings, warm sauces or toast nuts to dress up cakes or ice cream. Warm pie or cake a few seconds by mirowave for fresh from the oven flavor.

Be creative. Using these recipes as inspiration, invent some new desserts of your own with package mixes, toppings, fresh or canned fruits, or new combinations with canned pudding and pie filling.

CHOCOLATE SOUFFLE

10 servings
2-quart souffle dish

2 *squares semi-sweet chocolate*
3 *tablespoons butter*
¼ *cup flour*
½ *cup sugar*
1¼ *cups milk*
⅛ *teaspoon vanilla or 1 tablespoon rum*
6 *eggs, separated*
1 *teaspoon cream tartar*

In a 1½-quart bowl MICROWAVE the butter and chocolate on '8' until melted. Stir in flour, sugar, and milk. MICROWAVE on HIGH for 3 MINUTES or until thick, stirring once. Stir to blend and cool slightly. Add vanilla or rum.

Separate eggs. Beat egg yolks into the thickened sauce. Beat egg whites with cream tartar until stiff but not dry.

Gently fold sauce into egg whites. Pour into 6 to 8-cup souffle dish. Add a 2'' collar of freezer wrap, dull side in, or brown paper. (Don't use waxed paper or parchment or the souffle won't climb. Also, use a double thickness for a more stable collar.) PROGRAM TO MICROWAVE on '6' for 2 MINUTES, then '3' for 15 MINUTES, then '2' for 3 MINUTES. Rotate once if necessary. Serve with chocolate sauce.

NOTE: The top will look creamy, not dry.

CHOCOLATE SAUCE

2 *squares semi-sweet chocolate*
1 *tablespoon cream*
¼ *cup Kahlua*

In a 2-cup measure MICROWAVE the chocolate on '8' until melted. Stir in cream until smooth. Stir in Kahlua. Pour over souffle.

DESSERT BASICS

Cakes cook in the microwave oven in one-sixth to one-third the time needed conventionally. If the cake is to be turned out for layering and frosting, line the bottom of the baking dish with waxed paper for easy removal.

To line a round cake dish, tear off an 8 or 9-inch length of waxed paper. Fold and cut as shown.

A waxed paper lining is not necessary if the cake is to be served from the dish.

A few moist spots may appear on the surface of the cake, but the cake is done if the top springs back when lightly touched, or when a wooden pick inserted in the center comes out clean.

When baking conventionally, use your microwave oven to scald milk, soften butter, melt chocolate and prepare cooked frostings and fillings.

Pastry shells cooked by microwave are especially tender and flaky, but they do not brown.

Since they cook from all sides, smooth puddings, fillings and custards can be made quickly with only occasional, rather than frequent or constant stirring.

Baked fresh fruits and compotes keep their fresh flavor and texture when cooked.

PEACH SPICE PUDDING CAKE

12 servings
12 x 8-inch baking dish

1 *package lemon pudding*
1 *can (16-ounces) sliced peaches, drained*
1 *package (9-ounces) spice cake mix (one-layer size)*

Prepare pudding according to directions on page 221.

Pour pudding in (12 x 8-inch) baking dish. Arrange peach slices over pudding.

Prepare cake mix according to package directions. Pour over peaches and pudding. MICROWAVE 10 MINUTES on HIGH, or until a wooden pick inserted in cake center comes out clean, rotating dish ½ turn after 5 minutes.

Serve warm or cool, with whipped cream, if desired.

HARVEY WALLBANGER CAKE

12 servings
Ceramic bundt pan

1 *package (2 layer size) orange cake mix*
1 *package (3¾-oz.) instant vanilla pudding mix*
¾ *cup orange juice*
½ *cup oil*
4 *eggs*
¼ *cup vodka*
¼ *cup Galliano*

Evenly oil a ceramic bundt pan.

In a large mixing bowl, combine all ingredients and beat for 4 minutes on medium speed with electric mixer.

Remove 1½ cups of batter, reserve for cupcakes. Pour remaining cake batter into prepared pan. PROGRAM TO MICROWAVE on '6' for 2 MINUTES, '4' for 25 to 30 MINUTES, or until wooden pick inserted in center comes out clean. Rotate once during cooking time, if necessary. Batter will run over sides of pan slightly.

Let stand in pan for 10 minutes. Turn out on plate and glaze while warm.

GLAZE:

1 *cup confectioners' sugar*
1 *tablespoon orange juice*
1 *tablespoon vodka*
1 *tablespoon Galliano*
1 *tablespoon white corn syrup*

Combine ingredients in bowl. Stir until smooth.

Harvey Wallbanger Cake

FRESH APPLE CAKE

2 8-inch layers
2 8-inch round cake dishes
lined with waxed paper

½ *cup butter*
2 *cups sugar*
2 *eggs*
1 *teaspoon vanilla*
3 *medium cooking apples, grated (core, do not peel)*
1 *cup chopped nuts*
2½ *cups all-purpose flour*
2 *teaspoons baking soda*
1 *teaspoon cinnamon*
½ *teaspoon salt*

In a large mixing bowl, cream butter and sugar with an electric mixer. Add eggs and vanilla, beat well. Stir in nuts and apples. Add dry ingredients. Mix well. Pour batter into two 8'' round glass pans lined with wax paper.

PROGRAM TO MICROWAVE each layer on HIGH for 4 MINUTES, then on '6' for 4 to 5 MINUTES, or until a wooden pick inserted in the center comes out clean.

Allow cake to cool in pans on rack for 10 minutes.

TO FROST CAKE:

1 *8-ounce package cream cheese, softened*
1 *cup confectioners' sugar*
1 *teaspoon lemon juice*
1 *apple, cored and sliced (do not peel)*
1 *tablespoon sugar*
1 *teaspoon cinnamon*

Combine cream cheese, powdered sugar and lemon juice. Cream until smooth.

With ¼ of the frosting, frost the top surface of the bottom layer, make a thin layer of apples and frost with another ¼ of the frosting. Place other layer of cake on top. Using the remaining frosting, frost the top of the cake. Mix the sugar and cinnamon together. Coat apple slices in the sugar and cinnamon mixture. Garnish surface with coated apple slices.

NOTE: For easier spreading, use a wet knife when frosting the cake.

CHOCOLATE FUDGE CAKE

2 8-inch layers
1-cup measure
8-inch round cake dish
lined with waxed paper

3 *squares unsweetened chocolate*
⅔ *cup butter or margarine, softened*
2 *cups sugar*
4 *eggs*
1 *teaspoon vanilla*
2½ *cups cake flour*
1¼ *teaspoons soda*
½ *teaspoon salt*
1⅓ *cups ice water*

Place chocolate in 1-cup measure. MICROWAVE on HIGH, or until melted. Set aside to cool.

Cream together butter, sugar, eggs and vanilla in large mixing bowl, beat until light and fluffy. Blend in chocolate.

Mix in flour, soda and salt alternately with ice water, beating after each addition until mixture is smooth.

Pour half the batter into 8-inch cake dish. MICROWAVE 6 MINUTES, 30 SECONDS to 7 MINUTES on HIGH, or until a wooden pick inserted in center comes out clean. Let stand 5 minutes. Turn out on cake rack. Cool. Prepare and bake second layer. Cool.

CHOCOLATE ICING

Frosts 2 8-inch layers or
1 dozen cupcakes
2-quart batter bowl

¼ *cup cocoa*
⅔ *cup milk*
2 *cups sugar*
⅓ *cup butter or margarine*
1 *teaspoon almond or vanilla extract*

Blend cocoa and milk in 2-quart bowl to make a smooth paste. Mix in sugar and butter. MICROWAVE 8 MINUTES on HIGH, stirring after every 2 minutes. Cool thoroughly.

Add almond extract. Beat vigorously until frosting reaches spreading consistency.

213

First Prize Cake

IRELAND'S FUDGE PIE

6 servings
9-inch pie plate

1 *cup sugar*
3 *tablespoons cocoa*
½ *cup flour*
1 *stick butter*
1 *teaspoon vanilla*
2 *eggs*

Mix all ingredients together and pour into pie pan sprayed with non-stick spray. Place pie pan on inverted saucer. MICROWAVE 8 to 12 MINUTES on '6'. Serve in slices. Serve hot, topped with ice cream.

TRIPLE FUDGE BUNDT CAKE WITH GLAZE

9-inch cake
9-inch pottery bundt cake dish

1 *package (23½-ounces) Triple Fudge Bundt Cake mix*

Prepare cake according to package directions. Reserve ¼ cup batter to make 2 cup cakes. Pour remaining batter into bundt cake dish. MICROWAVE 25 to 30 MINUTES on '4', or until wooden pick inserted in center comes out clean, rotating dish twice during cooking period. Let stand 8 to 10 minutes before turning out on cake rack.

Prepare glaze according to directions on package. Drizzle over cooled cake.

FIRST PRIZE CAKE

8 servings
3 8-inch cake dishes

1 *box pineapple cake mix*
4 *eggs*
½ *cup cooking oil*
1 *can mandarin oranges (with juice)*

Frosting:

1 *small can crushed pineapple*
1 *box pineapple instant pudding*
1 *small container whipped cream*

Mix together cake mix, eggs, oil and oranges (with juice) and beat for 4 minutes. Pour into three glass cake pans (lined with waxed paper). Microwave 7 MINUTES on '8'. While cake is cooking, pour the dry instant pudding over the pineapple. Let stand until cake is cooled. Blend whipped cream into pudding.

YELLOW CAKE MIX

13 x 9-inch baking dish

1 *package (18½-ounces) yellow cake mix*

Prepare cake according to directions on package. Pour cake mix into (13 x 9-inch) baking dish. MICRO-WAVE 16 to 20 MINUTES on '8'.

FRUIT COCKTAIL TORTE

6 to 8 servings
8 x 8-inch baking dish

¾ *cup sugar*
1 *egg*
1 *can (16-ounces) fruit cocktail, drained*
1 *cup flour*
1 *teaspoon soda*
¼ *teaspoon salt*
½ *cup firmly packed brown sugar*
½ *cup chopped nuts*

Combine sugar and egg in medium bowl. Beat well. Stir in fruit, flour, soda and salt until mixed. Spread in (8 x 8-inch) baking dish. Combine brown sugar and nuts. Sprinkle over torte. MICROWAVE 8 to 10 MINUTES on HIGH, or until top springs back when lightly touched, rotating dish ½ turn after 5 minutes.

CAKES AND CUPCAKES FROM A MIX 🔲

Microwave cakes usually rise higher than those cooked conventionally, so it is important not to fill containers over half full. Use any extra batter for cupcakes. Often cakes will have a slightly uneven top. This will vary with the type of cake and the brand of cake mix used. Most types of mixes bake well on high, but generally chocolate cakes do better at a lower setting. Below you will find some sample recipes using cake mixes, as well as a chart to guide you to times and settings.

PREPARATION INSTRUCTIONS FOR CAKE MIXES

SIZE OF CAKE	CHOCOLATE		OTHER FLAVORS	
	Setting	Time	Setting	Time
8" round	6	8-10 min.	High	5-6 min.
8 x 8" square	6	8-10 min.	High	5½-6½ min.
1 cupcake	6	45 sec. 60 sec.	High	25-35 sec.
2 cupcakes	6	1-1¼ min.	High	35-45 sec.
4 cupcakes	6	1½-2 min.	High	1-1½ min.
6 cupcakes	6	2½-3 min.	High	1½-2½ min.

CAKE MIX CUPCAKES

Doubled paper baking cups
or paper-lined custard cups

1 *package cake mix*

Prepare batter according to directions on package. Fill baking cups ½ full.

Arrange cupcakes in center of oven with 1-inch spaces between. Follow cooking time on chart. Cupcakes are done when wooden pick inserted in center comes out clean.

NOTE: Some cupcakes may be done sooner than others.

RASPBERRY SWIRL BUNDT CAKE

9-inch cake
9-inch pottery bundt cake dish

1 *package (23½-ounces) Raspberry Swirl Bundt Cake mix*

Prepare cake according to package directions. Pour batter into bundt cake dish. MICROWAVE 16 to 18 MINUTES on '6', or until wooden pick inserted in center comes out clean, rotating dish once during cooking period. Let stand 8 to 10 minutes before turning out on cake rack.

Prepare glaze according to directions on package. Drizzle over cooled cake.

NOTE: Follow directions above when preparing Pound and Lemon-Blueberry Bundt cakes.

PINEAPPLE UPSIDE DOWN CAKE

9 servings
8 x 8-inch baking dish

¼ *cup butter or margarine*
½ *cup firmly packed brown sugar*
1 *can (8½-ounces) sliced pineapple, drained and juice reserved*
 Maraschino cherries
1 *package (9-ounce) yellow cake mix (1-layer size)*
½ *cup (reserved) pineapple juice*
2 *eggs*

Combine butter and brown sugar in (8 x 8-inch) baking dish. MICROWAVE 1 MINUTE, 30 SECONDS to 2 MINUTES on HIGH, or until butter and sugar melt. Stir.

Arrange pineapple rings in syrup. Place maraschino cherry in center of each pineapple ring.

Blend cake mix, pineapple juice and eggs in medium mixing bowl on low speed of electric mixer. Beat on medium speed two minutes. Pour evenly over fruit. MICROWAVE 8½ to 10 MINUTES on HIGH, or until wooden pick inserted in center comes out clean, rotating dish ½ turn after 5 minutes. Immediately invert onto serving plate and remove dish.

Serve warm or cooled to room temperature, with whipped cream, if desired.

Mocha Torte

MOCHA TORTE

8 to 10 servings
3(8-inch) round cake dishes,
lined with waxed paper

1 *package (18-ounces) chocolate cake mix*
2 *tablespoons cinnamon*
½ *teaspoon cloves*
Mocha Filling, below

Blend dry cake mix, cinnamon and cloves in large mixing bowl. Prepare cake according to package directions. Divide batter among 3(8-inch) round cake dishes. One at a time. MICROWAVE 4 MINUTES, 30 SECONDS to 5 MINUTES on '6', or until wooden pick inserted in center comes out clean.

Let stand 5 minutes. Immediately turn out on cake rack. Cool.

Mocha Filling

Fill and frost 3 (8-inch) round cake layers
1-quart bowl

1 *package (3¾-ounces) instant vanilla pudding mix*
2 *tablespoons instant coffee*
2 *cups prepared whipped topping mix*

Blend dry pudding mix and coffee in 1-quart bowl. Prepare pudding according to package directions. Let stand 20 minutes to set.

Gently fold pudding into topping.

Fill layers and frost top of Mocha Torte, using ⅓ of filling for each layer. Garnish with shaved semisweet or unsweetened chocolate. Refrigerate until ready to serve.

APPLESAUCE-SPICE CAKE

2-layer cake
8-inch cake dish, lined with waxed paper

½ *cup shortening*
2 *cups sugar*
2 *eggs*
2½ *cups all-purpose flour*
1½ *teaspoons soda*
1½ *teaspoons salt*
¼ *teaspoon baking powder*
¾ *teaspoon cinnamon*
½ *teaspoon cloves*
¼ *teaspoon nutmeg*
1 *cup raisins*
½ *cup chopped walnuts*
1½ *cups applesauce*
½ *cup water*

Cream shortening and sugar together. Beat in eggs. Add flour, soda, salt, baking powder, cinnamon, cloves, nutmeg, raisins, and nuts. Stir in applesauce and water. Place half of the batter into 8-inch cake dish lined with waxed paper. MICROWAVE 6 MINUTES, 30 SECONDS to 7 MINUTES on HIGH, or until cake springs back when touched lightly. Let stand 5 minutes before turning out onto cake rack.

Repeat with second layer.

BUTTERSCOTCH FROSTING

Frosts 8 or 9-inch layer cake
2-quart casserole

1½ *cups firmly packed brown sugar*
½ *cup granulated sugar*
½ *cup cream*
1 *teaspoon vanilla*
2 *tablespoons butter or margarine*

Blend sugars and cream in 2-quart casserole. MICROWAVE 5 to 6 MINUTES on HIGH, or until sugar is dissolved and mixture is no longer grainy, stirring after 3 and 4 minutes.

Immediately add butter and vanilla. Stir until butter melts. Cool thoroughly. Beat to spreading consistency. Thin with a little cream if necessary.

PASTRY FOR ONE-CRUST PIE

9-inch pie crust
9-inch pie plate

1 *cup all-purpose flour*
½ *teaspoon salt*
⅓ *cup plus* 1 *tablespoon shortening*
3 *to* 4 *tablespoons cold water*
  Yellow food coloring

Measure flour and salt into mixing bowl. Cut in shortening thoroughly. Add a few drops of yellow food coloring to water. Sprinkle water over mixture, one tablespoon at a time, stirring lightly with fork.

Roll out pastry to fit 9-inch pie plate. Trim and flute edge. Prick sides and bottom with fork. MICRO-WAVE 4 to 5 MINUTES on '8', or until crust appears flaky. Cool.

PASTRY SHELL FROM MIX

1 *pie crust stick or mix*

Using pie crust stick or mix, prepare recommended amount for one 9-inch single pastry shell as directed on package. Follow above directions.

GRAHAM CRACKER CRUST

9-inch crust
1-quart bowl
9-inch pie plate

⅓ *cup butter or margarine*
1½ *cups graham cracker crumbs*
⅓ *cup firmly packed brown sugar*

Place butter in 1-quart bowl. MICROWAVE on HIGH until butter is melted. Add graham cracker crumbs and sugar. Mix thoroughly. Press mixture firmly and evenly against bottom and sides of (9-inch) pie plate. MICROWAVE 1 MINUTE, 30 SECONDS to 2 MINUTES, 30 SECONDS on HIGH, or until hot. Cool.

Variations:

VANILLA WAFER CRUST

Substitute 1½ cups vanilla wafer crumbs for graham cracker crumbs.

CHOCOLATE WAFER CRUMB CRUST

Substitute 1½ cups chocolate wafer crumbs for graham cracker crumbs.

COCONUT CRUST

2 *tablespoons butter or margarine, softened*
1½ *cups flaked coconut*

Spread softened butter evenly on bottom and sides of (9-inch) pie plate. Sprinkle coconut over butter. Press firmly to form even crust. MICROWAVE 1 MINUTE to 1 MINUTE, 30 SECONDS on HIGH.

Pie Crusts: Back Row: Graham Cracker Crust, Chocolate Wafer Crust, Vanilla Wafer Crust
Front Row: Plain Pastry Crust, Crust with food coloring added

Strawberry Pie

STRAWBERRY PIE

9-inch pie
1-quart bowl
9-inch pie plate

9-*inch baked pastry shell*
1½ *quarts fresh strawberries*
3 *tablespoons cornstarch*
¾ *to 1 cup sugar*
1 *cup water*
1 *teaspoon butter or margarine*

Clean and hull berries. Measure ⅔ cup of berries and mash in 1-quart measure. Add water and ¾ to 1 cup sugar, depending on sweetness of berries. MICRO-WAVE 5 to 6 MINUTES on HIGH, or until mixture is boiling.

Soften cornstarch in small amount of water and add to mixture. MICROWAVE 2 to 3 MINUTES on HIGH, or until mixture thickens, stirring once. Stir in butter. Cool.

Fill baked pie shell with remaining strawberries. Pour cooled glaze over top. Garnish with whipped cream.

Variation:

Soften 1 package (8-ounces) cream cheese. Spread evenly in bottom of pie shell before adding straw-berries.

VANILLA CREAM PIE

9-inch pie
2-quart bowl or casserole

9-*inch baked pastry shell*
¾ *cup sugar*
3 *tablespoons cornstarch*
    Pinch salt
2 *cups milk or light cream*
3 *egg yolks, slightly beaten*
2 *tablespoons butter or margarine*
1 *teaspoon vanilla*
3 *egg whites*
¼ *teaspoon cream of tartar*
6 *tablespoons sugar*

Combine sugar, cornstarch and salt in 2-quart bowl. Gradually stir in milk. MICROWAVE 8 MINUTES on '8', or until thickened, stirring twice with wire whisk.

Stir a little of the hot mixture into egg yolks. Blend warmed yolks into hot mixture. MICROWAVE 2 MINUTES on '8', or until custard coats a metal spoon, stirring once.

Stir in butter and vanilla until butter melts. Cool. Pour into baked pie shell.

Beat egg whites with cream of tartar until foamy. Gradually beat in sugar. Continue beating until stiff peaks form. Gently spread meringue over cream filling, sealing meringue to edges of crust. Brown under conventional broiler.

NOTE: Sweetened whipped cream may be substituted for meringue.

Variations:
BANANA CREAM PIE
Slice 2 ripe bananas into bottom of baked pie shell, or graham cracker crust. Pour Vanilla Cream filling over bananas. Top with meringue.

CHOCOLATE CREAM PIE
Follow above recipe, but increase sugar to 1 cup. Melt 2 squares (1-ounce each) unsweetened choco-late. Add with vanilla.

COCONUT CREAM PIE
Stir in 1 cup flaked coconut with butter. Sprinkle ⅓ cup coconut over meringue before browning.

BUTTERSCOTCH PIE
Substitute ¾ cup firmly packed brown sugar for granulated sugar. Increase butter to ⅓ cup.

PUMPKIN PIE

9-inch pie
9-inch pie plate

1 *baked pastry shell, (page 217)*
2 *whole eggs*
1 *can (15-ounces) pumpkin*
½ *cup firmly packed brown sugar*
1 *teaspoon cinnamon*
½ *teaspoon nutmeg*
¼ *teaspoon ginger*
¼ *teaspoon cloves*
½ *cup evaporated milk*

Break eggs into 1½-quart bowl. Beat lightly. Add pumpkin and mix thoroughly. Add remaining ingredients, one at a time, beating well after each addition.

Pour mixture into baked pastry shell. MICROWAVE 18 MINUTES on '6', or until almost set. Let stand 30 minutes. Garnish with swirl of whipped cream, if desired.

NOTE: Standing time is important, as center of pie will continue to cook until firm.

LEMON MERINGUE PIE

9-inch pie
9-inch pie plate
1-quart measure

9-*inch baked pastry shell or graham cracker crust*
1½ *cups sugar*
⅓ *cup corn starch*
1½ *cups boiling water*
3 *egg yolks, slightly beaten*
3 *tablespoons butter or margarine*
1 *tablespoon grated lemon rind*
3 *tablespoons lemon juice*
3 *egg whites*
¼ *teaspoon cream of tartar*
6 *tablespoons sugar*

Combine sugar, corn starch and boiling water in 1-quart measure. MICROWAVE 3 to 4 MINUTES on HIGH, or until thick and clear, stirring once with wire whip.

Stir a little of the hot mixture into egg yolks. Add warmed yolks to hot filling. MICROWAVE 1 MINUTE on HIGH. Add butter, lemon rind and lemon juice. Cool. Pour into baked pie shell.

Beat egg whites with cream of tartar until foamy. Gradually beat in sugar. Continue beating until stiff peaks form. Gently spread meringue over lemon filling, sealing meringue to edges of crust. Brown under conventional broiler.

PUMPKIN CHIFFON PIE

9-inch pie plate

Crust:
1½ *cups crushed graham cracker crumbs*
⅓ *cup firmly packed brown sugar*
⅓ *cup butter or margarine, melted*
¾ *teaspoon cinnamon*

Filling:
½ *cup sugar*
1 *envelope unflavored gelatin*
¾ *teaspoon cinnamon*
½ *teaspoon ginger*
½ *teaspoon nutmeg*
½ *teaspoon salt*
3 *eggs, separated*
½ *cup milk*
1¼ *cup canned pumpkin*
¼ *cup sugar*
Whipped topping (optional)

In 9-inch pie plate, mix graham cracker crumbs, brown sugar and cinnamon until well blended. Add melted butter and mix well. Press into crust. MICROWAVE 1 MINUTE, 30 SECONDS to 2 MINUTES on HIGH, set aside.

In 1-quart mixing bowl, combine sugar, gelatin, spices and salt. Mix well. In small dish, combine milk and egg yolks, mix well. With wire whisk, gradually stir into gelatin mixture. Add pumpkin and mix well. MICROWAVE 8 to 10 MINUTES on '8', or until thickened. Stir 2 to 3 times during cooking. Refrigerate until cool but not set.

In large mixing bowl, beat egg whites with remaining sugar until soft peaks form. Gently fold chilled pumpkin mixture into egg whites. Pour into cooled crust. Refrigerate until set. Garnish with whipped topping, if desired.

PECAN PIE

9-inch pie
9-inch pie plate

9-*inch baked pastry shell*
3 *eggs, slightly beaten*
⅔ *cup sugar*
½ *teaspoon salt*
⅓ *cup butter or margarine, melted*
1 *cup light corn syrup*
1 *cup pecan halves*

Beat eggs, sugar, salt, butter and corn syrup in medium bowl using a rotary beater. Stir in pecan halves. Pour into 9-inch baked pastry shell. MICROWAVE 15 MINUTES on '6', or until filling is set, rotating dish ½ turn after 3 minutes. Let cool, covered with foil, for 15 minutes. Garnish with whipped cream, if desired.

EGG NOG PIE

9-inch pie
Medium mixing bowl

1½ cups milk
1 tablespoon gelatin
2 tablespoons cold water
4 egg yolks
½ cup sugar
2 teaspoons cornstarch
⅛ teaspoon salt
1 tablespoon butter or margarine
¾ teaspoon vanilla
½ teaspoon nutmeg
3 egg whites
Nutmeg
1 9-inch baked pie shell
Whipped cream

Soak gelatin in water. In medium mixing bowl scald milk. MICROWAVE 2 to 3 MINUTES on HIGH, or until hot. In small mixing bowl, mix together egg yolks, sugar, cornstarch and salt, and add to milk. MICROWAVE 3 to 4 MINUTES on '6', or until thickened. Stir in butter, vanilla, nutmeg and gelatin. Chill in refrigerator until cool. Beat egg whites until fluffy. Blend into egg yolk and milk mixture, fill pie shell and chill until set.

Sprinkle with nutmeg and top each slice with whipped cream if so desired.

TAPIOCA FLUFF

5 servings
1½-quart casserole

1 egg, separated
3 tablespoons sugar
⅛ teaspoon salt
2 cups milk
3 tablespoons minute tapioca
2 tablespoons sugar
¾ teaspoon vanilla

Combine egg yolk, 3 tablespoons sugar, salt, milk and tapioca in 1½-quart casserole. Let stand 3 minutes to soften tapioca.

Beat egg white until foamy in 2-quart bowl. Gradually beat in sugar. Continue beating until egg white holds soft peaks. Set aside.

Place tapioca mixture in oven. MICROWAVE 8 to 10 MINUTES on '8', or until mixture has thickened, stirring twice.

Fold tapioca mixture into meringue carefully but thoroughly. Stir in vanilla. Cool slightly and chill.

BAKED CUSTARD

6 servings
1½-quart casserole
1-quart measure
8 x 8-inch baking dish

3 eggs
4 tablespoons sugar
¼ teaspoon salt
½ teaspoon vanilla
1⅔ cups milk
Nutmeg

Beat eggs lightly in 1½-quart casserole. Mix in sugar, salt and vanilla, stirring well.

Measure milk into 1-quart measure. MICROWAVE 3 to 4 MINUTES on HIGH, or until about to boil. Stir gradually into egg mixture. Sprinkle with nutmeg.

Place casserole in (8 x 8-inch) baking dish. Pour 1 cup very hot water into baking dish. MICROWAVE 9 MINUTES on '6', or until custard is almost set. Custard will become firm as it cools. Serve chilled.

CHOCOLATE PUDDING

6 servings
Custard cup
1½-quart casserole

1 tablespoon butter or margarine
2 squares unsweetened chocolate
½ cup sugar
3 tablespoons corn starch
¼ teaspoon salt
1¾ cups milk
1 egg yolk, slightly beaten
1 egg white
1 teaspoon vanilla or almond extract

Combine butter and chocolate in custard cup. MICROWAVE 45 SECONDS to 1 MINUTE on HIGH, or until melted. Set aside.

Mix sugar, corn starch and salt together in 1½-quart casserole. Gradually stir in milk. Blend in melted chocolate mixture. MICROWAVE 6 to 7 MINUTES on '8', or until thickened, stirring once with wire whip.

Stir a little of the hot mixture into egg yolk. Blend warmed yolk into hot mixture. MICROWAVE 1 MINUTE, 30 SECONDS on '8', or until custard coats a metal spoon.

Beat egg white in small bowl until stiff peaks form. Gently fold into custard. Fold in vanilla. Cool.

FANTASTIC CHOCOLATE FONDUE

2 cups
1-quart bowl or ceramic fondue pot

¾ cup whipping cream
1 package (11½-ounces) milk-chocolate chips
3 tablespoons kirsch or brandy
¼ to ½ teaspoon cinnamon
1½ cups fresh strawberries
2 medium bananas, cut into ½-inch slices
1½ cups fresh pineapple cubes
6 slices pound cake, ¾-inch thick, cut in 1-inch squares

Pour cream in bowl or fondue pot. Add 1½ cups chocolate chips. MICROWAVE 1 MINUTE on HIGH, or until chocolate melts. Stir to blend chocolate and cream.

Add remaining chocolate chips. MICROWAVE 30 SECONDS on HIGH. Stir in liqueur and cinnamon. Keep mixture warm in fondue pot or chafing dish, or reheat as needed.

Serve with fruits and cake on bamboo skewers or fondue forks.

PUDDING OR CUSTARD MIX

4 servings
1-quart measure

2 cups milk
1 package (3¾-ounces) pudding or custard mix

Measure milk into 1-quart measure. Add mix, stirring until dissolved. MICROWAVE 4 MINUTES on HIGH, or until pudding starts to boil, stirring every minute. Pudding thickens as it cools.

NOTE: Pudding may be cooked without stirring, and then beaten with wire whisk until smooth.

6 serving package:
Mix in 1½-quart bowl and MICROWAVE 7 MINUTES on HIGH, or until mixture starts to boil.

RHUBARB CRISP

9 servings
8 x 8-inch baking dish

1 cup all-purpose flour
½ cup rolled oats
1 cup firmly packed brown sugar
½ cup butter or margarine
1¾ pounds rhubarb, cut in ½-inch pieces (4 cups)
1 cup sugar
¼ cup all-purpose flour
½ teaspoon cinnamon
½ cup water

Mix together flour, oats and sugar in large bowl. Stir in butter with fork to make a crumbly mixture. Set aside.

Combine rhubarb, sugar, flour, cinnamon and water in (8 x 8-inch) baking dish. Stir to mix well. Cover with plastic wrap. MICROWAVE 3 MINUTES on HIGH.

Sprinkle topping evenly over rhubarb mixture. Do not cover. MICROWAVE 8 MINUTES on HIGH, or until topping is golden and crusty, and rhubarb is tender.

APPLE CRISP

8 servings
8 x 8-inch baking dish

1 cup all-purpose flour
1 cup rolled oats
1 cup firmly packed brown sugar
½ cup butter or margarine
1¾ pounds tart apples, ½-inch diced (4 cups)
1 cup sugar
¼ cup all-purpose flour
½ teaspoon cinnamon

Mix together flour, oats and sugar in large bowl. Stir in butter with fork to make a crumbly mixture. Set aside.

Combine apples, sugar, flour and cinnamon in (8 x 8-inch) baking dish. Stir to mix well. Sprinkle topping over apple mixture.

MICROWAVE 10 to 12 MINUTES on HIGH or until apple mixture starts to bubble through topping.

FRUIT BRULE

6 to 8 servings
10 x 6-inch baking dish

1 *can (16-ounces) pitted black cherries, drained*
1 *can (17-ounces) figs, drained*
1 *can (16-ounces) pears, drained*
1 *can (16-ounces) apricots, drained*
   Juice and grated rind of one orange
   Juice and grated rind of one lemon
1½ *cups firmly packed brown sugar*

Combine fruits, juices and rinds in (10 x 6-inch) baking dish. Sprinkle brown sugar over top. MICROWAVE 15 MINUTES on HIGH, or until mixture is hot and syrupy, stirring once after 7 minutes.

Serve hot or cold, garnished with dairy sour cream, if desired.

APPLESAUCE

6 servings
1½-quart casserole

4 *medium cooking apples, peeled, cored*
   and quartered
½ *cup water*
¾ *cup sugar*
½ *teaspoon cinnamon*

Place apples and water in 1½-quart casserole. Cover. MICROWAVE 10 MINUTES on HIGH, or until apples are tender, stirring well after 5 minutes.

Mash apples with fork. Stir in sugar and cinnamon. Cool.

Variation:

RHUBARB SAUCE

Substitute 4 cups rhubarb cut in ½-inch pieces for apples. Adjust sugar to taste.

BANANA BOATS

4 servings
8 x 8-inch baking dish

2 *ripe bananas, peeled*
3 *tablespoons brown sugar*
1 *tablespoon butter or margarine, cut in pieces*
1 *tablespoon chopped walnuts*

Split bananas lengthwise and place in (8 x 8-inch) baking dish, cut sides up. Sprinkle brown sugar over bananas. Dot with butter. Scatter nuts on top. MICROWAVE 30 SECONDS on HIGH, or until sugar melts. Garnish with whipped cream or chocolate syrup, if desired.

HOLIDAY FRUIT PUDDING

16 servings
3-quart casserole or bowl

1 *package (8-ounces) dried apples*
1 *package (12-ounces) dried pears*
1 *package (12-ounces) dried peaches*
1 *package (16-ounces) dried prunes, pitted*
1 *can (20-ounces) pineapple chunks and juice*
⅓ *cup red wine*
½ *cup water*
1 *can (21-ounces) cherry pie filling*
1 *cup chopped walnuts*

Combine dried fruits, pineapple chunks and juice, red wine and water in 3-quart casserole.

Spread cherry pie filling over mixture. Sprinkle with chopped walnuts. Cover. MICROWAVE 20 to 25 MINUTES on HIGH, or until fruits are tender. Serve warm or chilled.

NOTE: Fruit pudding may be stored in refrigerator up to two weeks, tightly covered.

BEAUTIFUL BAKED APPLE

1 serving
Custard cup

1 *cooking apple*
1 *to 1½ tablespoons brown sugar*
2 *teaspoons butter or margarine*
   Cinnamon

Peel a rim of apple skin from top of apple to allow steam to escape. Core apple. Combine brown sugar and butter. Fill cavity. Place apple in custard cup. Sprinkle cinnamon over cavity and peeled portion of apple. MICROWAVE 2 MINUTES on HIGH, or until apple is almost tender. Let stand 5 minutes to complete cooking.

NOTE: When cooking several apples at a time, add 1 additional minute per apple.

SPICED APRICOTS

6 servings
2-quart casserole

1 *pound dried apricots*
½ *cup sugar*
2 *cups water*
½ *teaspoon cinnamon*
6 *whole cloves*

Wash apricots. Place in 2-quart casserole. Add sugar, water and spices. Cover. MICROWAVE 15 to 20 MINUTES on HIGH, or until fruit is tender and flavors have blended.

Pears in Red Wine

PEARS IN RED WINE

4 servings
1-quart measure
Serving dish or casserole large enough
to hold pears upright

4 *ripe pears, d'Anjou or Comice*
1 *cup red wine*
½ *cup water*
1 *cup sugar*
1 *teaspoon ginger*

Arrange pears in serving dish so that they stand upright. Set aside. Combine wine, water, sugar and ginger in 1-quart measure. MICROWAVE 3 to 5 MINUTES on HIGH, or until boiling.

Pour sauce over pears. Cover with plastic wrap. MICROWAVE 4 to 5 MINUTES on HIGH, or until pears have softened but still hold their shape. Let stand 5 minutes, covered.

HOT AMBROSIA COMPOTE

6 servings
2-quart casserole

½ *cup flaked coconut (plain or toasted)*
¼ *cup graham cracker crumbs*
1 *can (13-ounces) pineapple chunks, drained*
1 *can (16-ounces) sliced peaches, drained*
1 *can (11-ounces) mandarin oranges, drained*
½ *cup sliced fresh green grapes, or 1 can*
(8-ounces) green grapes, drained
8 *to 10 maraschino cherries, halved*
1 *can (13-ounces) apricots, drained*

Combine all ingredients in 2-quart casserole. MICROWAVE 5 to 6 MINUTES on HIGH, or until bubbly. Spoon into serving dishes. Garnish with whipped cream, if desired.

QUICK CURRIED FRUIT DESSERT

6 servings
12 x 8-inch utility dish

2 *cans (16 ounces) fruits for salad*
1 *can (16 ounces) dark sweet cherries*
1 *can (20 ounces) pineapple chunks*
1 *large banana*
⅓ *cup brown sugar*
¼ *cup all-purpose flour*
1 *to 2 teaspoons curry powder*
¾ *cup melted buter or margarine*

Drain canned fruit thoroughly and mix together. Cut banana into ½-inch chunks and stir into fruit. Mix brown sugar, flour and curry powder together and sprinkle over top. Drizzle melted butter over the top. MICROWAVE 10 MINUTES on HIGH.

BANANAS FOSTER

4 servings
1-quart casserole

2 *tablespoons butter or margarine*
2 *large bananas, quartered*
2 *tablespoons brown sugar*
½ *teaspoon cinnamon*
2 *tablespoons banana or orange liqueur*
2 *tablespoons rum*

Place butter in 1-quart casserole. MICROWAVE on HIGH until butter melts. Roll bananas in butter.

Mix brown sugar and cinnamon together. Sprinkle over bananas. MICROWAVE 2 MINUTES, 30 SECONDS to 3 MINUTES on HIGH, or until sugar begins to melt. Remove from oven.

Pour liqueur and rum over hot bananas. Ignite. When flame dies down serve bananas and sauce on ice cream or a thin slice of pound cake.

Candies & Cookies

Candy making is easy and fast with a microwave oven. Because microwave heats from all sides, candies need only minimum attention. They cook smooth and creamy without constant stirring. With a heat control microwave oven, you can bring mixtures to a boil on high, then reduce the settings so they bubble without boiling over.

Bar cookies cook quickly by microwave, whether you bake them from a mix or from 'scratch'. Have them often for desserts, a coffee break or snacks. They're the perfect choice when you're asked to bake something for a meeting or potluck supper. Use our recipes as a guide, and adapt your favorite bar cookies to microwave baking.

Two recipes for individual cookies are given in this section. Some cookie doughs are not suitable for microwave baking because they cook unevenly or do not set. If you wish to convert cookie recipes to microwave, test one cookie when you are baking conventionally. Large batches of cookies should be done conventionally.

CANDY BASICS

Sugar becomes very hot when boiled. Be sure to use a container which can withstand high temperatures, and be careful when removing the bowl from the oven.

Traditional candy recipes call for a temperature test. If you test with a candy thermometer, do not use it in the oven while cooking. You may prefer to use the cold water tests given in our recipes.

CARAMEL NUT POPCORN CLUSTERS

15 to 20 clusters
3-quart mixing bowl

40 *caramel squares (approximately* 14 *ounces)*
 2 *tablespoons light cream*
 2 *quarts popped popcorn (lightly salted)*
 1 *cup salted peanuts*

Combine caramel squares and cream in small bowl. MICROWAVE 2 MINUTES 30 SECONDS to 3 MINUTES on '8', stirring several times, or until caramel is smooth.

In large bowl, mix popcorn and peanuts together, add carmel sauce gradually, stir until combined.

Drop by spoonfuls onto waxed paper. Let cool.

TOFFEE TEMPTERS

16 small pieces
8 x 8-inch baking dish

½ *cup butter or margarine, softened*
½ *cup firmly packed brown sugar*
 1 *cup flour*
 1 *package (6-ounces) semi-sweet chocolate pieces*
½ *cup chopped nuts (optional)*

Thoroughly mix butter, shortening and sugar in medium bowl. Blend in flour.

Spread evenly in (8 x 8-inch) baking dish. MICROWAVE 5 MINUTES on HIGH, or until set, rotating dish ¼ turn after each minute. Immediately sprinkle chocolate pieces on crust. Let stand 2 to 3 minutes until chocolate softens. Spread evenly. Sprinkle with nuts, if desired. Cut into squares while warm.

SUGAR AND SPICE PECANS

16 *ounces shelled pecans*
 2 *tablespoons butter or margarine*
¼ *cup granulated sugar*
 1 *tablespoon cinnamon*
¼ *teaspoon nutmeg*
¼ *teaspoon cloves*

In 4 to 5-quart casserole place pecans, MICROWAVE 7 MINUTES on HIGH, stirring 2 to 3 times.

While nuts are cooking, combine sugar, cinnamon, nutmeg and cloves in small bowl. Stir until blended.

To hot pecans add butter. Stir until butter is melted and pecans are lightly coated. (If necessary, MICROWAVE 10 to 20 SECONDS on HIGH to melt butter.)

Add sugar and spice mixture to nuts. Stir well until evenly coated.

Allow to cool. Store in covered container.

Candies clockwise from upper left: Caramel Nut Popcorn Clusters, Chocolate Drop Candy, Citrus Sugared Nuts, Toffee Tempters. Center: Sugar and Spice Pecans.

SUNSHINE DIVINITY

2½ dozen pieces
3-quart bowl or casserole

2 cups sugar
½ cup light corn syrup
⅓ cup water
2 egg whites
1 teaspoon vanilla
¾ cup finely chopped candied cherries
¾ cup chopped nuts

Combine sugar, corn syrup and water in 3-quart bowl. Stir until sugar dissolves. MICROWAVE 5 MINUTES on HIGH, or until mixture is clear.

Stir thoroughly. MICROWAVE 8 MINUTES on HIGH, or until a small amount dropped in very cold water forms a hard ball (260°).

While syrup is cooking, beat egg whites until stiff peaks form. When syrup is ready, beat egg whites with electric mixer while slowly pouring in a thin stream of hot syrup. Add vanilla. Beat until candy loses its gloss. (About 6 to 8 minutes.) Fold in fruit and nuts.

Drop from buttered teaspoon onto waxed paper or spread in a buttered (10 x 8-inch) pan. Cut into squares when cooled.

NOTE: Do not make divinity when humidity is high, as it will not set. Do not use candy thermometer in the microwave oven.

BUTTERSCOTCH YULE LOG

2 dozen pieces
1-quart bowl

1 6-ounce package butterscotch chips
⅓ cup sweetened condensed milk
½ teaspoon vanilla
⅓ cup chopped pecans
1 egg white, slightly beaten
2 cups pecan halves

Place butterscotch chips in 1-quart bowl, MICROWAVE 1 to 2 MINUTES on HIGH, or until melted. Stir halfway through. Add milk and vanilla. Stir well. Add chopped pecans. Mix well. Chill (15 to 20 minutes) until firm enough to form into log. On waxed paper, form into log. Roll tightly in waxed paper for uniform shape. Mark log lengthwise with tines of fork. Brush with egg white. Press pecan halves into log to cover surface. Wrap in wax paper. Chill. Cut into ½-inch slices.

NATURE'S OWN CANDY ❄

5 dozen pieces
10 x 8-inch baking dish

½ cup (1 stick) butter or margarine
¾ cup firmly packed light brown sugar
1½ cups quick-cooking oatmeal
1 cup flaked coconut
1 cup coarsely chopped walnuts
½ cup toasted wheat germ
⅓ cup sesame seeds
½ cup snipped dried apricots
⅓ cup honey
1 teaspoon cinnamon

Combine butter and brown sugar in (10 x 8-inch) baking dish. MICROWAVE 1 MINUTE, 30 SECONDS on HIGH, or until melted.

Add all remaining ingredients and mix thoroughly. Spread evenly in baking dish. MICROWAVE 6 MINUTES on HIGH, or until bubbly, stirring every 2 minutes.

Turn mixture out onto a sheet of waxed paper. Spread evenly to 1-inch thickness. Allow candy to cool completely and break into bite-sized pieces, or cool only until mixture can be handled comfortably. Form into 1-inch balls. Cool.

FANTASTIC FUDGE

64 pieces
2-quart batter bowl

¾ cup evaporated milk or light cream
1 tablespoon butter or margarine
1½ cups sugar
16 marshmallows, cut in half
1 package (12-ounces) chocolate chips
1 cup chopped nuts
1 teaspoon vanilla

Combine evaporated milk, butter, sugar and marshmallows in 2-quart bowl. MICROWAVE 3 to 4 MINUTES on HIGH, or until marshmallows puff and mixture begins to boil. Stir.

Reduce setting. MICROWAVE 3 to 4 MINUTES on '6', or until mixture boils and sugar dissolves completely. Stir in chocolate chips, nuts and vanilla. Beat until smooth. Spread in buttered (8 x 8-inch) baking dish. Cool. Cut into 1-inch squares.

Top tier: Peanut Brittle (page 229)
Middle tier: Fantastic Fudge and Nature's Own Candy (page 226)
Bottom tier: Sunshine Divinity (page 226) and Penuche (page 229)

NEVER-FAIL FUDGE

2 dozen pieces
10 x 8-inch utility dish

1 *package (1-pound) confectioners sugar*
½ *cup cocoa*
½ *cup butter or margarine*
¼ *cup milk*
½ *cup finely chopped nuts*
1 *teaspoon vanilla*

Mix sugar and cocoa together in (10 x 8-inch) utility dish. Drop butter onto sugar mixture in 4 or 5 pieces. Pour in milk, MICROWAVE 2 to 3 MINUTES on HIGH, or until bubbly. Stir lightly.

Thoroughly stir in nuts and vanilla so nuts are evenly distributed. Spread fudge evenly in dish. Refrigerate 1 hour. Cut into squares.

SCOTCH ROCKY ROAD CANDY

24 pieces
1-quart measure

¼ *cup butter or margarine*
1 *package (6-ounces) semi-sweet chocolate chips*
1 *package (6-ounces) butterscotch chips*
1 *package (10-ounces) miniature marshmallows*
½ *cup coarsely chopped nuts*

Combine butter, chocolate and butterscotch chips in 1-quart measure. MICROWAVE 2 to 3 MINUTES on HIGH, or until chips have softened and can be stirred easily. Beat with a fork until well blended.

Mix marshmallows and nuts in 2-quart casserole. Pour in melted mixture. Mix thoroughly. Drop by spoonfuls onto waxed paper. Refrigerate until firm.

FONDANT

3 dozen 1-inch pieces
3½ to 4-quart casserole

2 cups sugar
1½ cups, plus 2 tablespoons water
⅛ teaspoon cream of tartar
2 tablespoons light corn syrup
1 tablespoon butter or margarine
1 teaspoon vanilla

Butter the sides of a 3½-quart casserole. Combine sugar, water, cream of tartar and corn syrup in casserole. MICROWAVE 22 to 26 MINUTES on HIGH, or until a small amount dropped in very cold water forms a soft ball (238°).

Immediately pour syrup into large platter. Let cool until warm to touch. Using a wooden spoon, work fondant from outside toward center until it forms a creamy white mass.

Work in butter and vanilla. Continue working until fondant begins to harden. Drop by teaspoonfuls onto wax paper. Let stand until firm. Store in closed container.

CHOCOLATE DROP CANDIES

2½ dozen pieces candy
2-quart bowl

1 6-ounce package real chocolate chips
1 cup miniature marshmallows
1 cup M & M's
1 cup peanut-butter chips
1 cup almond brickle chips
1 cup nuts
1 cup raisins

Place chocolate chips in 2-quart mixing bowl, MICROWAVE 3 MINUTES on HIGH. Stir till smooth. Choose any combination of the above to equal 4 cups. Stir in melted chocolate chip mixture. Drop by spoonfulls onto wax paper. Cool.

Bring sugar mixture to boil. DO NOT USE THERMOMETER IN OVEN.

A drop in cold water forms a soft ball or candy thermometer reads 238°.

Immediately pour onto large platter. Let cool until bottom of dish feels warm.

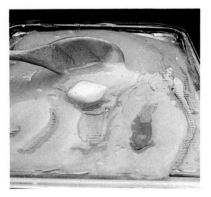

Add butter and vanilla.

Stir in food coloring with spoon. Mixture will be opaque.

Drop by spoonfuls onto waxed paper or foil and let cool.

CRISPY TREATS

18 to 24 bars
12 x 8-inch utility dish

3 tablespoons butter
½ cup peanut butter
5 cups mini marshmallows
5 cups cocoa rice or 5 cup plain rice
    cereal

In a medium mixing bowl, place butter and peanut butter. MICROWAVE 30 SECONDS to 1 MINUTE on HIGH, or until butter is melted.

Add marshmallows, mix well. MICROWAVE 2 MINUTES to 2 MINUTES, 30 SECONDS on HIGH or until all marshmallows melt when stirred. Stir twice during cooking time. Add cereal, mix well until cereal is coated.

Press out on waxed paper or into utility dish.

Let cool. Cut into squares.

PENUCHE

1½ dozen pieces
3-quart casserole

2½ cups firmly packed brown sugar
  ¾ cup milk
  1 tablespoon butter or margarine
  1 tablespoon light corn syrup
    Pinch salt
  1 teaspoon vanilla
  ⅓ cup chopped nuts

Blend together sugar, milk, butter, corn syrup and salt in a 3-quart casserole. MICROWAVE 5 MINUTES on HIGH, or until sugar is dissolved. Stir well. MICROWAVE 6 MINUTES on HIGH, or until a small amount dropped in very cold water forms a soft ball (240°).
Cool to lukewarm. Using a wooden spoon, beat vigorously until mixture begins to thicken. Stir in vanilla and nuts. Continue beating until candy is thick and difficult to work. Spread evenly in buttered (8 x 8-inch) pan. Cool until firm. Cut in squares.

NOTE: Do not use candy thermometer in the microwave oven.

PEANUT BRITTLE

1½ pounds
2-quart batter bowl

2 cups sugar
1 cup light corn syrup
1 cup water
2 cups shelled unroasted peanuts
¼ teaspoon salt
1 teaspoon butter or margarine
1 teaspoon soda

Combine sugar, corn syrup and water in 2-quart batter bowl. MICROWAVE 18 to 20 MINUTES on HIGH, or until a small amount dropped in very cold water forms a soft ball (240°).

Stir in peanuts and salt. MICROWAVE 7 to 9 MINUTES on HIGH, or until a small amount dropped in very cold water separates into hard, brittle threads (290°). Immediately stir in butter and soda. Mix well. Spread evenly and thinly on large buttered cookie sheet. Cool, lifting occasionally with spatula to prevent sticking. Break into pieces when cool.

NOTE: Do not use candy thermometer in microwave oven.

CITRUS SUGARED NUTS

18 ounces shelled walnut halves or pieces
½ cup powdered sugar
2 teaspoons lemon rind
2 tablespoons orange rind

Place walnuts in 3 to 6 quart casserole, add water to cover. MICROWAVE 10 to 15 MINUTES on HIGH, or until water boils. Remove cover, boil for 4 minutes.

Drain walnuts, return to casserole. MICROWAVE uncovered 6 to 10 MINUTES on HIGH, or until dry.

While walnuts are still hot, add sugar, lemon rind and orange rind. Mix well until walnuts are coated.

NOTE: Gift Idea — Put nuts into decorative glass containers for holiday gift giving.

Basic Cookie

GINGER JOYS

3 to 4 dozen
1-quart casserole
12 x 8-inch baking dish

½ cup vegetable shortening
½ cup sugar
½ cup light molasses
1½ teaspoons vinegar
1 egg, well beaten
3 cups all-purpose flour
½ teaspoon soda
½ teaspoon ginger
½ teaspoon cinnamon
¼ teaspoon salt

Blend shortening, sugar, molasses and vinegar together in 1-quart casserole. MICROWAVE 2 MINUTES on HIGH, or until mixture begins to boil, stirring once. Let stand ½ hour to cool.

Stir in egg. Combine flour, soda, ginger, cinnamon and salt in 1-quart measure. Mix together lightly. Stir into cooled mixture. Mix thoroughly. Refrigerate several hours.

Place a sheet of waxed paper on inverted (12 x 8-inch) baking dish. Form dough into 1-inch balls. Place 6 to 8 on waxed paper. MICROWAVE 2 MINUTES on HIGH, or until set. Let stand 1 minute. Cool.

COOKIE BASICS

Individual cookies and bars do not brown when baked by microwave. Select recipes with ingredients which add color, such as spices or chocolate. You may also use toppings, frostings or a sprinkling of powdered sugar. Over-baked bar cookies are hard and dry. A few moist spots may appear on the surface, but bars are done when a wooden pick inserted in the center comes out clean, or when a light touch on the center leaves no imprint.

BASIC COOKIE RECIPE

2½ dozen cookies
Wax paper or cookie sheet

½ cup butter or margarine
½ cup sugar
1 egg
1½ cups all-purpose flour
½ teaspoon cream of tartar
¼ teaspoon baking soda
¼ teaspoon salt
½ teaspoon almond flavoring

Soften butter. Cream butter, sugar and egg until well blended. Add flour, cream of tartar, soda, salt and almond flavoring to butter mixture. Beat until well blended. Chill until firm.

Use one tablespoon of dough per cookie, roll into ball. Bake 9 at a time. MICROWAVE 2 to 3 MINUTES on HIGH or until set.

Variations:

CHOCOLATE CHIP

Substitute ½ cup brown sugar for granulated sugar, substitute ½ teaspoon vanilla for almond flavoring and add 1 cup chocolate chips.

PEANUT BUTTER CHIP

Substitute ½ cup brown sugar for granulated sugar, substitute ½ teaspoon vanilla for almond flavoring and add 1 cup peanut butter chips.

BUTTERSCOTH CHIPS

Substitute ½ cup brown sugar for granulated sugar, substitute ½ teaspoon vanilla for almond flavoring and add 1 cup butterscotch chips.

CHOCOLATE

Substitute ½ teaspoon vanilla for almond flavoring. Add 2 teaspoons cocoa.

LEMON

Substitute 2 teaspoons lemon juice for almond flavoring. Add 1 teaspoon lemon rind (grated).

PUMPKIN BARS ❄️

36 bars
Two 8 x 8-inch glass baking dishes

4 *eggs*
1 *cup salad oil*
2 *cups sugar*
1 *can (15-ounces) pumpkin*
2 *cups all-purpose flour*
2 *teaspoons baking powder*
1 *teaspoon soda*
½ *teaspoon salt*
2 *teaspoons cinnamon*
½ *teaspoon ginger*
½ *teaspoon cloves*
½ *teaspoon nutmeg*

Blend eggs, oil, sugar and pumpkin together in large mixing bowl. Measure flour, baking powder, soda, salt, cinnamon, ginger, cloves and nutmeg into 1-quart measure. Mix together lightly with a fork. Stir into pumpkin mixture.

Divide batter equally into two (8 x 8-inch) glass baking dishes. One at a time, MICROWAVE 5 MINUTES, 30 SECONDS to 6 MINUTES on HIGH, or until wooden pick inserted in center comes out clean. Let stand until thoroughly cooled. Top with Cream Cheese Frosting.

CREAM CHEESE FROSTING

2 *packages (3-ounces each) cream cheese*
½ *cup butter or margarine*
1 *tablespoon cream or milk*
1 *teaspoon vanilla*
4 *cups confectioners sugar (sift if lumpy)*

Combine cream cheese and butter in medium mixing bowl. MICROWAVE 1 to 2 MINUTES on '2', or until soft but not melted.

With a fork, stir in cream and vanilla. Gradually add sugar until frosting reaches spreading consistency. Frost pumpkin bars. Cut into 2-inch squares.

BROWNIES

16 to 18 squares
8 x 8-inch baking dish

1 *package (13-ounces) brownie mix*

Prepare batter as directed on package. Spread into (8 x 8-inch) baking dish. MICROWAVE 7 MINUTES to 8 MINUTES, 30 SECONDS on '6', or until firm to touch. Cool. Cut in 2-inch squares.

CANDIED ORANGE DATE BARS ❄️

20 bars
2-quart bowl
8 x 8-inch baking dish

Filling:
½ *pound candied orange slices, cut in thirds*
½ *cup pitted dates, cut up*
¼ *cup sugar*
1 *tablespoon all-purpose flour*
½ *cup boiling water*

Batter:
½ *cup butter or margarine*
1 *cup firmly packed brown sugar*
2 *eggs*
1¾ *cups all-purpose flour*
1 *teaspoon baking soda*
   Pinch salt
1 *teaspoon vanilla*
1 *cup chopped walnuts*

Combine orange slices, dates, sugar and flour in 2-quart bowl. Toss lightly to distribute sugar and flour. Pour boiling water over fruit. MICROWAVE 2 MINUTES, 30 SECONDS to 3 MINUTES on HIGH, or until thick. Set aside.

Mix butter, sugar and eggs thoroughly. Blend in flour, soda, salt and vanilla. Beat well. Stir in nuts.

Spread half of batter in (8 x 8-inch) baking dish. Cover evenly with filling. Top with remaining batter. (It will not cover completely.) MICROWAVE 7 MINUTES, 30 SECONDS to 8 MINUTES on HIGH, or until almost no imprint remains when touched in center.

LEMON BUTTER DESSERT SQUARES

6 to 8 servings
8 x 8-inch baking dish

1 *cup all-purpose flour*
½ *cup butter or margarine*
¼ *cup powdered sugar*
2 *eggs*
1 *tablespoon all-purpose flour*
½ *teaspoon baking powder*
1 *cup granulated sugar*
   Grated rind and juice of 2 lemons

Blend flour, butter and powdered sugar together. Press lightly into bottom of (8 x 8-inch) baking dish. MICROWAVE 3 MINUTES on HIGH, or until firm.

Beat eggs until light. Stir in flour, baking powder, granulated sugar, lemon rind and juice. Pour over baked layer. MICROWAVE 6 MINUTES on HIGH, or until top is set and custard like.

Jams, Preserves & Relishes

The microwave oven makes small batches of jams, preserves or relishes quickly and easily so that you can always have fresh jam or jelly. Preserves and jellies are traditional at breakfast, but try serving savory ones with hot dinner rolls as a compliment to meats. Prepare hot strawberry jam to serve as an ice cream topping.

By following the methods given in these recipes, you can prepare your favorite preserves and jellies in the microwave oven. Be sure to reduce the setting after the mixture boils to prevent over-boiling and eliminate the need for constant watching.

GRAPE JELLY

2 cups
2-quart batter bowl

2 *cups grape juice*
2 *teaspoons lemon juice*
1 *cup sugar*
1 *package powdered fruit pectin (1¾-ounces)*

Combine all ingredients in a 2-quart batter bowl and MICROWAVE 15 to 18 MINUTES on HIGH, or until jelly leaves a coating on a spoon dipped into the mixture. It will thicken more as it cools. Pour into glasses. Cover with plastic wrap and store in refrigerator. Jars can be sterilized in the normal manner, filled with the hot jelly and sealed.

Grape Jelly is quick and easy in a microwave.

SPICY APPLE JAM

4 ½-pint jars with lids
2 quart batter bowl

2 *cups apple juice*
2½ *cups sugar*
1 *package (1¾-ounce) fruit pectin*
2 *tablespoons lemon juice*
1 *cup cinnamon candy bits or ½ cup red hots*

Stir apple juice, sugar and fruit pectin together. MICROWAVE 5 to 7 MINUTES on HIGH, or until mixture boils. Stir in lemon juice and candy, stirring constantly until candy bits are dissolved. MICROWAVE 7 to 10 MINUTES on '6', or until thickened. Skim and pour into 4 ½-pint sterilized jars. Seal.

GRAPEFRUIT AND SAVORY JELLY

Three ½-pint jars with lids
2-quart batter bowl

½ *cup boiling water*
2 *teaspoons dried summer savory*
1 *cup grapefruit juice*
1 *package (1¾-ounces) powdered fruit pectin*
  Green food color
3¼ *cups sugar*

Pour boiling water over savory in small bowl. Cover. Let stand 15 minutes. Strain through cheese cloth into measuring cup. Add more water, if needed, to make ½ cup.

Combine savory water, grapefruit juice and pectin in 2-quart bowl. MICROWAVE 5 to 7 MINUTES on HIGH, or until mixture boils. Tint light green with food color. Stir in sugar.

Reduce setting. MICROWAVE 6 to 8 MINUTES on '6', or until slightly thickened, stirring once to dissolve sugar. Skim. Pour into hot sterilized jars. Seal.

Testing jelly for doneness

Bring jelly to a full boil in the microwave.

When done, boiling jelly will coat a spoon dipped into it.

AROMATIC APPLE JELLY

4 ½-pint jars
2-quart batter bowl

2 *cups apple juice*
1 *package (1¾-ounces) powdered fruit pectin*
1 *tablespoon aromatic bitters*
2 *tablespoons lemon juice*
    Red food color
3½ *cups sugar*

Stir apple juice and pectin together in 2-quart batter bowl. MICROWAVE 5 to 7 MINUTES on HIGH, or until mixture boils. Add bitters, lemon juice and a few drops red food color. Stir in sugar.

Reduce setting. MICROWAVE 6 to 8 MINUTES on '6', or until mixture is slightly thickened, stirring once to dissolve sugar. Skim. Pour into hot sterilized jars. Seal.

WINE JELLY

4 ½-pint jars with lids
2-quart batter bowl

2 *cups Rose wine*
3 *cups sugar*
½ *of a 6-ounce bottle fruit pectin*

Combine wine, sugar and fruit pectin, stir. MICROWAVE 12 MINUTES on HIGH, or until mixture boils and then MICROWAVE 15 MINUTES on '5'. Stir. Skim off any foam with a metal spoon. Pour into sterilized jars, cool and seal. The jelly may be MICROWAVED 1 MINUTE on HIGH, and used as a glaze for a roast turkey or goose.

This jelly makes a good glaze for poultry. To use as a glaze, MICROWAVE 1 to 2 MINUTES on HIGH, or until jelly melts. Brush on poultry.

STRAWBERRY REFRIGERATOR JAM

1½ cups
2-quart batter bowl

2 cups (1-pint) strawberries, washed and
    hulled
1½ cups sugar
2 teaspoons powdered fruit pectin

Slice strawberries into 2-quart bowl. Mash well. Stir
in sugar and pectin thoroughly. MICROWAVE 3 to
4 MINUTES on HIGH, or until mixture comes to a
full rolling boil.

Reduce setting. MICROWAVE 5 MINUTES on
'6', or until mixture is slightly thickened. It will
thicken more as it cools. Pour into glasses. Cover
with plastic wrap. Store in refrigerator. For a thicker
jam, add 1 teaspoon pectin.

NOTE: Fresh strawberry jam in a pretty glass makes
a thoughtful gift for your hostess, a new neighbor or
a good friend. The recipe makes enough jam to fill a
large coffee mug or 2 wine glasses.

1 package (10 to 12-ounces) frozen strawberries
may be substituted for fresh. Add 1 teaspoon pectin.

MILD PEACH CHUTNEY

Two 1-pint jars with lids
3-quart casserole

1 large unpeeled apple, cored and chopped
1 cup chopped celery
¼ cup chopped green pepper
1 tablespoon finely chopped onion
2 cans (16-ounces each) sliced cling peaches
    with juice
½ cup seedless raisins
¾ cup cider vinegar
½ cup sugar
½ teaspoon salt
¼ teaspoon ginger
    Dash cayenne pepper

Combine all ingredients in 3-quart casserole. Stir
well. Cover. MICROWAVE 5 MINUTES on
HIGH, or until mixture boils.

Reduce setting. MICROWAVE 45 MINUTES on
'5', or until syrup is thickened and chutney is desired consistency, stirring 2 or 3 times.

Ladle into hot sterilized jars. Cover tightly. Cool.
Store in refrigerator. Serve with meats.

NOTE: Be sure mixture is boiling before reducing
setting to '5'.

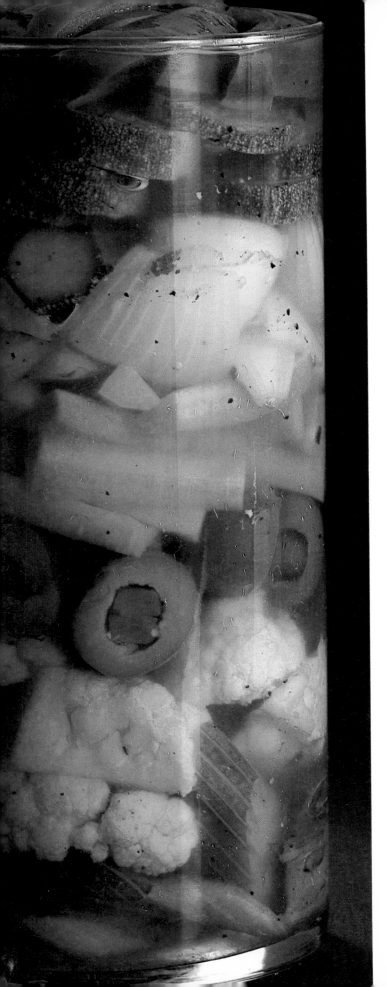

ANTIPASTO RELISH

6 servings
3-quart casserole

½ *small head cauliflower, cut in flowerets*
   and sliced
2 *carrots, pared, cut in 2-inch strips*
2 *stems celery, cut diagonally in 1-inch pieces*
   (1 cup)
1 *small onion, cut in ¾ inch squares*
1 *green pepper, cut in 2-inch strips*
1 *jar (3-ounces) stuffed green olives, drained*
¾ *cup wine vinegar*
½ *cup olive or salad oil*
1 *to 2 tablespoons sugar*
1 *teaspoon salt*
½ *teaspoon oregano leaves*
¼ *teaspoon pepper*
¼ *cup water*

Combine all ingredients in 3-quart casserole. MI-CROWAVE 8 to 10 MINUTES on HIGH, or until mixture has come to a rapid boil, stirring twice.

Reduce setting. MICROWAVE 4 to 6 MINUTES on '6'. Cool. Refrigerate at least 24 hours. Drain well before serving.

Will keep several days in refrigerator, covered. Serve as appetizer, salad, or garnish for meats.

NOTE: Pitted ripe olives, medium zucchini cut in 1-inch pieces, or other crisp, fresh vegetables may be substituted for part of ingredients above.

CRANBERRY-ORANGE RELISH

8 to 10 servings
3-quart casserole

1 *pound fresh cranberries*
2 *medium oranges*
2 *cups sugar*
1 *cup chopped nuts (optional)*

In blender, chop quartered seeded oranges. Pick over cranberries and wash. Place oranges, cran-berries, sugar and nuts (if desired) in a 3-quart cas-serole. Stir to mix well. Cover. MICROWAVE 15 to 20 MINUTES, or until cranberries are soft. Stir every 5 minutes.

HOT GINGERED PEARS

2 to 3 pint jars
2-quart batter bowl
12 x 8-inch baking dish

2 cans (1-pound, 13-ounces each) pear halves
24 whole cloves
2 cinnamon sticks (2-inches)
¼ teaspoon nutmeg
4 teaspoons lemon juice
1 teaspoon grated lemon peel
1 teaspoon grated orange peel
2½ tablespoons chopped crystallized ginger
⅛ teaspoon ground ginger
2 tablespoons butter or margarine

Drain pears well, reserving 1½ cups syrup. In 2-quart bowl, combine reserved syrup, 10 cloves, cinnamon sticks and nutmeg. MICROWAVE 4 to 6 MINUTES on HIGH, or until mixture boils.

Reduce setting. MICROWAVE 4 MINUTES on '6'. Remove and discard cloves. Add lemon juice, lemon and orange peels, gingers and butter. Mix well. MICROWAVE 4 to 6 MINUTES on '6', or until slightly thickened.

Arrange pear halves in (12 x 8-inch) baking dish. Insert 1 or 2 cloves in each. Pour hot syrup over pears. MICROWAVE 5 MINUTES on '6', basting pears with syrup several times.

Serve hot or cold. Will keep in jars several days, refrigerated.

PARTY CORN RELISH

2 cups
1½-quart casserole

1½ cups sugar
½ teaspoon salt
½ teaspoon celery seed
¼ teaspoon mustard seed
½ cup white wine vinegar
¼ teaspoon hot pepper sauce
1 can (12-ounces) whole kernel corn
2 tablespoons chopped green pepper
1 small onion, chopped
1 tablespoon chopped pimiento

Combine sugar, salt, celery seed, mustard seed, vinegar and pepper sauce in 1½-quart casserole. Cover. MICROWAVE 2 to 3 MINUTES on HIGH, or until sauce just starts to boil. Stir in corn, green pepper, onion and pimiento. Combine. Cool. Refrigerate at least 6 hours to blend flavors.

PICKLED BEETS

2 cups
1-quart measure

1 can (16-ounces) sliced beets
Vinegar
1 tablespoon sugar
½ teaspoon salt
½ teaspoon celery seed
1 to 2 whole cloves
Small cinnamon stick

Drain liquid from beets into 1-quart measure. Set beets aside. Add equal amount of water to beet juice. MICROWAVE 1 to 2 MINUTES on HIGH, or until boiling.

Stir in sugar, salt, celery seed, cloves and cinnamon. MICROWAVE 1 MINUTE on HIGH, or until sugar is dissolved. Add beets. Refrigerate at least 12 hours to blend flavors.

Variation:
Add ½ to 1 cup sliced onions with beets. Stir in 1 tablespoon dairy sour cream just before serving.

EASY SPICED PEACHES

2 to 3 pint jars
2-quart batter bowl
12 x 8-inch baking dish

2 cans (1-pound, 13-ounces each) peach halves
2 tablespoons cider vinegar
1 teaspoon whole allspice
1 teaspoon whole cloves
4 cinnamon sticks (2½-inches)

Drain peaches well, reserving 1½ cups syrup. In 2-quart bowl, combine reserved syrup, vinegar; allspice, cloves and cinnamon sticks. MICROWAVE 4 to 6 MINUTES on HIGH, or until mixture boils.

Reduce setting. MICROWAVE 4 MINUTES on '6'. Remove and discard cloves.

Arrange peach halves in (12 x 8-inch) baking dish. Pour hot syrup over peaches. MICROWAVE 5 MINUTES on '6', basting peaches several times.

Serve hot or cold. Peaches will keep in jars several days, refrigerated.

Convenience Foods

Microwave cooking makes convenience foods even more convenient. Mixes, ready-prepared frozen and canned foods save you preparation time. The microwave oven saves you cooking and heating time.

Some convenience foods have become so basic to the American cooking style that they are considered ingredients. Canned and frozen soups and sauces, meats, fish and vegetables, evaporated and condensed milks, gravy and seasoning mixes appear in recipes throughout this cookbook.

In the Casserole section there are sample recipes for the preparation of dehydrated mixes, such as "add-meat" dinners and macaroni and cheese. The Vegetable section includes charts for cooking frozen vegetables and sample recipes for dehydrated potato mixes. Directions and time charts for cooking macaroni, spaghetti and noodles are in the Rice and Pasta chapter.

In the Dessert and Baking sections you'll find basic instructions for preparing mixes in the microwave oven, sample recipes to illustrate the method and time charts for different types of mix cakes, cupcakes, quick breads and muffins. There are also recipes which call for mixes as ingredients.

The charts on the following pages list some readily available frozen, canned and dehydrated convenience foods. Instructions are given for defrosting, heating or cooking them. Time and setting charts are provided for different heat control microwave ovens. Standing times are important since foods will continue to heat after removal from the oven.

These charts can serve as guide lines for handling similar convenience foods, as well as frozen or canned foods prepared in the home. A special chart for defrosting homemade frozen casseroles follows the convenience food guide.

Convenience foods come in several types of packages. Foods frozen in pouches may be defrosted or heated right in the pouch. Slit or puncture the pouch before heating to allow steam to excape, and open carefully when done. You may also remove pouched foods from the package and heat them in casseroles or serving dishes covered with plastic wrap.

Foods frozen or canned in glass jars may be heated right in the jar with the lid removed. Foods frozen in aluminum foil trays need not be removed to another dish, although you may wish to do so for faster heating. If the lid is foil, remove it and replace it with plastic wrap. Non-foil lids can be loosened and left resting on top of the tray to cover lightly. Check paper lids for foil linings. Turn down any rough edges on the tray.

Slit or puncture frozen food pouches before heating or defrosting to allow steam to escape.

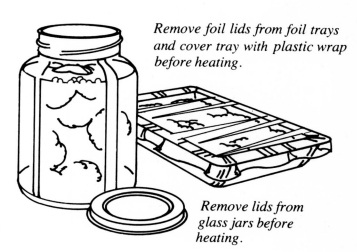

Remove foil lids from foil trays and cover tray with plastic wrap before heating.

Remove lids from glass jars before heating.

Convenience Foods

Frozen Foods/Defrosting

ITEM	SIZE	COOKING CONTAINER	MINUTES	SETTING	SPECIAL INSTRUCTIONS
Beef pattie in bun (2 per package)	8¼ oz.	Place on paper napkin	2 - 3	4	
Brownies	13 oz.	Original tray, loosen lid	1 - 1½	4	Let stand 3 minutes
Cake, frosted	20½ oz.	Original tray	2 - 2½	4	Let stand 3 - 5 minutes
Coffee cake (streusel type)	10⅞ oz.	Original package, loosen lid	2 - 2½	4	Let stand 3 minutes
Donuts	2 donuts	Place on paper plate or napkin	1	4	Let stand 3 minutes
Eggs, frozen	8 fl. oz.	Original carton, open	4 - 5	4	Shake well, let stand 10 minutes
Hamburger buns	8 buns	Original package, open	2 - 3	4	Let stand 2 minutes
Pancake batter	7 oz.	Original carton, open	3 - 5	4	Shake, let stand 10 minutes
Strawberries, whole	16 oz.	Covered casserole	2 - 3	High	Let stand 5 minutes

Frozen Foods/Reheating

ITEM	SIZE	COOKING CONTAINER	MINUTES	SETTING	SPECIAL INSTRUCTIONS
Chicken Ala King	5 oz.	Plastic pouch, slit	3 - 4	High	
Chicken, batter fried	16 oz.	Original tray, loosen lid	13	High	Turn after 8 minutes
Corn, peas, beans, in butter sauce	10 oz.	Plastic pouch, slit, or 1-qt. casserole	5 - 6	High	

Frozen Foods/Reheating   *continued*

ITEM	SIZE	COOKING CONTAINER	MINUTES	SETTING	SPECIAL INSTRUCTIONS
Fish fillets, fried	14 oz.	Place on roasting rack	5 - 6	High	Rearrange after 3 minutes
Fondue, Swiss	10 oz.	Plastic pouch, slit	6	6	Stir well before serving
Green peppers, stuffed	14 oz.	Original pkg. cover with plastic wrap	18 - 20	8	
Lasagna	50 oz.	Original tray, loosen lid	20 - 22	8	
Omelets, Western	10 oz. (two omelets)	Glass or pottery plate	4 - 5	6	Turn once
Pizza roll appetizers	6 oz.	Browning dish, preheat 4 min. on High, add 1 Tbsp. oil	1 - 2	High	Turn once
Pork ribs, (cooked)	32 oz.	Original pkg. cover with plastic wrap	15	8	Rearrange after 10 minutes
Potatoes, baked, stuffed	12 oz.	Original pkg. open one end	8 - 9	High	
Potatoes and celery in white sauce	10 oz.	Plastic pouch, slit or 1-qt. covered casserole	5 - 6	High	
Potatoes, shoestring	10 oz.		5 - 6	High	
Potatoes, fried	10 oz.	Preheat browning dish on High 4 min. add 1 Tbsp. oil and potatoes	5 - 6	High	Stir after 2 minutes
Tater Tots	16 oz.		3 - 5	High	Stir after 2 minutes

Convenience Foods

Frozen Dinners/Reheating

ITEM	SIZE	COOKING CONTAINER	MINUTES	SETTING	SPECIAL INSTRUCTIONS
Meatballs, with gravy and mashed potatoes	9¼ oz.	Original tray, loosen lid	6 - 7	8	
Mexican style dinner	11 oz.	Original tray, loosen lid	6 - 7	8	
Salisbury steak with gravy	32 oz.	Original tray, loosen lid	23 - 25	8	Rearrange after 8 minutes
Spaghetti and sauce	14 oz.	Remove from pouch, place in 1-qt. casserole	8 - 9	6	
Tuna-noodle casserole	11½ oz.	Original pkg. remove cover from tray	9 - 10	High	
Turkey or beef dinner	11½ oz.	Original pkg. loosen lid	10 - 12	8	Stir before serving

Frozen Foods/Cooking

ITEM	SIZE	COOKING CONTAINER	MINUTES	SETTING	SPECIAL INSTRUCTIONS
Chicken Kiev	6½ oz.	8 x 8 baking dish lightly covered with plastic wrap	15 - 18	6	Rearrange after 10 minutes
Mixed vegetables	16 oz.	Covered casserole	8 - 10	High	Stir before serving
Spinach souffle	12 oz.	Original pkg. loosen lid	13 - 15	8	

Canned Foods

ITEM	SIZE	COOKING CONTAINER	MINUTES	SETTING	SPECIAL INSTRUCTIONS
Beans, baked	21 oz.	Covered casserole	6 - 7	8	Stir before serving
Beef ravioli	40 oz.	Covered casserole	10	8	
Beef stew	24 oz.	Covered casserole	10	8	Stir once
Cabbage, stuffed with beef, soy	16 oz.	Covered casserole	7 - 8	8	Rearrange once
Chili with beans	15 oz.	Covered casserole	5 - 6	High	Stir once

Canned Foods *continued*

ITEM	SIZE	COOKING CONTAINER	MINUTES	SETTING	SPECIAL INSTRUCTIONS
Corn, peas, cut beans	17 oz.	Covered casserole	3 - 4	High	Stir before serving — Larger cans, increase time 1-1½ min.
Ham, patties (refrigerated)	4 patties	Plate	3 - 3½	8	Turn once
Hash, corned beef	15 oz.	Covered casserole	5 - 6	High	Stir before serving
Pork, sliced with gravy	12½ oz.	Covered casserole	5 - 6	8	Stir before serving
Potato salad, German style	15 oz.	Covered casserole	5 - 6	High	Stir before serving
Soup, chunky style	19 oz.	Covered casserole	5 - 6	High	Stir before serving
Soup, condensed cream style (diluted)	10¼ oz.	Covered casserole	5 - 6	High	Stir before serving
Spaghetti	15 oz.	Covered casserole	5 - 6	High	Stir before serving

Dehydrated Foods

ITEM	SIZE	COOKING CONTAINER	MINUTES	SETTING	SPECIAL INSTRUCTIONS
Onion soup, dry mix	1¼ oz.	Medium mixing bowl, covered	13 - 14	High	Stir before serving
Wine sauce mix	1 oz.	Medium mixing bowl, covered	4½ - 5	High	Stir before serving
Hamburger Helper	See recipes in Casserole section (page 148 - 167).				
Tuna Helper					
Macaroni and cheese					
Scalloped potatoes					
Hash browns					

Homemade Casseroles Frozen - Precooked

ITEM	MINUTES	SETTING	SPECIAL INSTRUCTIONS
1-quart	12 - 18	4	Cover Stir once
2-quart	25 - 30	4	Cover Stir once

Drying Flowers

The microwave oven dries flowers in minutes, with a fresher appearance and color than flowers dried by traditional methods. Microwave-dried flowers are also less perishable.

Microwave-drying of flowers requires a drying agent to absorb moisture and hold the flower in its natural shape. Three different agents may be used.

1. Silica Gel, available in most hobby shops, is best for drying smooth petals, such as orchids.

2. An equal mixture of borax and corn meal can be used.

3. Kitty litter is inexpensive and easiest to use.

All three drying agents can be used over again. Rubber or plastic gloves will protect your hands from the drying agents.

1. Select fresh flowers or leaves. Flowers should be just at the peak of bloom. Flowers which have their prime will continue to turn brown. Clip stem of flower to ½-inch long.

2. Select a glass or paper container large enough to hold the flower and deep enough so that the drying agent covers the entire bloom. Small flowers may be dried individually in small bowls; up to three may be dried in the oven at once. Use a casserole for large flowers.

3. Spread a ½-inch layer of drying agent in the bottom of container. Place flower in agent, bloom up. With a spoon, carefully sprinkle drying agent between and over the petals, making sure that each petal is covered, but not bent out of shape by the weight of the agent.

4. Place a 1-cup measure full of water and the flower container in the microwave oven. The separate container of water provides moisture and keeps the flowers from becoming too dry.

MICROWAVE on HIGH, depending upon the size and type of flower. (See chart.)

Let flower stand in the agent 4 to 12 hours, or when container is cool to the touch. (See chart.) When removing flower from the agent, tap flower gently until all granules of the drying agent are removed. Tape wires or floral sticks to the remaining ½-inch of flower stem.

DRYING LEAVES

Fall leaves dried in the microwave oven retain their beautiful color. Select a branch of 3 leaves, with the largest leaf about 4-inches wide. Clean leaves carefully. Invert a 12 x 8-inch baking dish on the oven floor. Cover with a paper towel. Place the branch on the towel. Cover with another paper towel. MICROWAVE 1 MINUTE, 30 SECONDS on HIGH. Turn branch over and cover with towel. MICROWAVE 1 MINUTE, 30 SECONDS on HIGH. To dry larger branches, increase oven time.

FLOWER	NUMBER IN CONTAINER	MICROWAVE ON HIGH	ROTATE POSITION	LET STAND IN DRYING AGENT
Azaleas	Several Clusters	2 min.	Every ½ Minute	10 hours
Carnations (2 containers at once)	1	3 min.	Every Minute	12 hours
Dogwood Cluster	2-3	3 min.	Every Minute	8 hours
Rose (Medium) (full bloom)	1	2½ min.	Every ½ Minute	12 hours
Rose (Minature) (use cardboard platter)	Several	1½ min.	Every ½ Minute	5 hours
Pansy (use cardboard platter)	5-8	2 min.	Every ½ Minute	4 hours
Chrysanthemum (Large) (use pyrex bowl)	1	3 min.	Every Minute	12 hours
Chrysanthemum (Single Bloom) (Use cardboard platter)	3-5	2½ min.	Every ½ Minute	10 hours
Zinnia (Large)	1	2½ min.	None	10 hours

Recipe Index